Early Psychoanalytic Religious Writings

Contemporary Psychoanalytic Studies

Editor

Jon Mills
Adelphi University

Associate Editors

Gerald J. Gargiulo
Keith Haartman
Ronald C. Naso

Editorial Advisory Board

Howard Bacal, Alan Bass, John Beebe, Christopher Bollas, Mark Bracher,
Marcia Cavell, Nancy J. Chodorow, Walter A. Davis, Peter Dews,
Michael Eigen, Irene Fast, Bruce Fink, Peter Fonagy, Leo Goldberger,
Oren Gozlan, R.D. Hinshelwood, Otto F. Kernberg, Joseph Lichtenberg,
Todd McGowan, Nancy McWilliams, Jean Baker Miller, Thomas Ogden,
Owen Renik, Joseph Reppen, William J. Richardson, Peter L. Rudnytsky,
David Livingstone Smith, Donnel Stern, Frank Summers, M. Guy Thompson,
Wilfried Ver Eecke, Brent Willock, Robert Maxwell Young

VOLUME 29

The titles published in this series are listed at *brill.com/cps*

Early Psychoanalytic Religious Writings

Edited by

H. Newton Malony
Edward P. Shafranske

BRILL
RODOPI

LEIDEN | BOSTON

Cover illustration: *Man walking between two seas*, used with permission by iStock.com/francescoch.

Library of Congress Cataloging-in-Publication Data

Names: Malony, H. Newton, editor. | Shafranske, Edward P., editor.
Title: Early psychoanalytic religious writings / edited by H. Newton
  Malony, Edward P. Shafranske.
Description: Leiden ; Boston : Brill Rodopi, [2021] | Series: Contemporary
  psychoanalytic studies, 1571–4977 ; volume 29 | Includes bibliographical
  references and index. |
Identifiers: LCCN 2020023189 (print) | LCCN 2020023190 (ebook) | ISBN
  9789004426740 (hardback) | ISBN 9789004429222 (ebook)
Subjects: LCSH: Psychoanalysis and religion.
Classification: LCC BF175.4.R44 E34 2021 (print) | LCC BF175.4.R44
  (ebook) | DDC 150.19/5--dc23
LC record available at https://lccn.loc.gov/2020023189
LC ebook record available at https://lccn.loc.gov/2020023190

Typeface for the Latin, Greek, and Cyrillic scripts: "Brill". See and download: brill.com/brill-typeface.

ISSN 1571-4977
ISBN 978-90-04-42674-0 (hardback)
ISBN 978-90-04-42922-2 (e-book)

Copyright 2021 by Koninklijke Brill NV, Leiden, The Netherlands.
Koninklijke Brill NV incorporates the imprints Brill, Brill Hes & De Graaf, Brill Nijhoff, Brill Rodopi,
Brill Sense, Hotei Publishing, mentis Verlag, Verlag Ferdinand Schöningh and Wilhelm Fink Verlag.
All rights reserved. No part of this publication may be reproduced, translated, stored in a retrieval system,
or transmitted in any form or by any means, electronic, mechanical, photocopying, recording or otherwise,
without prior written permission from the publisher.
Authorization to photocopy items for internal or personal use is granted by Koninklijke Brill NV provided
that the appropriate fees are paid directly to The Copyright Clearance Center, 222 Rosewood Drive, Suite
910, Danvers, MA 01923, USA. Fees are subject to change.

This book is printed on acid-free paper and produced in a sustainable manner.

This book is dedicated to H. Newton Malony (1931–2020) – a gracious scholar and leader in the psychology of religion

Contents

Note on Original Publications IX

1 The Psychoanalytic Study of Religion: Past, Present, Future 1
   Edward P. Shafranske

2 Two Contributions to the Research of Symbols (*Zwei Beitrage zur Symbolforschung.* Imago IX, 1923, 122–126) 30
   Karl Abraham

3 If Moses were an Egyptian ... (International Journal of Psycho-Analysis, XX, 1939, 1–32) 36
   Sigmund Freud

4 The Dogma of Christ (*Die Entwicklung des Christusdogma.* Imago XVI, 1930, 305–373) 43
   Erich Fromm

5 Two Traditions from Pascal's Childhood (*Zwei Überlieferungen aus Pascals Kinderjahren.* Imago XI (3), 1925, 346–351) 101
   Imre Hermann

6 A Psychoanalytic Study of the Holy Spirit (*Eine Psychoanalytische Studie über den Heiligen Geist.* Imago IX (1), 1923, 58–72) 108
   Ernest Jones

7 Is the Mark of Cain Circumcision? A Critical Contribution to Biblical Exegesis (*Ist das Kainszeichen die Beschneidung?* Imago V, 1919, 290–293) 115
   Ludwig Levy

8 The Illusion of the Future: A Friendly Dispute with Professor Sigmund Freud (*Die Illusion einer Zukunft.* Imago XIV, 1928, 149–184) 119
   Oskar Pfister

9 The Fifth Commandment (*Das fünfte Gebot.* Imago IX, (1), 1923, 129–130) 149
   Sandor Rado

VIII CONTENTS

10 The Three Foundational Elements of Religious Feeling (The Mass
    Psychology of Fascism [*Die Massenpsychologie des Faschismus*] 1933,
    Chapter VII: Sex Economy in the Fight Against Mysticism)   152
       Wilhelm Reich

11 Freud's Journal IMAGO – 1912 to Present   159

12 The Future of an Illusion, The Illusion of the Future: An Historic
    Dialogue on the Value of Religion between Oskar Pfister and Sigmund
    Freud (Reprinted with Permission from *The Journal of the History of the
    Behavioral Sciences*, 15(2), 1979, 177–186)   161
       H. Newton Malony and Gerald O. North

    Index   177

Note on Original Publications

Except for Freud (1939) and Reich, this collection of articles were taken from the pages of the journal IMAGO in the 1920s. IMAGO is the journal established by Freud in 1912 that remains in publication. The articles are written by a number of early psychoanalysts and reflect a wide interest in relating analysis to religion. They represent Freud's interest in establishing such a means of dialogue.

This selection also includes an account of Freud's friendship with Oskar Pfister, a Swiss pastor who became an analyst. Pfister wrote the review of Freud's *The Future of an Illusion* IMAGO titled *The Illusion of the Future* that is included in this volume.

CHAPTER 1

The Psychoanalytic Study of Religion: Past, Present, Future

Edward P. Shafranske

> [T] hose ideas – ideas which are religious in the widest sense – are prized as the most precious possession of civilization, as the most precious thing it has to offer its participants. It is far more highly prized than all the devices for winning treasures from the earth or providing men with sustenance or preventing their illnesses, and so forth. People feel that life would not be tolerable if they did not attach to these ideas the value that is claimed for them. And now the question arises: What are these ideas in the light of psychology? Whence do they derive the esteem in which they are held? And to take a further timid step, what is their real worth?
>
> FREUD, 1927/1964, p. 20

We begin with Freud's words, with his acknowledgment of the value culture ascribes to religion and, in the same breath, his challenge to its merits. The questions that Freud posed have relevance not only for the psychology of individual religious experience but, as we will see, form the basis of his critique of culture and influenced early psychoanalytic exploration of religion.

1   The Psychoanalytic Impulse

Psychoanalysis aims to understand religious experience from the perspective of the complex dynamics of the mind. Its vantage examines religious beliefs and experiences as products of ever-present psychodynamics. These dynamics operate for the most part outside of conscious awareness and bear the imprint of countless human interactions. Freud's anthropology (and psychoanalysis, *in toto*) would be incomplete without considering the function of religion in the life of the individual (Vergote, 2002, p. 6) and in the transmission of cultural forms and ethics. Conversely, the study of religion or spirituality would be lacking without a means to examine the unconscious psychological and developmental vicissitudes that contribute to its potency. As an "initiator of discourse"

© KONINKLIJKE BRILL NV, LEIDEN, 2021 | DOI:10.1163/9789004429222_002

(Foucault, 1970) on society and culture, Freud employed "psychoanalytic perspectives to diagnose the psychological roots of cultural trends, unearthed archaic patterns in 'civilized' behavior and illuminated the relationship of the individual to society" (cf. Fischer, 1991, p. 108). Throughout this volume we see attempts to interrogate the manifest content found in Biblical and religious texts and to mine unconscious meaning by applying psychodynamic principles obtained in clinical psychoanalysis. These early works of Freud and others established applied psychoanalysis in which a critical analysis of individual and cultural experience could be undertaken which incorporated an appreciation of unconscious phantasy and psychodynamics.

Although incapable of authoring an objective opinion regarding the truth claims of religion or the veridical status of beliefs (Rizzuto & Shafranske, 2013), Freud's cultural texts initiated an approach to investigate the *psychological means* by which transcendent realities are apprehended or imaginatively created and to examine how culturally given religious forms influence individual and corporate subjectivities. In addition, the psychoanalytic perspective illuminates the possibility that human tensions, struggles, and compromises may be given expression through the cultural idiom of religion and other cultural texts. Contemporary psychoanalytic scholarship builds on this foundation, offering critique and extending Freud's theory of the genesis of personal religiousness as well as illustrating the pervasive influence of unconscious wishes and fantasies in human affairs. Such investigations necessarily fall into the temptation to reduce religious experience exclusively to the categories, methods, and models employed within the psychoanalytic paradigm. Such reductionism results in an emphasis on the intrapsychic functions religion performs outside of consciousness. Freud (1913b/1964), although confident in his discoveries, appears to have understood the inherent limitations in his approach and so concluded that, "There are no grounds for fearing that psycho-analysis ... will be tempted to trace the origin of anything so complicated as religion to a single source" (p. 100). The essential meaning of the findings derived from psychoanalytic inquiry ultimately rests on the fundamental faith perspective of the interpreter (cf. Wulff, 1997, p. 276) – for the theist such studies illuminate the psychological processes that shape one's relationship to transcendent *realities*, and for the atheist, religion is unclothed to be a cultural artifact, a *delusion*. No matter the resolution of this fundamental question, "Without psychoanalysis," as Robert Jay Lifton (2000) noted, "we don't have a psychology worthy of address to [individual] history and society or culture" (p. 222), of which religion holds a central position.

In this chapter Freud's seminal contributions to the psychoanalytic study of religion are discussed with multiple intents – to present a summary of his analysis and critique of religion, to consider his ideas in light of contemporary

THE PSYCHOANALYTIC STUDY OF RELIGION: PAST, PRESENT, FUTURE 3

psychoanalytic scholarship, and to provide context to examine the contributions of his contemporary psychoanalytic colleagues.[1]

2 Preliminary Considerations

Psychoanalysis takes as its primary method a clinical approach in which religious material obtained within the treatment setting is analyzed, paying particular attention to the patient's web of associations, which reveal wishes, defenses, and fantasy as well as the influences of internalized objects and cultural forms within the context of transference. Applied scholarship, such as Freud's contributions, involves the use of psychoanalysis as a hermeneutical method in which cultural texts are reinterpreted and meanings are reconstituted. Knowledge and theory, derived primarily from clinical experiences, are applied to cultural phenomena, in an attempt to "unfreeze" the symbolic potential embedded in language and ritual (Obeyesekere, 1990). In both clinical and applied contexts, the problem of meaning is "the central disclosure of psychoanalysis" and involves apprehending the "multivocal relations within a symbolic sphere" (Kovel, 1988, p. 89). In these endeavors, analysts, beginning with Freud, have labored to understand the unconscious constituents of individual and cultural experience in which wish and illusion play dominant roles. For Freud, clinical experiences illuminated the ways in which psychological conflicts, originating in early development, come to be represented and repetitively expressed within the mind as unconscious fantasy and discharged through behavior, as exemplified in the cases of neuroses and in religious beliefs and rituals. This clinical discovery provides the foundation on which Freud constructed a psychoanalytic account of the psychological underpinnings of religion. Although Freud assumed that the origins of religion were found in prehistory and transmitted through phylogeny (Ritvo, 1990), his ideas today are better appreciated through an understanding of ontogeny and through the application of semiotics.

In light of its focus on non-material essences in the formation of conscious and unconscious meaning, psychoanalysis is best situated among the historical-hermeneutic sciences rather than considered an empirical-analytic science (Habermas, 1971) as Freud had originally intended. Such an epistemological stance is advantageous for the psychoanalytic study of religion, which involves the analysis of the psychological function and appearance of religious forms

---

1 This chapter draws from substantially from Shafranske, E. P. (1995). Freudian theory and religious experience. In R. Hood, Jr. (Ed.). *Handbook of the psychology of religious experience* (pp. 200–230). Birmingham: Religious Education Press.

within individual and cultural existence (DiCenso, 1999, p. 1). Its purview does not permit investigation of the correspondence between such religious forms and objective reality or history; rather, it performs a study of symbolization and its motivation, inspecting the mental processes that mediate between the subject and the real. Its findings are therefore delimited and require the posit, as Ricoeur (cf. 1970, p. 242) suggested, of the double possibility of "faith" and "nonfaith" in which the question of the actuality of transcendent realities is suspended.

In addition, much of Freud's theory is conveyed through inventive literary expositions[2] and speculative essays, which offer insights into unconscious psychological dynamics rather than establish historical truth. Ultimately, Freudian theory, itself, is embedded in and limited by the specific historical/cultural context in which it germinated. Freud's oeuvre reflects the assumptions of his time, i.e., materialism, Aristotelian faith in the ability to obtain knowledge of reality, and the valuation of reason over subjectivity,[3] as well as a form of psychological essentialism based on his belief in the universality of the Oedipus complex. These works present a case for the coherence of psychic life, in which "unconscious wishes and fantasies are not constructed within particular cultural worlds, but are universal, a common ground of meaning that articulates or 'expresses' itself with some limited variations within different historical and cultural contexts" (cf. Toews, 1999, p. 99).

Freud's texts outline the central role religion plays in what Obeyesekere (1990) refers to as "the work of culture [whereby] symbolic forms existing on a cultural level get created and recreated through the minds of people" (p. xix). Beyond the sociological perspective of the social construction of reality, psychoanalysis amplifies the dynamic nature of these processes in which religion instills powerful moods and motivations. In a complementary fashion, culture reflects the mental contents of its citizens, which are then expressed and transmitted in the symbolic forms which culture supplies to be introjected by future generations. These dynamics involve the civilizing forces of moral systems in which desire becomes known within a specific cultural context and is expressed, sublimated, or repressed.

---

2 For example, Freud initially titled, *Moses and Monotheism*, *The Man Moses, A Historical Novel* (Jones, 1957, p. 206) and he referred to *Totem and Taboo* as his construction.

3 Freud remained committed throughout his life to a scientific view that emphasized positivism and correspondence of mental phenomena to physical (biological) substrates and was informed by the theories of Darwin, Haekel and Lamark and his teachers, including Brucke, Helmholtz, Du Bois-Raymond, and Claus (Gay, 1988; Ritvo, 1990; Sulloway, 1979; Solms, 1998).

3 Freud's Critique of Religion

Rather than a simple exposition, Freud's analysis deftly offered a critique of religion that simultaneously advanced his views regarding the universality of the Oedipus complex and the role of irrational unconscious libido-driven forces in human existence.[4,5] In these studies, Freud returned to the "cultural problems" that had been a fascination in his youth (1935/1964) and, in keeping with his commitment to a positivist worldview, he searched for the material causality of the idiographic and universal origins of religion. In applying psychoanalytic principles to religious texts, Freud could advance his knowledge of psychodynamics and argue that religion was the product of illusion fueled by ever-present wishes orchestrated within the context of Oedipal dynamics, embedded within the core of civilization. This provided a means to expand the reach of psychoanalysis beyond the narrow clinical context to a universal human dimension. Religious faith involved both a commitment to an illusion as well as an irrational renunciation of instinct drives, both of which posed the greatest threat to rationality and to the advancement of civilization (Gay, 1988). He begins his argument by drawing a correspondence between neurosis and religion and then posits a common cause for psychic conflict, which is rooted in phylogeny, expressed within religion, and appears within individual development.

4 The Correspondence between Neurosis and Religion

With the publication of "Obsessive Actions and Religious Practices" in 1907, Freud began his formal analysis of religion by drawing a comparison between "neurotic ceremonials and the sacred acts of religious ritual" (p. 119). Although allowing for differences in their manifest content, he posits an essential correspondence between the two practices. He proposes that each in character is the result of an unconscious compromise formation[6] in which "an unconscious

---

4 Freud's critique also served more personal motivations in providing a rationale for his formidable rejection of God and the compromise formation it served (see Ana-Maria Rizzuto, 1998, for a detailed account) as well as serving "sweet revenge" on Carl Jung, "the crown prince who had proved so brutal to him and treacherous to psychoanalysis" and who had rejected Freud's dual drive theory (Gay, 1988, p. 326).

5 The following discussion draws liberally from Shafranske (1995).

6 Freud (1923, 1925, 1926) proposes that unconscious compromise formations are attempts to resolve conflicts between the psychic agencies (id, ego, and super-ego) and the outside world. Conflicts ensue from the demands for instinctual expression (pleasure-seeking) and external

sense of guilt" (1907, p. 123) and "the qualms of conscience brought on by their neglect" (1907, p. 119) are expiated and instinctual drives are suppressed through the performance of ritual acts. The role of unconscious conflict is proposed somewhat similarly in Reik's interpretation of the mark of Cain as a form of unconscious self-punishment (see Levy, this volume). Freud (1907/1964, p. 127) describes, "neurosis as an individual religiosity and religion as the universal obsessional neurosis" in which a shared etiology is found in the renunciation of instinctual wishes. Considering the implicit moral prescriptions, particularly in respect to sexual ethics, transmitted through the authority of religion, Freud (1908/1964) concluded, "the single steps [in the progression of civilization through renunciation of instincts] were sanctioned by religion" (p. 187). He questions the price exacted on wish fulfillment in service of the reality principle and cultural advancement. However, of particular concern for Freud are the conflicts associated with renunciation enacted under the influence of irrational forces, originating in prehistory and embedded within the Oedipus complex, which result in the development of the psychoneuroses. It is this concern that becomes the centerpiece of his critique; however, further descriptions of the causes and motives that govern compliance with the demands for renunciation were required to establish the prime motives at the heart of monotheistic religion. In *Totem and Taboo, Moses and Monotheism, Civilization and Its Discontents*, and *The Future of an Illusion*, Freud constructs an historical narrative, drawing primarily from anthropology,[7] evolutionary theory,[8] and clinical observations, which renders a psychoanalytic account of the epigenesis of civilization, in which religion plays a central role, and its parallel within individual development.

5   Phylogeny: The Primal Cause

At the time of writing *Totem and Taboo*, Freud had already formulated a number of clinical insights and was prepared to shift focus from an exclusive *proximate*-causal theory to an *ultimate*-causal theory, which would extend the

---

reality, including its internalized aspects within the super-ego; compromises involve a dynamic balancing act between expression and inhibition, involving repression and may result in psychogenic symptom formation and neurosis (See Brenner, 1994, 2002 for a contemporary discussion).

7 Freud drew upon the studies of totemic religion conducted by anthropologists James G. Frazer, W. Robertson Smith, and Edward B. Tyler.

8 Freud was influenced by the theories of both Darwin and Lamark (Ritvo, 1990; Sulloway, 1979) as well as by the model of embryology in vogue at the time in which a parallel was suggested between the early development of an individual member of the species and the evolution of the species.

THE PSYCHOANALYTIC STUDY OF RELIGION: PAST, PRESENT, FUTURE 7

insights of psychoanalysis from the consulting room and the specific culture in which he practiced to a general theory of human behavior (Sulloway, 1979, pp. 365–367). Evidence obtained from an examination of culture could further justify his claim of the discovery of a universal construct, the Oedipus complex, situating the development of the individual to that of the species, in keeping with Darwin's law of recapitulation and reflecting embryonic stages of cultural evolution (Ritvo, 1990). Further, Freud had to account for the practice of exogamy and the emergence of Oedipus complex. His answer was found in the anthropological studies of totems.

Social order becomes instituted through the establishment of the totem, usually in the form of an animal, which symbolically differentiates the members of the clan from others, involves the indwelling of ancestral spirits, and is associated with the prohibition of sexual relations between members of the clan.

He regarded the taboos of primitive peoples to be analogous to the obsessional symptoms of neurotics. "Further, he" posited that "There are men still living who, as we believe, stand very near to primitive man, far nearer than we do, and whom we therefore regard as his direct heirs and representatives" (Freud, 1913b/1964, p. 1). From the anthropological studies of such "savages," Freud inferred the mental contents and practices of primitive peoples. Homans (1989, p. 283) considers this Freud's equation: savage = children = neurotic. He comments that this annuls the notion of timelessness and "ushers in the full-scale temporalization of life" (p. 284).

Freud traced their development to particular epochs in the history of the species and divined the origin of the Oedipus complex to an historical event at the crossroads of civilization. In keeping with Darwin's thesis, this event concerned the murder of the tyrannical father by the primal horde. This act of parricide led to a disruption of the horde and eventuated in the establishment of a rudimentary social order built around two basic totemic laws concerning incest and killing the totem animal. This act of parricide was not an isolated event but rather consisted of a series of experiences within a given epoch of human existence. The murdered father became symbolized in the totem animal, which held the authority within the horde. Through the sacrifice of the totem animal, the sons "could attempt, in their relation to this surrogate father, to allay their burning sense of guilt, to bring about a kind of reconciliation with their father" (Freud 1913b/1964, p. 144). Freud drew upon his clinical experience in which he observed the child's use of animals as displacements of the ambivalently held father. Freud (1913b/1964, p. 145) concluded that:

> Totemic religion arose from the filial sense of guilt, in an attempt to allay that feeling and to appease the father by deferred obedience to him. All later religions are seen as attempts to solve the same problem. They vary

according to the stage of civilization at which they arise and according to the methods that they adopt; but all have the same end in view and are reactions to the same great event with which civilization began and which, since it occurred, has not allowed a moment's rest.

From his model of "neurosis, early trauma, defense, latency, and outbreak of neurosis and partial return of repressed material," Freud (1939/1964, p. 80) constructs an analogous process in the essence of religious symbolism, beliefs, and functions. Religious ceremonies were enactments, which contained the representations of the original murderous act. Levy (this volume) argues that "prehistory explains phenomena which touch on all the peoples of the world" (p. 116). This prehistory is in the symbolic fabric of religious mythology and ritual – tracing from prehistory to contemporary religious practices. Freud agreed with Robertson-Smith's interpretations of the Christian Lord's Last Supper and Mass as a derivative of the totemic sacrificial meal. Keeping in mind the rituals of neurotics, Freud could conjecture that such religious ceremonies served defensive purposes and contained and represented the unconscious memory of the original act.

The injunctions following the epoch of parricide gave birth to civilization, religion, and the Oedipus complex (See Bergmann 1992 for an alternative view implicating the sacrifice of children and its impact on religion and culture). Freud took from Robertson-Smith the principle of exogamy which protected the horde from a repetition of parricide. Freud suggests that each person, through inherited psychic endowment, carries under the veil of repression, the original Oedipal "sin." Etched forever in the unconscious, the mnemonic image of the father prompted the formation of deistic religion and attracted generations removed from the historical event to the commemorative ritual of the totem meal. Religion is not only repentance, it is also the disguised remembrance of the triumph over the father, hence a covert filial revolt; this filial revolt is hidden in other features of religion, principally in "the son's efforts to put himself in the place of the father-god" (Ricoeur, 1970, p. 242).

Through this formulation Freud placed religion within the context of phylogeny. The progressions of the totemic meal from animal sacrifice to the Christ sacrifice in the Catholic Mass represented not so much changes in the essence of the ritual as illustrations of the progression of civilization away from the prehistorical to the more abstract and symbolic. The functions of commemoration, appeasement, and renunciation of instinct remained integral to the cultural compromise the Oedipus complex expressed through religion.

Freud was able to assert a historical context for the universality of the Oedipus complex in keeping with the evidence provided by religion. Judeo-Christian

THE PSYCHOANALYTIC STUDY OF RELIGION: PAST, PRESENT, FUTURE 9

beliefs and ceremonies contained and represented the history of the species and the contents of archaic inheritance. The transmission of this history was a product of inheritance. The influence of Lamarck is obvious as Freud (1923a/1964, p. 38) concluded: "Thus in the id, which is capable of being inherited, are harbored residues of the existences of countless egos; and when the ego forms the super-ego out of the id, it may perhaps only be reviving shapes of former egos and bringing them to resurrection." Rice (1990, p. 147) comments:

> It should be noted that when Freud speaks of acquired characteristics he is not referring to physical aspects of the human organism but to the memory-traces of external events which, through repetition, become permanently embedded in the unconscious *id* through which, after a presumed saturation point is reached, is transmitted to further generations. It is the *id* of the progenitor that is inherited by the offspring.

Such a view is in keeping with 19th century preformationist embryology, "which taught that organisms existed fully formed from the beginning" (Ritvo, 1990, p. 18). This notion was popularized by Haeckel, in "ontogeny recapitulates phylogeny" (Ritvo, 1990; See also, Hoffer, 1992), and appears directly in *Beyond the Pleasure Principle*, "embryology in its capacity as a recapitulation of developmental history" (Freud, 1920/1964, p. 26). Rieff (1961, pp. 199–201) captures the importance of Freud's emphasis on inherited characteristics:

> Freud rejected the conscious transmission of culture for what he considered a more profound continuity. The deepest ancestral secrets are not rationally preserved and disseminated by parents and teachers; they are remembered ... On the conscious surface of a culture, the repressed content of the past is something 'vanished and overcome in the life of a people.' But this is just what defines the impact of memory: one's reaction to it, against it. Prototypical events – the primal crime and its repetitions, like the murder of Moses or the murder of Christ – take on the weight of tradition when they are repressed, and the reaction to them is, of course, unconscious. History, as the trail of the prototype, became for Freud a process of the 'return of the repressed,' distorting extensively yet eternally recapitulatory.

Freud locates religious thinking as a primitive form of thinking of a forgotten epoch in prehistory. Extending the thesis first explicated in his 1907 paper, Freud draws an analogy between the compulsions of obessional neurotics and the rituals of totemic religion now within the context of the repressed primal event. Freud was able to reconcile the gap between the *private* character of the "religion of the neurotic" and the *universal* character of the "neurosis of the religious man" through the phylogenetic hypothesis. (cf. Ricoeur, 1970, p. 233) Further, in linking contemporary religious practices to the domain of the id, Freud could establish the universality of the Oedipus complex.[3] This accomplishment would safeguard the primacy of sexuality in human motivation and pathogenesis. Freudian psychoanalysis would be maintained.

In *Moses and Monotheism*, Freud (1939) returned to the thesis of *Totem and Taboo*. He sought to bring into line a further explication of the development of religion from animism, through the prophetic stage to monotheism. Freud deduced a repetition of the original parricide within the more immediate history of Judaism. Moses was the historical figure upon whom a mythology emerged which served to bring Judaism into existence. To encapsulate his argument: Moses was, in fact, an Egyptian; he introduced a strict, monotheistic religion to the Jewish people; for this he was murdered; after a period of time the tribes reunited under the tenets of monotheism which reflected Moses' original credo. The reemergence of monotheism occurs, in a fashion similar to that of the totem meal. After a period of social unrest, a compromise formation appears in which the murdered father, and now the murdered father-substitute, Moses, are commemorated and the parricide is symbolically undone. The resolution of the murder of Moses and the original sin is found in the form of a Messiah to expiate the murderous deeds. We see, in this explication, the Oedipal story retold now in a later epoch in history.

> It is worth noticing how the new religion dealt with the ancient ambivalence in relation to the father. Its main content was, it is true, reconciliation with God the Father; atonement for the crime committed against him; but the other side of the emotional relation showed itself in the fact that the son, who had taken atonement on himself, became a god himself beside the father and actually, in place of the father. Christianity, having arisen out of a father-religion [Judaic monotheism], became a son-religion. It has not escaped the fate of having to get rid of the father. (Freud 1939/1964, p. 136)

Religion bears the imprint of these events and the ambivalence of its resolution through its rituals. Contained within religion exists the original deed and its legacy of the conflict between the father and the son. Freud (1913b/1964, p. 145) spoke of this earlier in *Totem and Taboo*, another feature which was already present in totemism and which has been preserved unaltered in religion. The tension of ambivalence was too great for any contrivance to be able to counteract it; or it is possible that psychological conditions in general are unfavorable to getting rid of these antithetical emotions. However that be, we find that the ambivalence implicit in the father-complex persists in totemism and in religions generally. Totemic religion was not only comprised of expressions of remorse and attempts at atonement, it also served as a remembrance of the triumph over the father.

The emergence of Judaic monotheism marked a significant turn in the development of civilization. This turn consisted of the prohibition against making an image of God. For Freud (1939/1964, p. 113), "it meant that a sensory perception was given second place to what may be called an abstract idea; it was a triumph of intellectuality over sensuality, or strictly speaking, an instinctual renunciation." As we will develop in a moment, this turn from God representation toward abstraction foreshadowed, for Freud, an epoch in which instinctual renunciation would be achieved not through a relationship with a god but rather solely through the application of ethical precepts. Rizzuto (1979, p. 28) succinctly captured the essence of this conceptual shift, "Freud is no longer concerned with images or ancestral 'precipitates' but with ideas."

Christianity, Freud assessed, retreated from Judaic monotheism in remaining fixed to a figure of God, Christ the Son of God. Recall Freud's earlier remark that "religions are subject to reforms which work retroactively and aim at a re-establishment of the original balance of values" (Freud, 1907/1964, p. 167). It is the Messiah of Christianity who is then sacrificed, to be commemorated in the Mass. The distinction that Freud is drawing has to do with the substitution of an idea of God for that of a representation or image of God. That Judaism maintained an ethical monotheism suggested a slight movement away from reliance upon a wish fulfilling, God imago. The unifying thesis in these texts concerns the unconscious memory of the original parricide and the Oedipus complex, which bears the imprint in perpetuity within the psyches of the horde's descendents. This event is the origin of civilization's progress and simultaneously the progenitor of psychological conflict.

Freud (1939/1964) posits the centrality of this event for the development of neurosis and "bridges the gulf between individual and group psychology" (p. 100). It was through his analysis of religion that Freud was able to point to the universality of the Oedipus complex in both the individual and in the culture. Freud (p. 99) writes in *Moses and Monotheism*,

The work of analysis has, however, brought something else to light which exceeds in its importance what we have so far considered. When we study the reactions to early traumas, we are quite often surprised to find that they are not strictly limited to what the subject himself has really experienced but diverge from it in a way which fits in much better with the model of a phylogenetic event and, in general, can only be explained by such an influence. The behavior of neurotic children towards their parents in the Oedipus and castration complex abounds in such reactions, which seem unjustified in the individual case and only become intelligible phylogenetically – but their connection with the experience of earlier generations ... Its evidential value seems to me strong enough for me to venture one further step and to posit the assertion that the archaic heritage of human beings comprises not only dispositions but also subject-matter – memory-traces of the experience of earlier generations. In this way the compass as well as the importance of the archaic heritage would be significantly extended.

The veracity of Freud's account has been challenged repeatedly. Freud was not unaware of the difficulties in putting forth his historical hypothesis. It is evident in his correspondence during the writing of this work that Freud was aware of the problem of "poetic license versus historical truth" and originally intended *Moses and Monotheism* to be subtitled "Ein historischer Roman" (A Historical Novel). He wrote to Arnold Zweig, "Where there is an unbridgeable gap in history and biography, the writer can step in and try to guess how it all happened" (Yersuhalmi, 1989, p. 377). Bolstered by his discoveries of the Oedipus complex in clinical psychoanalysis, Freud applied psychoanalytic thinking to the figure of Moses. We may also discern in *Moses and Monotheism* the workings of Freud's own mind in his resolution of the Oedipus complex. Freud (1935/1964, p. 71), in a postscript to *An Autobiographical Study*, reveals that "two themes run through these pages: the story of my life and the history of psychoanalysis. They are intimately interwoven." Freud (1914/1964, p. 233) is, perhaps, unconsciously self-referential, in ascribing to Michelangelo's Moses, "the highest achievement that is possible in a man, that of struggling against an inward passion for the sake of a cause to which he has devoted himself." *Moses and Monotheism* brings to a close Freud's longstanding interest of Moses and explicates, perhaps, the nature of his identification with this historical figure[4]. Meissner (1984, p. 50) suggested: "In a sense, Freud's writing of *Moses and Monotheism* was the final attempt to work through and resolve this deep-seated conflict and ambivalence about his father. Jacob [Freud] had destroyed

Freud's image of the omnipotent father, and Freud never forgave him. The work was an act of rebellion and revenge, a rising up against the religion of the father and a smashing of it with the power of the mind." Echoing the primordial theme, perhaps, we may find the Freud's attempt at Oedipal resolution: the father-religion of Judaism and Christianity yields to the son-religion of psychoanalysis. We turn now to Freud's examination of individual psychodynamics and religious experience.

6   The Ontogenetic Contribution to Religion

Complementing Freud's phylogenetic explanation of the origins of religion is his discussion of ontogeny, the development of the individual member of the species. In "A Phylogenetic Fantasy," Freud (1915/1964, p. 10) considers the relationship between phylogeny and ontogeny:

> [O]ne can justifiably claim that the inherited dispositions are residues of the acquisition of our ancestors. With this one runs into (the) problem of the phylogenetic disposition behind the individual or ontogenetic, and should find no contradiction if the individual adds new dispositions from his own experience to his inherited disposition on the basis of earlier experience.

His description of individual development is anchored within the structure of the Oedipus complex which as we've seen finds its genesis in the prehistory of humanity. Freud's analysis of religion concerns religious practices, religious experience, and religious ideas. As we have discussed Freud (1907/1964, 1913b/1964, 1939/1964) viewed religious practices from the perspectives of analogy to the individual neurosis and repetition of totemic ritual. Religious practices are seen as processes of atonement and undoing related to ancestral paracide and the psychodynamics of obsessive actions [see for example Freud's (1913a/1964, pp. 9–82) case of Schreber]. We turn now to his examination of religious experience and religious ideas.

7   Religious Experience

Having declared an "infidel Jew," and, although, by his own admission, emotionally moved by religious art and architecture and fascinated by superstition and the "uncanny," Freud (1928, p. 170; 1919) reported having never had an experience he considered religious (See Gay, 1987; Parsons, 1999). Our discussion commences with Freud's analysis of his friend Rolland's description of religious experience.

> This, he says, consists of a peculiar feeling, which he himself is never without, which he finds confirmed by many others, and which he may suppose is present in millions of people. It is a feeling which he would like to call a sensation of "eternity," a feeling as of something limitless, unbounded as it were, "oceanic." This feeling, he adds, is a purely subjective fact, not an article of faith; it brings with it no assurance of personal immortality, but it is the source of the religious energy
>
> FREUD 1930/1964, p. 64

Freud reports that he cannot discover such an experience in himself and admits that it is not easy to deal scientifically with such feelings. He goes on to consider such feelings within the context of the ego's relation to the world. Freud conjectures that the child seeks an object cathexis with the mother, in part, to ensure her protection from the dangers of the external world. The origin of religious inclination is found in the child's helplessness in the face of the crushing powers of nature. He suggests that the primary ego-feeling, described by Romain Rolland, as limitlessness and a bond with the universe, finds its origin in the child's nascent ego relating prior to the formation of the more sharply demarcated ego-feeling of maturity (Freud, 1930/1964, 1936/1964; See also Fisher, 1991). Freud (1930/1964) writes:

> a feeling can only be a source of energy if it is itself the expression of a strong need. The deviation of religious needs from the infant's helplessness and the longing for the father aroused by it seems to me incontrovertible, especially since the feeling is not simply prolonged from childhood days, but is permanently sustained by fear of the superior power of Fate. I cannot think of any need in childhood as strong as the need for the father's protection. Thus the part played by the oceanic feeling, which might seek something like the restoration of limitless narcissism, is ousted from a place in the foreground. The origin of the religious attitude can be traced back in clear outlines as far as the feeling of infantile helplessness (p. 72).

The "oceanic" feeling is located within childhood and is understood as a telling complement of the regressive, wish fulfilling aspect upon which religion is based. Such infantile feelings are far more intense and inexhaustibly deep than those of adults; only religious ecstasy can bring back that intensity[5] (cf. Freud, 1939/1964, p. 134). Kovel (1990) argues that Freud's view is unnecessarily reductionistic.

> What is not possible – within the framework of Freud's worldview – is that the experience can have any transcendent qualities ... The infantile version of the oceanic experience is simply that – a *version*, or to use another term, an occasion (p. 71) ... Thus we need not assume that later occasions of the oceanic experience are somehow produced by the memory of the first one (p. 76).

Freud's reading of such experiences was delimited to interpretations based on wish fulfillment within the individual and universal context of the Oedipus complex. Explications of alternative versions of the meanings of religious experience were left to future writers, e.g. Meissner (1984). These feelings contribute and set the stage for the development of religious ideas (Freud 1930/1964, p. 72).

8   Religious Ideas

For Freud (1927/1964) religious ideas are illusions tethered to human desire. In keeping with his analysis of religious practices and religious experience, wish fulfillment is progenitor, as well, of religious sentiment and belief. Within the context of ontogeny, as the child shifts attachment from the mother to the father, who is perceived as stronger and better able to protect the child from the forces of nature, ideas of the father-god are formed. The construction of the god imago is a product not only of ontogeny, however, but phylogeny as well.

> To begin with, we know that God is a father-substitute; or, more correctly, that he is an exalted father; or, yet again, that he is a copy of a father as he is seen and experienced in childhood – by individuals in their own childhood and by mankind in its prehistory as the father of the primitive and primal horde ... *the ideational image belonging to his childhood is preserved and becomes merged with the inherited memory-traces of the primal father to form the individual's idea of God"*
>
> FREUD 1923a/1964, p. 85, italics added

Freud saw the creation of the father-god as serving an important function in the economics of the resolution of the Oedipus complex. In dealing with the rivalry of the Oedipus complex, an ambivalence exists in the wish to maintain the bond with the father-protector. This is accomplished through projection in which the child shifts cathexis to a now more powerful father-god with whom the Oedipal drama is played out. "It is an enormous relief to the individual psyche if the conflicts of its childhood arising from the father-complex – conflicts which it has never wholly overcome – are removed from it and brought to a solution which is universally accepted" (Freud 1927/1964, pp. 38–39). In his somewhat autobiographical reflection, "On Schoolboy Psychology," Freud (1914/1964) writes: "Of all the imagos of a childhood which, as a rule is no longer remembered, none is more important for a youth or a man than that of his father ... A little boy is bound to love and admire his father, who seems to him the most powerful, the kindest and the wisest creature in the world. God himself is after all only an exaltation of this picture of a father as he is represented in the mind of early childhood".

Religion finds its dynamic impetus in motives similar to the child's investment in the father. The individual comes to realize that in many respects he or she will remain a child forever, helpless to the forces of nature. Realizing "that he can never do without protection against strange superior powers, [he] lends those powers the features belonging to the figure of his father; he creates for himself the gods whom he dreads, whom he seeks to propitiate, and whom he nevertheless entrusts with his own protection ... [This reaction to helplessness is] "precisely the formation of religion" (1927, p. 24). Religion is an illusion, which stems from the individual's wish for protection and favor and out of fear of destruction and injury. "By representing the hostile presence of nature in human form, man treats nature as a being that can be appeased and influenced; by substituting psychology for a science of nature, religion fulfills the deepest wish of mankind" (Ricoeur, 1970, p. 251). The essence of religion does not derive from the content of its beliefs but rather from the strength of the wish. Freud goes beyond Feuerbach's (1841) thesis, "God is merely the projected essence of man," in identifying the psychodynamics of the propelling force of the wish. Grotstein (1999) suggests such religious ideation, for example, the person of Jesus reflects transhistorical and archetypal dimensions.

Freud (1927/1964, p. 31) wrote: "Thus we call a belief an illusion when a wish-fulfilment is a prominent factor in its motivation, and in doing so we disregard its relations to reality, just as the illusion itself sets no store for verification." Freud does not state that illusion is necessarily false; he intends, however, to place emphasis on wish fulfillment which is expressed within the structure of belief. At this level of analysis Freud does not assume a pejorative view but rather understands religious inclination within a psychoanalytic appreciation of wish fulfillment. Religious beliefs express, using Ricoeur's phrase, "a semantics

THE PSYCHOANALYTIC STUDY OF RELIGION: PAST, PRESENT, FUTURE   17

of desire." In other words, he does not fault religion its motivational wellspring. Freud did not overstate his case by attempting to disprove the validity of religious beliefs; he never crossed the line between arguments of persuasion and those of scientific assertion. Grunbaum (1987, p. 152) claims that Freud "did *not* fall prey to the well-known genetic fallacy." He drew short of claiming a disproof of religion, "all I have done – and this is the only thing that is new in my exposition – is to add some psychological foundation to the criticisms of my great predecessors" (Freud, 1927/1964, p. 35). That religious beliefs find motivation from human desires and psychodynamics does not constitute disproof. Critics sympathetic to religion, e.g., Meissner (1984) and Kung (1979), do not object to examination of the psychodynamic vicissitudes that contribute to faith.

It is only when religion asserts truth claims, as Hood (1992) noted, that Freud takes up the cause of reality, proposing religion to be a delusion. Freud (1925/1964, p. 72) concluded: "Later, I found a formula which did better justice to [religion]: while granting that its power lies in the truth it contains, I showed that the truth was not a material but a historical truth." Freud's argument again rests on the phylogenetic thesis.

Freud places the ontogenesis of religious experience and religious beliefs within the same context: the fulfillment of the infantile wish for protection and favor and to expiate guilt. Although not addressing Freud's phylogenetic hypothesis, Pfister (1928, this volume) considers the role of fear and guilt issuing in part from Freud's notions of Oedipal dynamics. In this location, the adult believer, and a culture built upon religious illusion, is fixed within the developmental sequence of the Oedipal child. In his placement of religion within the context of the child's relationship with the father, he amplifies the importance of the Oedipus complex for both the individual and for civilization. The ambivalence of this period and the inclination to the regressive pull of the pleasure principle supersedes the mature attention to the reality principle. Further, religious inclination is based, as well, on the influence of inherited prehistory. The dynamics of religious belief extend beyond personal history to the history of civilization. Freud's understanding of the complementary forces of ontogeny and phylogeny contribute to his critique of religion and culture.

9   The Problem of Religion and the Renunciation of Instinct

We turn, now, from Freud's explication to his critique of religion. He, "invite[s] the reader to take a step forward and assume that in the history of the human species something happened similar to the events in the life of the individual. That is to say, mankind as a whole also passed through conflicts of a sexual-aggressive nature, which left permanent traces, but which were for the most part warded off and forgotten; later, after a long period of latency, they came to life again and created phenomena similar in structure and tendency to neurotic symptoms"[6] (Freud, 1939/1964, p. 80). His thesis rests on the merits of the proposed relationship between ontogeny and phylogeny. "What is today an act of internal restraint was once an external one, imposed perhaps, by the necessities of the moment; and, in the same way, what is now brought to bear upon every growing individual as an external demand of civilization may someday become an internal disposition to repression" (Freud, 1913b/1964, pp. 188–189).

The problem with religion, for Freud, is that it establishes the renunciation of instinct based on an illusion tied to Oedipus complex and residue from prehistory. "It now became the task of the gods to even out the defects and evils of civilization, to attend to the sufferings which men inflict on one another in their life together and to watch over the fulfillment of the precepts of civilization, which men obey so imperfectly" (Freud, 1927/1964, p. 22). Responsibility for one's fate is entrusted to the gods; wish supersedes personal responsibility. The disposition of the instinctual life is meted out not only within the Oedipal complex of personal history but within one of phylogenic origin, as well. "Instinctual renunciation [occurs] through the presence of the authority, which replaced and continued that of the father" (Freud, 1939/1964, p. 120). Further, instinctual renunciation becomes internalized as a psychological structure. This ego ideal of super-ego is formed through the process of identification of one's parents. "When we were little children we knew these higher natures, we admired them and feared them; and later we took them into ourselves" (Freud, 1923a/1964, p. 36). This internalization enjoins the pre-existing, archaic heritage. Renunciation of instinctual life finds its origin in the confluence of ontogeny and phylogeny, within the personal history of the individual and the prehistory of civilization.

For Freud this meant that the basis of personal intentionality was not located in the reasoning capacities of the individual but rather was found in archaic prehistory. As long as these forces held sway in the lives of individuals, civilization could not progress. As in individual neurosis, the conflicts and resolutions of the past preempted further development. The culture was fixated and mired within the throes of the Oedipal conflicts of a long-forgotten time. Further, the problem with religion was that it was potentially a Trojan horse and may eventually undermine the civilization and social order which it supports (cf. Roazen 1968, p. 160; See also Trilling, 1955; Rieff, 1966; DeLuca, 1977). Ricoeur (1970) concludes:

> The striking thing about this history is that it does not constitute an advance, a discovery, a development, but is a sempiternal repetition of its own origins. Strictly speaking, for Freud there is no history of religion: religion's theme is the indestructibility of its own origins; religion is precisely the area where the most dramatic emotional configurations are revealed as unsurpassable (p. 243).

While acknowledging the positive influence of religion on culture, For Freud (1927/1964, p. 44), asserted that there was a greater risk in maintaining the "present attitude towards religion than [in giving] it up."

> Religion has clearly performed great services for human civilization. It has contributed much to the taming of asocial instincts. But not enough. It has ruled society for many thousands of years and has had time to show what it can achieve. If it had succeeded in making the majority of mankind happy, comforting them, in reconciling them to life and in making them into vehicles of civilization, no one would dream of attempting to alter the existing conditions.
>
> FREUD, 1927/1964, p. 47

Cultural progression, which for Freud was based on instinctual renunciation, was forestalled as long as the renunciation was based on religious, father-god prohibitions rather than on a thoughtful, deliberate and rational assessment.

The end result of renunciation based on religion is that the restriction of instinctual expression: (1) occurs within the vicissitudes of a personal and primeval Oedipal setting; (2) is achieved not through a rational assessment which would foster healthy pride but rather through the expression of the wish for favor and through oppression and repression; and (3) may be overly restrictive due to sexual and aggressive wishes being apprehended within the context of the aforementioned dynamics (Jay, 1973). Wishes are not transformed within the course of their appearance but rather are wishfully maintained, repressed, or inappropriately acted upon. Religion does not lead to the reality principle but rather maintains the "wished for" benevolence to allow for the expression of such instinctual drives. "Its essence is the pious illusion of providence and a moral world order, which are in conflict with reason" (Meng and Freud, 1963,

p. 129). The dynamics of religion were seen as analogous to the psychodynamics of neurosis in which both originated in the compromise formations under the sway of the unresolved Oedipus complex [See for example Freud's (1918/1964, p. 114–11) case of the Wolf Man].

This view led to a strident assay of religion and a juxtaposition of psychoanalysis and religion. Of the powers within culture that "may contest the very soil of science," he judged, "religion alone is the serious enemy" (1933, p. 160). As we have seen, in anchoring culture to the wish fulfillments that religious illusions offer, Freud argued that religion prohibited rationality from asserting its influence in human affairs. Human activity was swayed by the regressive pull of infantile wishes which religion nurtured. Faith and religious belief were inimical, in Freud's thinking, to reason and objectivity. "Religion, was quite simply the enemy" of the progression of society (Gay 1988, p. 533). Jones reflected Freud's thinking on this matter in responding:

> "Obviously" the study of religion "is the last and firmest stronghold of what may be called the anti-scientific, anti-rational, or anti-objective Weltanschauung, and no doubt it is there we may expect the most intense resistance, and the thick of the fight"
>
> JONES to FREUD, August 31,1911, as cited in GAY (1988, p. 534).

What Freud called for was a religion of science to supersede the old religion of illusion [Freud to Eitington, 1927, as cited in Gay (1987, p. 12)]. Freud called for an evaluation of instinctual expression in accordance to the reality principle. Logos (reason) and Anake (necessity) were to be the guiding principles of the progress of civilization. This progress clearly reflected Freud's own resolutions of psychic conflict. Van Herik (cf. 1982, p. 59) argues that Freud establishes his critique on a gender-biased formula in which renunciation is seen as progressive and fulfillment as regressive. Further, "intellectual primacy is not only the psychological but also the masculine and the cultural ideal" (Van Herik, 1982, p. 166). As we have seen, Freud's discussion of religion went beyond an assessment of its psychological constituents. In fact, individual religious experience, or what today we might refer to as God representation, took a back seat to Freud's critique of culture. He wrote: "my discoveries are a basis for philosophy. There are few who understand this; there are few who are capable of understanding this" [Freud, cited in Van Herik (1982, p. 9)]. Religion was for Freud the stumbling block civilization would have to master to develop further. As Gay (1987, p.56) summarized:

Freud would have been the first to admit that his indefatigable harassment of that illusion, religion, was anything but disinterested, anything but detached scientific investigation. Immersed as he was in European culture, he wove his commitment to the supremacy of science into the very texture of his intellectual style.

Freud (1933/1964, p. 161) was aware that science "can be no match for [religion] when it soothes the fear that men feel of the vicissitudes of life, when it assures them of a happy ending and offers them comfort in unhappiness." Freud, having endured much suffering through his own life (see Schur, 1972; Gay, 1982), seems to have found through the life of the intellect a means of personal resolution. In these cultural texts we may discern his application of psychoanalysis to a critique of culture and glean an understanding of Freud's personal solutions to the problems in living.

10   Conclusion and Commentary

Freud demonstrated through his cultural texts the utility of applying psychoanalytic theory and clinical method to investigations beyond the consulting room. These expositions on religion contributed not only to an examination of unconscious dynamics in religious observance and belief but also provided, in Freud's view, additional support for the tenets of psychoanalysis. First, the universality of the Oedipus complex could be demonstrated through the study of the religious beliefs and ceremonies of primitive peoples and their analogous ceremonies in contemporary religious observance. The parallels between the past and the present, the primitive and the contemporary, suggested to Freud the existence of a universal intrapsychic dynamic. The thread of the Oedipus complex, which he perceived as woven throughout the history of the individual and the culture, was clarified in his speculation concerning the origins of Judeo-Christian religion. As in neurosis, the cultures beliefs and practices were shaped by long repressed conflictual events; however, derivatives of the events could be discovered through an analysis of the symbolism contained within the rituals. *Totem and Taboo* and *Moses and Monotheism*, in particular, present the findings of such an analysis. Second, clinical experience furnished empirical evidence of the workings of unconscious mental processes which contributed to Freud's appraisal of religion as a disguised wish fulfillment and illusion. The latent content of religious ideas and practices could be inferred in keeping with the principles of psychoanalysis as practiced in the consulting room. These investigations served one hierarchical purpose: the demonstration of unconscious psychic determinism within human existence. Through these texts Freud could assert the workings of primeval history in the unconscious life of the individual. He could peer into the heart of the culture through his inspection and analysis of religious experience. His view that religion contains truth, but that this truth was of the veracity of a past event, and not the material truth of the existence of a deity, paralleled his understanding of neurosis and prepared the way for his radical critique of culture and "after education" (Freud 1925/1964, p. 72).

In his critique, Freud placed religion at the nexus of cultural development. He viewed religion as contributing to an immature mode of instinctual renunciation that was established in the Oedipal complex and was in response to the repressed guilt and anxiety originating in prehistory. Freud (1927/1964) called for:

> a re-ordering of human relations ... which would remove the sources of dissatisfaction within civilization by renouncing coercion and the suppression of instincts, so that, undisturbed by internal discord, men might devote themselves to the acquisition of wealth and its enjoyment (p. 7).

For Freud, religion was the cultural expression of neurosis. The influence of the rational was overshadowed by the claims of the irrational. Civilization was held captive by the dynamics of oedipal conflict enshrined within religion. This examination concludes with a final question to which we now turn: "What is the value of Freud's critique of religion today?"

As we have seen, Freud's critique was established on the interplay between phylogeny and ontogeny. His acceptance of the phylogenetic hypothesis remained immutable throughout his life. Anna Freud remarked in a letter to Lucille Ritvo, "Personally, I remember very well how imperturbed my father was by everyone's criticism to his neo-Lamarkianism. He was quite sure that he was on safe ground" (Ritvo, 1990, frontispiece). The phylogenetic basis of Freud's understanding of religion is untenable. Although an appreciation of evolutionary biology in psychological functioning is developing [See Slavin & Kriegman, 1992], Freud's reliance upon specific Lamarkian principles of inherited characteristics is not supported. His view of religion as the cultural expression of an archaic event, *as transmitted through biological inheritance*, is unfounded. It was Freud's examination of ontogeny that has been the springboard for contemporary psychoanalytic study of religion.

THE PSYCHOANALYTIC STUDY OF RELIGION: PAST, PRESENT, FUTURE

Ontogeny was conceived by Freud as psychosexual development culminating in the resolution of the Oedipus complex. In a footnote to *Three Essays on Sexuality*, Freud (1905/1964) asserted:

> It has been justly said that the Oedipus complex is the nuclear complex of the neuroses, and constitutes the essential part of their content ... Every new arrival on this planet is faced by the task of mastering the Oedipus complex ... With the progress of psycho-analytic studies the importance of the Oedipus complex has became more and more clearly evident; its recognition has become the shibboleth that distinguishes the adherents of psycho-analysis from its opponents (p. 226).

In keeping with this view, Freud's critique of religion rests firmly on the cornerstone of the Oedipus complex. Belief in god finds its origin in the child's desire for maternal protection and care. From this origin, religious belief evolves into the form of a father-god in keeping with the increased focus and conflict with the father within the Oedipal constellation. Is Freud correct in his reduction? In my view, Freud was both correct and limited in this assessment. He was correct in illustrating the dynamics of identification and projection in God-representational processes. He was also correct in placing emphasis on God-representational processes in the oedipal phase. Further, there are instances in clinical practice in which the leitmotif of the Oedipal, ambivalently held God the Father, articulates accurately an individual's God representation, its dynamic origin and the compromise formations that it serves. As salient as this model is, it is inadequate to describe the legion of self and object representations and the multiple dynamics which are contained in religious experience. Freud's view was limited by his unidimensional understanding of the Oedipus complex.

Freud brought both the method and theory of psychoanalysis to bear on Feuerbach's critique of religion as a human enterprise of projection. Psychoanalysis views these processes of identification and projection within the context of unconscious conflict. It is its approach to religion as a solution to an intrapsychic conflict as well as a response to humanity's ontological situation that marks a significant contribution. Freud's analysis leads to an appraisal of the function of God-representations and religion, in toto, along topographic, structural, economic, genetic and dynamic lines. This perspective posits religious experience to be a dynamic, multi-dimensional process. For example, within the structural approach, the influence of religion, vis-a-vis, processes of internalization and projection, may be seen to contribute significantly to super-ego functioning. Religious experience, seen in this light, is far more than theistic beliefs; rather, as an ingredient of the structure of the psychic apparatus it contributes to the psychological equilibrium of the human organism. Religion participates silently in the mental operations, which dictate behavior and consequence. Religious ideas and object relations serve a multiverse of functions. This view expands the horizon of inquiry into the nature of religious experience. In Freud's analysis, however, this horizon was contained within the Oedipus complex. This leads to a consideration of the Oedipus complex: its universality and comprehensiveness.

For Freud the Oedipus complex referred to specific libidinal and aggressive conflicts centered around the gradual triangulation of child's relationship with his or her parents. Anthropological studies for the most part have not substantiated Freud's thesis of the universality of the Oedipus complex; debate continues to ensue regarding the interpretation of such investigations [See Malinowski, 1927; Spiro, 1982]. The failure to support the universality of the Oedipus complex necessarily calls into question the claim that all religious experience bears the mark of Oedipus. This leads to a second concern regarding the comprehensiveness of the Oedipus complex as a template for understanding religious experience.

The Oedipus complex remains for many psychoanalysts today the cornerstone of psychoanalytic work and theory [See Panel, 1985; Feldman, 1990; Greenberg, 1991; Loewald: 1979; Wisdom: 1984]; however, for many theorists it refers to processes that go beyond the categories of drive theory. For example, Loewald (1983, p. 439) points to its function as "a watershed in individuation" in which drive conflict is seen within the context of the developing self. In his view emphasis is placed on object relations that become internalized as structures of the self within the oedipal phase. Chasseguet-Smirgel (1988), although not convinced of its phylogenetic nature, nervertheless views the Oedipus complex as an innate schema through which the capacity for establishing categories and classifying impressions leads to structure formation. Kohut (1977, 1984), although rejecting the psychobiology of drive theory, maintains the importance of the Oedipus complex in terms of the parents' attunement to the child's emerging Oedipal self. When we examine the validity of the Oedipus complex as a template for religious experience we must first establish which Oedipus complex do we mean?

Freud's understanding of the Oedipus complex is restrictive and inadequate to capture *all* of the facets of development and conflict. Toews (1999) finds that,

Freud assumed a universality apparently incompatible with contemporary notions of cultural otherness, difference, heterogeneity, and pluralism. With the theory of the Oedipus complex (however variable and flexible, it might work itself out in individual cases) Freud affirmed the ultimately homologous character of processes of acculturation in all humsan cultural formations across space and time; the production of the human was presented as a single plot with variations (p. 111).

However limited, his theory does articulate important constituents of God-representational processes as related to drive conflict and structural theory. He locates religious belief and experience within the intrapsychic realm of conflict and compromise and demonstrates the utility of God-representations in the economy of psychic operation and structure. Although Freud did not develop a comprehensive understanding of object relations, his inquiries into internalization and the processes leading to the formation of the super-ego anticipated a more complete explication of the internal world of objects.[7] Was Freud incorrect in positing that a God-representation is a displacement from the Oedipal father vis-a-vis processes of identification and projection? No, Freud was not wrong, however, he was limited by the metapsychology that he invented. His limitation lies in the narrowly conceived catalogue of meanings for religious experience posited by drive theory. In a more contemporary view of psychological functioning, considering multiple developmental lines within the realms of pre-Oedipal and Oedipal experience, religious experiences are seen to hold the potential to express a host of meanings and serve a number of functions. Rizzuto (1979), in her landmark study, *The Birth of the Living God*, proposed that the formation of the image of God is an object representational process that originates within the transitional space and that occurs, shaped by ever-present psychodynamics throughout the life of the individual. Although God-representations may derive in part from the processes which Freud described in terms of identification and projection of the father, her understanding goes beyond Freud's in asserting that "[God-representation] is more than the cornerstone upon which it was built. It is a *new* original representation which, because it is new, may have the varied components that serve to soothe and comfort, provide inspiration and courage – or dread and terror – far beyond that inspired by the actual parents" (Rizzuto, 1979, p. 46). It may be concluded that Freud initiated an inquiry into the psychodynamics, which are involved in God-representations.

His view of wish fulfillment as the basis for religious illusions represents a partial understanding. If the notion of wish is construed beyond the parameters of drive, then Freud's thesis accounts for many aspects of religious motivation. Psychoanalysis does not have the ability to reduce all religious motivation and experience to the determinants of wish. Nor would a demonstration of such an occurrence establish or deny the veracity of religious beliefs or experience. Psychoanalysis provides a unique perspective and method, however, to examine a particular class of influences. This leads us to his critique of culture. Does religion serve the function of renunciation? A definitive answer cannot be found outside of an individual's psychodynamics. Freud's analysis of the function of religion as renunciation, and his comparison of religious practices to the obsessive actions of neurotics, in certain instances yields a valid appraisal. However, as Meissner (1991, 1992, 1996) and Vergote (1988) have convincingly argued, it is not religion per se but rather how an individual is religious that determines the function of religious belief and practice. It is within the consulting room that the nature of the influence of religion in the resolution of conflict and the formation of identity can be surmised.

Freud's contributions to the study of religion are significant in terms of the perspective that he offers; it is one which posits the crucial influence of unconscious processes in religious experience. Although Freud's reliance on phylogeny and his exclusive focus on the Oedipus complex is inadequate, in light of our current knowledge, these speculative texts, nevertheless, demonstrate the potential of applied psychoanalysis in which insights gleaned from clinical investigation may be employed in the study of culture. His contributions offer a perspective and a method of inquiry into the unconscious constituents of religious experience. His significance lies not in his definitive analysis of religion and culture but rather in commencing the psychoanalytic study of religion.

References

Bernstein, R.J. (1998). *Freud and the legacy of Moses*. Cambridge: Cabridge University Press.

Bingham, K.A. (2003). *Freud and faith*. Albany, NY: State University of New York Press.

Blass, R.B. (2003). The puzzle of Freud's puzzle analogy: Reviving a struggle between doubt and conviction in *Moses and monotheism*. *International Journal of Psychoanalysis, 84,* 669–682.

Blass, R.B. (2004). Beyond illusion: Psychoanalysis and the question of religious truth. *International Journal of Psychoanalysis, 85,* 615–634.

Brenner, C. (1994), The mind as conflict and compromise formation. *Journal of Clinical Psycho-Analysis, 3,* 473–496.

THE PSYCHOANALYTIC STUDY OF RELIGION: PAST, PRESENT, FUTURE 27

Brenner, C. (2002). Conflict, compromise formation, and structural theory. *Psychoanalytic Quarterly, 71,* 397–418.

DiCenso, J. (1994). Symbolism and subjectivity: A Lacanian approach to religion. *Journal of Religion, 74*(1), 45–64.

DiCenso, J. (1996). Totem and Taboo and the constitutive function of symbolic forms. *Journal of the American Academy of Religion, 64*(3), 557–574.

DiCenso, J. (1999). *The other Freud. Religion, culture and psychoanalysis.* London: Routledge.

Earle, W.J. (1997). Illusions with futures. In J.L. Jacobs & D. Capps (Eds.), *Religion, society, and psychoanalysis* (pp. 218–229). Boulder, CO: Westview Press.

Fink, B. (1997). *A clinical introduction to Lacanian psychoanalysis.* Cambridge, MA: Harvard University Press.

Fisher, D.J. (1991). *Cultural theory and psychoanalytic tradition.* New Brunswick, NJ: Transaction Publishers.

Foucault, M. (1970). *The order of things: An archeology of the human sciences.* New York: Random House.

Freud, S. (1907/1964). Obsessive actions and religious practices. In J. Strachey (Ed. & Trans.), *The standard edition of the complete psychological works of Sigmund Freud* (Vol. 9, pp. 115–127). London: Hogarth Press. (Original work published 1907).

Freud, S. (1908/1964). 'Civilized' sexual morality and modern nervous illness". In J. Strachey (Ed. & Trans.), *The standard edition of the complete psychological works of Sigmund Freud* (Vol. 9, pp. 181–204). London: Hogarth Press. (Original work published 1908).

Freud, S. (1913/1964). On beginning the treatment. In J. Strachey (Ed. & Trans.), *The standard edition of the complete psychological works of Sigmund Freud* (Vol. 12, pp. 121–144). London: Hogarth Press. (Original work published 1913).

Freud, S. (1913/1964). Totem and taboo. In J. Strachey (Ed. & Trans.), *The standard edition of the complete psychological works of Sigmund Freud* (Vol. 13, pp. 1–162). London: Hogarth Press. (Original work published 1913).

Freud, S. (1927/1964). The future of an illusion. In J. Strachey (Ed. & Trans.), *The standard edition of the complete psychological works of Sigmund Freud* (Vol. 21, pp. 5–56). London: Hogarth Press. (Original work published 1927).

Freud, S. (1930/1964). Civilization and its discontents. In J. Strachey (Ed. & Trans.), *The standard edition of the complete psychological works of Sigmund Freud* (Vol. 21, pp. 167–172). : Hogarth Press. (Original work published 1930).

Freud, S. (1933/1964). The question of a weltanschauung. New introductory lectures, Lecture XXXV. In J. Strachey (Ed. & Trans.), *The standard edition of the complete psychological works of Sigmund Freud* (Vol. 22, pp. 158–182). London: Hogarth Press. (Original work published 1933).

Freud, S. (1935/1964) Postscript. In J. Strachey (Ed. & Trans.), *The standard edition of the complete psychological works of Sigmund Freud* (Vol. 20, pp. 71–74). London: Hogarth Press. (Original work published 1935).

Freud, S. (1939/1964). Moses and monotheism. In J. Strachey (Ed. & Trans.), *The standard edition of the complete psychological works of Sigmund Freud* (Vol. 23, pp. 3–139). London: Hogarth Press. (Original work published 1939).

Gardiner, S. (1993). *Irrationality and the philosophy of psychoanalysis*. Cambridge, England: Cambridge University Press.

Grotstein, J.S. (2000). *Who is the dreamer who dreams the dream*. Hillsdale, NJ: The Analytic Press.

Jonte-Pace, D. (2001). *Speaking the unspeakable. Religion, misogyny and the uncanny mother in Freud's cultural texts*. Berkeley, CA: University of California Press.

Kovel, J. (1988). *The radical spirit*. London: Free Association Books.

Kristeva, J. (1980). *Desire in language: A semiotic approach to literature and art*. New York: Columbia University Press.

Kristeva, J. (trans. M. Waller) (1984). *Revolution in poetic language*. New York: Columbia University Press.

Kristeva, J. (trans. L.S. Roudiez) (1984). *Tales of love*. New York: Columbia University Press.

Laplance, J. (1999). *Essays on otherness*. London: Routledge.

Lifton, R.J. (2000). Whose psychohistory? In P. Brooks & A. Woloch (Eds.), *Whose Freud? The place of contemporary psychoanalysis in contemporary culture* (pp. 222–228). New Haven, CT: Yale University Press.

Meissner, W.W. (1984). *Psychoanalysis and religious experience*. New Haven, CT: Yale University Press.

Obeysekere, G. (1990). *The work of culture*. Chicago: The University of Chicago Press.

Parsons, W.B. (1999). *The enigma of the oceanic feeling*. New York: Oxford University Press.

Paul, R.A. (1996). *Moses and civilization. The meaning behind Freud's myth*. New Haven, CT: Yale University Press.

Raschke, C. (1997). God and Lacanian psychoanalysis. In J.L. Jacobs & D. Capps (Eds.), *Religion, society, and psychoanalysis* (pp. 230–239). Boulder, CO: Westview Press.

Ricoeur, P. (1970). *Freud and Philosophy: An Essay on Interpretation.* translated by D. Savage, New Haven: Yale University Press.

Ritvo, L. (1990). *Darwin's influence on Freud*. New Haven: Yale University Press.

Rizzuto, A-M., & Shafranske, E.P. (2013). Addressing religion and spirituality in treatment from a psychodynamic perspective. In K.I. Pargament, A. Mahoney, E.P. Shafranske (Eds.), *APA handbook of psychology, religion, and spirituality (Vol 2): An applied psychology of religion and spirituality* (pp. 125–146). Washington, DC US: American Psychological Association. doi:10.1037/14046-006

Shafranske, E.P. (1995). Freudian theory and religious experience. In R. Hood, Jr. (Ed.). *Handbook of the psychology of religious experience* (pp. 200–230). Birmingham: Religious Education Press.

Solms, M. (1998). Before and after Freud's *Project*. In R.M. Bilder & F.F. LeFever (Eds.), *Neuroscience of the Mind on the Centennial of Freud's Project for a Scientific Psychology*, Annals of the New York Academy of Sciences, Volume 843 (pp. 1–10). New York: New York Academy of Sciences.

Toews, J. (1999). Historicizing the psyche of psychohistory. In N. Ginsburg & R. Ginsberg (Eds.), *Psychoanalysis and culture at the millennium* (pp. 96–114). New Haven, CT: Yale University Press.

Van Herik, J. (1982). *Freud on femininity and faith*. Berkeley, CA: University of California Press.

Vergote, A. (2002). At the crossroads of the personal word. In M. Arieti & F. De Nardi (Eds.), *Psychoanalisi e religione* (pp.4–34). Torino, Italy: Centro Scientifico Editore. [Il significanto dell'esperienza religiosa.]

Wulff, D.M. (1997). *Psychology of religion: Classic and contemporary.* New York: John Wiley & Sons.

CHAPTER 2

Two Contributions to the Research of Symbols

Karl Abraham

Abstract

This article notes how the three bodily openings (the mouth, the anus, and the genitals) preoccupy children long before awareness of how the genitals include any sexual connotations. Abraham notes how these three appear in fairy tales and myths and become part of childhood dreams analyzed in the therapeutic process. He relates the fairy tale entitled "The magic table" in which a father rewards each of his three sons a magic gift after they finish learning a trade. One receives a table that can be filled with food. The second the gift of excreted gold and the third a stick that can overthrow all enemies. This fairy tale relates to the wishful fantasies involving the three erogenous zone that must be modulated and overcome in early childhood ego development. He notes how such fantasies are integral to the dynamics and resolution of the Oedipal Complex as understood in psychoanalytic theory. [Editors]

1 The Symbolic Meaning of the Number Three

For a long time we have been aware of the frequency of the number three in all products of human fantasy. We know, too, that it has been given different symbolic meanings. Particularly well-known is the meaning of "three" as a symbol for the male genitals, as well as the allusion contained in it to the trinity of father, mother and child. Time and again in the dreams of my analysands I have encountered another, lesser-known meaning in the number three. Here I have in mind a typical one, grounded in universal human conditions rather than the manifold possibilities of determinations of the symbolism of numbers peculiar to individuals.

There are three body openings which capture the attention of the child in strongest measure, because they serve the ingestion and engestion of substances as well as possess the most important erogenous functions: the oral, anal, and urogenital zones. They appear to me to be represented in dreams through the number three particularly when the establishment of genital primacy fails, and these three erogenous zones are in competition with each other. A neurotic female patient, whose dreams demonstrated to me this meaning

© KONINKLIJKE BRILL NV, LEIDEN, 2021 | DOI:10.1163/9789004429222_003

TWO CONTRIBUTIONS TO THE RESEARCH OF SYMBOLS

of the number three in especially vivid fashion, produced in her unconscious a maximum of oral-cannibalistic and anal wish fantasies.

I became interested in being able to identify this same meaning of three also in fairy-tales or myths, whose extensive psychological correspondence with individual fantasies has been unveiled to us by psychoanalysis. A very impressive parallel relative to this [sexual] meaning of the number three is offered to us in the fairy tale of "Tischlein deck dich!" [German for "The magic table" or "Little table set yourself!"]

A father sends his three sons into another country. Each learns a trade and, after the apprenticeship is over, receives a gift from his master: the oldest [receives] a little table that upon command will set itself with all the desired foods, the second an ass that defecates gold pieces at the words: Ass, stretch yourself! The third receives a sack with a cudgel (a stick) in it; at the command of the owner the cudgel comes out of the sack and beats any of its master's opponents, and likewise on command goes back into the sack.

The first gift signifies a wish fulfillment in the area of the oral zone. Indeed, every child wishes that the "omnipotence of his thoughts" could be capable of providing whatever he wants to eat whenever he wants it.

It is the same with the second gift! The admiration of excrement and its identification with gold is known to us from child psychology. We find in the second gift the realization of the wish to be able to procure for himself whatever riches he would like in the way of anal production.

The meaning of the third gift is not quite so clear, but will become comprehensible without difficulty when we remember the typical symbolic meaning of the stick. The sack with the stick then cannot be misconstrued, and the command which the owner of the gift gives the stick: "Cudgel out of the sack!" and "Cudgel in the sack!" reveals clearly the sense of erection and the opposite process. The third son thus receives the gift of unlimited potency which obeys the will absolutely.

The fairy-tale thus contains three wish fulfillments in metaphors for the three erogenous zones. It is interesting that the sequence is the same as that of the organizational stages of the libido discovered by Freud. In the first stage the mouth receives the dominant erogenous meaning, in the second the anus, in the third, definitive stage, the genitals.

It is further to be noted that the two older brothers make fun of the youngest at the beginning of the fairy-tale. The oldest, however, soon loses the miraculous little table to a deceitful innkeeper with whom he spends the night on the way home and brings home an ordinary table. At home he is derided by his father as he tries in vain to obtain delicious food from the table. It goes no better for the second brother with the ass. He, too, is deceived by the innkeeper and derided by the father. On the basis of the psychoanalytic research of fairy-tales it is to be assumed without further ado that both innkeeper and father signify the jealous father. Only the youngest son defeats the innkeeper through his masculinity, symbolized by the cudgel; it is also he who is given the father's approval at home.

Thus the fairy-tale confirms the real-life experience that it is not the infantile fantasies of oral or anal origin, but rather only the successful establishment of genital primacy constitutes the man. But it is particularly instructive for us through its symbolism of the number three.

2 The "Three way Intersection" in the Oedipus[1] Legend

In a short article on the symbolism of a neurotic rescue fantasy,[2] I attempted to demonstrate that this fantasy of rescuing one's father corresponds extensively to the Oedipus legend not merely in terms of its latent content. I endeavored to show that in the representation of this similar content, both creations of fantasy also employ a very similar symbolism which until now had not aroused our full attention. In the latent content of both creations of fantasy the son is a witness to the sexual intercourse of the parents; he seeks to prevent it by killing the father and thus rescuing the mother.

The encounter of the son with the father's carriage travelling at full speed (coitus-symbolism!) takes place in the Oedipus myth in a particular location. In different versions of the legend a "narrow pass" or a "crossroad" is mentioned. The narrow pass as a symbol of the feminine genitals would be in complete harmony with the rest of the symbolism. The explanation appears more difficult in the other case; "Odos sxiste," strictly speaking, means not "crossroad," but rather is most correctly translated as "fork in the road." In a translation of the tragedy of Sophocles we find the expression "three-way [intersection]." As much and as suitably as the "narrow pass" as a symbol fits our understanding, so little does the "three-way intersection" appear at first glance to be comprehensible from the same point of view.

Prof. Freud called my attention to this difficulty in detail when I sent him the above-mentioned article asking for his critique. One particular explanation seemed obvious in any case. The fork in the road – similar to the Heracles legend – could signify a doubt on the part of the wanderer, for Oedipus was indeed in dreadful doubt about his future when he met King Laios. But such an

---

1 For consistency, the following form will be used for Oedipus.

2 Cf. *Internat. Z. f. Psychoanalyse* v Ill. p. 7If. It is the fantasy of some neurotics to rescue the king (or other high-ranking personality) at the moment when his carriage's runaway horses put his life in greatest danger.

TWO CONTRIBUTIONS TO THE RESEARCH OF SYMBOLS

interpretation would be much too expedient, and certainly would not exhaust the latent content of this part of the myth. Moreover, it would not satisfy an objection: the locality is so described to us that there is room only for Oedipus or for Laios' carriage – at a fork in the road, however, passing would be easily possible. An interpretation of the oddity can satisfy us only if it also explains this peculiarity of the story.

With regard for these difficulties I considered this particular question thoroughly. Shortly afterwards a dream which I had to analyze with one of my [male] patients brought me an explanation of the three-way intersection which appears to me to satisfy all demands. The dream narrative runs:

> My mother has died and I take part in the burial. The scene then becomes unclear. I walk away and then return to the grave. Thereby I have the impression it is in Russia and Bolsheviks had desecrated it. A hole is drilled in the ground; I see something white in the depths like perhaps a shroud. Then the place changes again. Mother's grave is now in a place where two streets run together to form a wide highway. It sticks up just a little above the surrounding soil. As a result, carriages drive over it. These disappear and now I myself drive back and forth over it.

The analysis reveals the incestuous character of the dream. Pronounced necrophilic fantasies exist in the unconscious of the patient; only when the mother was dead could he take possession of her belongings. The act of violence against the mother (the drilling of the hole in the burial mound) is ascribed to the Bolsheviks because of censure; in our patients' dreams these often represent their own wish impulses which fly in the face of all conventional morals. According to the free associations of the dreamer, the shroud visible in the depths means the uncoveredness of the body; "dark" is associated with "white" (covering of hair). In place of the dreamer's own unconscious desire to do violence to his mother, we find the deed already done in the dream by other people, which is demonstrated in the linguistic relationship, in that we speak of a "desecration of a grave" [*Grabschändung*] as well as of the violation [*Schändung*] of a woman.

The indeterminate number of perpetrators ("Bolsheviks") return once again in the dream in the form of the many carriages which drive over the grave. If earlier the grave represented the mother who was violated by many men, the identification of mother and prostitute is now more than clear. The place in which several streets run together naturally exhibits particularly busy traffic. We remember here that places of the heaviest traffic are often used as symbols of prostitution (train station, warehouse, etc.). At the same time, however, we bear in mind the meaning of the street as a symbol of the feminine genitals, [and the meaning] of the carriage as a symbol of the masculine genitals. The "driving back and forth" over that place likewise is no longer to be misunderstood.

Another assertion of the manifest dream content, that the grave rises a little above the ground, is important. It becomes understandable from our patient's repressed fantasies of finding a protrusion (penis) on the female body. In many of his dreams the mother appears in a masculine [role], he himself in a feminine role; in the dream at hand he himself is the active member, under, of course, the singular condition that the mother is no longer alive.

The grave of the mother thus represents her body, and in particular her genitals. Both dream scenes refer to this. In the first scene the hole in the grave mound, and in the second scene the small protrusion above the ground was comprehensible to us in this sense. A particular allusion, hardly to be misunderstood any longer, reveals to us the place in which this shallow grave lies the two streets which come together to form a wide highway are the thighs which turn into the torso. The place where they run together is the genitals!

The dreamer thus comes to the way in which a number of men are busy with his mother. They disappear and he takes possession of her. But it [also] happened exactly this way in the Oedipus legend. Oedipus meets Laios (together with a number of other men) at the three-way intersection, slays him and the others, and then sets out on the path to his mother. If we understand the symbolism of the legend in this way, the struggle of Oedipus with Laios is a struggle for the genitals of the mother. Now we understand why it is that for father and son there is no giving way to one another.

We thus come to the unexpected outcome that the three-way intersection has the same meaning as the narrow pass. The former refers to the location of the female genitals, the latter to its shape. Nonetheless, each version contains a different tendency. The version with the three-way intersection (the place of busy traffic) contains with particular clarity the representation of the mother as prostitute. The encounter in the narrow pass expresses another notion, namely the fantasy of meeting with the father before birth in the mother's body (fantasy of intra-uterine observation of coitus). There is more about this in my above-mentioned article.

Editor's Note. Karl Abraham was a German psychoanalyst who Freud called his "best pupil." By this he could not have meant that he was Freud's best patient because we have no evidence that Abraham was ever analyzed by anybody. He did become one of the clearest explicators of analytic ideas about early childhood development. To that extent he clarified and amplified for Freud ideas that were more implicit than explicit. Although early childhood was his primary focus, Abraham's theorizing about manic-depressive psychosis was the primary rationale that led to Freud's paper on "Mourning and Melancholia" Abraham was already practicing psychoanalysis in the Jungian model before meeting Freud at a conference in Berlin. He became a close confidant and was often part of public meetings with Freud. Freud criticized Abraham's ideas privately but supported him publicly in his production of four books and 49 papers. His most important work was: *A Short History of the Development of the Libido, Viewed in Light of Mental Disorders.*

Although he was the son of a Jewish religious teacher, Abraham gave up Judaism and joined an anti-Zionist society. He only wrote one religious article and that concerned Amenhotep IV's Cult of Aton. Although he showed deep interest in philosophy and the symbols of libidinal development and ego defenses, he did not participate in Freud preoccupation with organized religion and did not relate his ideas in any way to the influence of parental religiousness.

CHAPTER 3

If Moses were an Egyptian . . .

Sigmund Freud

To deprive a people the man whom they take pride in as the greatest of its sons is not something that one will gladly or easily do, especially if one belongs to this people himself. But no example will move you to reset the truth in favor of supposed national interests, and one can also expect a gain in our understanding from the clarification of a fact may be expected to bring us gain in knowledge.

The man Moses, who was a liberator, legislator and founder of religion to the Jewish people, belongs to such remote times that one cannot avoid the question of whether he is a historical figure or a creation of the saga. If he lived, it was in the 13th, or maybe in the 14th century BC; we have no other information about him than from the holy books and the written traditions of the Jews. Therefore, even if the decision lacks ultimate security, the vast majority of historians have argued that Moses really lived and that the exodus from Egypt linked to him did indeed take place. It is rightly claimed that the later history of the people of Israel would be incomprehensible if this condition were not admitted. Today's science has become more cautious and is far more careful with traditions than in the early days of historical criticism.

The first thing that attracts our interest in the person of Moses is the name that is in Hebrew Moshe. One can ask; where does it come from? what does it mean? As is well known, the report in Exodus, Chap. 2 an answer. There it is said that the Egyptian princess, who saved the boy exposed in the Nile, gave him this name with the etymological reason: because I pulled him out of the water. This explanation alone is clearly inadequate. "The biblical interpretation of the name 'The one drawn from the water'", judges an author in the "Jewish Lexicon"[1] "is folk etymology with which the active Hebrew form ('Moshe' can at most mean 'the extractor') does not come in There are two other reasons to support this rejection. First, it is nonsensical to attribute an Egyptian princess a name derived from Hebrew, and second, the water from which the child was drawn is most likely was not the water of the Nile.

On the other hand, the assumption has long been made and from various sides that the name Moses comes from the Egyptian vocabulary. Instead of

---

1 Jüdisches Lexikon, begründet von Herlitz und Kirschner, Bd. IV, 1930, Jüdischer Verlag, Berlin.

listing all the authors who have expressed themselves in this way, I want to use the corresponding passage translated from a recent book by J. H. Breasted[2], an author whose "History of Egypt" (1906) is considered authoritative. "It is noteworthy that his (this leader) name, Moses, was Egyptian. It is simply the Egyptian word 'mose', which means 'child', and is the abbreviation of fuller forms of names such as B. Amen-mose, that is Amon-child or Ptah-mose, Ptah-child, which names are themselves abbreviations of the longer sentences: Amon (gave a child) or Ptah (gave a child). The name 'child' soon became a convenient replacement for the extensive full name and the name form 'Moses' is not uncommon on Egyptian monuments. The father of Moses had certainly given his son a name made up of Ptah or Amon and the name of God gradually fell out in everyday life until the boy was simply called 'Moses'. (The 's' at the end of the name Moses comes from the Greek translation of the Old Testament. It also does not belong to the Hebrew, where the name is 'Moshe'.) I have reproduced the passage literally and am in no way ready to take responsibility for sharing their details. I am also a little surprised that Breasted's list has just overridden the analog theophoric names that appear on the list of Egyptian kings such as Ah-mose, Thut-mose (Tothmes) and Ra-mose (Ramses).

Now one should expect that any of the many who recognized the name of Moses as Egyptian would have drawn the conclusion or at least considered the possibility that the bearer of the Egyptian name himself was an Egyptian. For modern times we allow such conclusions without hesitation, although at present one person does not have one name, but two, surnames and first names, and although changes in names and adjustments are not excluded under newer conditions. We are then by no means surprised to find it confirmed that the poet Chamisso is of French origin, Napoleon Buonaparte is Italian, and that Benjamin Disraeli is really an Italian Jew, as his name suggests. And for old and early times, one would think that such a conclusion from name to ethnicity should be far more reliable and actually appear to be mandatory. Nevertheless, as far as I know, no historian has reached this conclusion in the case of Moses, nor any of those who, like Breasted, are ready to assume that Moses was "familiar with the wisdom of the Egyptians".[3]

What stood in the way is not guessable. Perhaps respect for biblical tradition was insurmountable. Perhaps the idea that the man of Moses should have been something other than a Hebrew seemed too outrageous. In any case, it turns out that the recognition of the Egyptian name is not decisive for the assessment of Moses' descent, that nothing is inferred from it. If the question of

---

2 *The Dawn of Conscience*, London 1934, p. 350.

3 *The Dawn of Conscience*, London 1934, p. 334.

the nationality of this great man is considered significant, it would be desirable to provide new material to answer it.

This is what my little treatise does. Your claim for a place in the magazine "Imago" is based on the fact that your contribution has an application of psychoanalysis. The argument gained in this way will certainly only make an impression on the minority of readers who are familiar with analytical thinking and who appreciate the results. Hopefully it will seem important to you.

In 1909, O. Rank, at that time still under my influence, published a writing on my suggestion entitled "The Myth of the Birth of the Hero".[4] It deals with the fact that "almost all worshiping cultures ... early on their heroes, legendary kings and princes, founders of religion, founders of dynasties, empires and cities, briefly glorified their national heroes in poems and legends". "In particular, they have given the birth and youth history of these people fantastic features, whose astonishing similarity, sometimes even literal correspondence, among various, sometimes very separate and completely independent peoples has long been known and has been noticed by many researchers", for example in Dalton's technique, an "average saga" that highlights the main features of all these stories, you get the following picture:

> "The hero is the child of the most distinguished parents, usually a king's son.
>
> Difficulties precede its emergence, such as abstinence or prolonged infertility or secret intercourse between parents as a result of external prohibitions or obstacles. During pregnancy or earlier, there is a warning (dream, oracle) before birth that usually threatens the father.
>
> As a result, the newborn child is usually determined to be killed or abandoned at the instigation of the father or the person representing him; usually it is given to the water in a box.
>
> It is then rescued by animals or minor people (shepherds) and nursed by a female animal or minor woman.
>
> Growing up, it finds the distinguished parents in a very changeable way, takes revenge on the father on the one hand, is recognized on the other hand and achieves greatness and fame."

The oldest of the historical figures to whom this birth myth was linked is Sargon of Agade, the founder of Babylon (around 2800 BC). It is not without interest for us to reproduce the report attributed to him here:

---

4   Fifth issue of "Writings on Applied Soul Science", Mrs. Deuticke, Vienna. I am far from reducing the value of Rank's independent contributions to this work.

"Sargon, the mighty king, I am king of Agade. My mother was a vestal, I didn't know my father while my father's brother lived in the mountains. In my city Azupirani, which is located on the banks of the Euphrates, I became pregnant with the mother, the Vestalin.

She gave birth to me in secret. She put me in a reed jar, sealed my door with earth pitch, and let me down in the stream, which did not drown me. The stream led me to Akki, the water creator. Akki, the water creator, in the kindness of his heart, lifted me out. Akki, the water creator, raised me as his own son. Akki, the water creator, he made me his gardener. Istar became dear to me in my gardening office, I became king and 45 years of kingship."

The most familiar names in the series beginning with Sargon of Agade are Moses, Kyros, and Romulus. In addition, Rank has put together a large number of heroic characters belonging to poetry or legend, who are said to have the same youth history, either in their entirety or in well-known parts, as: Oedipus, Karna, Paris, Telephos, Perseus, Heracles, Gilgamesch, Amphion, and Zethos, etc.

The source and tendency of this myth have been made known to us by Rank's studies. I need only refer to it with brief indications. A hero is someone who courageously rose up against his father and ultimately won over him. Our myth continues this struggle to the primeval age of the individual, in that he has the child born against the will of the father and saved against his evil intent. The suspension in the box is an unmistakable symbolic representation of the birth, the box the womb, the water the birth water. In countless dreams, the parent-child relationship is represented by pulling out of the water or saving from the water. If folk fantasy attaches the birth myth discussed here to an outstanding personality, it wants to acknowledge the person concerned as a hero, and announce that he has fulfilled the pattern of a heroic life. The source of the whole poetry, however, is the so-called "family novel" of the child, in which the son reacts to the change in his emotional relationship with the parents, especially the father. The early years of childhood were dominated by a great overestimation of the father, who, according to king and queen, always meant only the parents in dreams and fairy tales, while later, under the influence of rivalry and real disappointment, the separation from the parents and the critical attitude towards the father began. The two families of the myth, the noble and the low, are both reflections of their own family as it appears to the child in successive lifetimes.

It can be said that these explanations fully understand both the spread and the uniformity of the myth of the hero's birth. It is therefore all the more worthy of our interest that the legend of Moses' birth and exposition occupies a special position, indeed contradicts the others in one essential point.

We start from the two families between which the saga lets the child's fate play. We know that they coincide in the analytical interpretation, but differ from each other only in time. In the typical form of the saga, the first family into which the child is born is the noble, usually a royal milieu; the second, in which the child grows up, the low or the low, as, incidentally, corresponds to the circumstances on which the interpretation is based. This difference is only blurred in the Oedipus stage. The child abandoned from one royal family is taken in by another royal couple. It is said that it is hardly a coincidence that the original identity of the two families shines through in the saga in this example. The social contrast of the two families opens up a second function to the myth, which, as we know, is intended to emphasize the heroic nature of the great man, which is particularly significant for historical figures. It can also be used to create a noble letter for the hero, to raise him socially. So Kyros is a foreign conqueror for the Medes, on the way of the suspension legend he becomes the grandson of the Med king. Similar to Romulus; if a person corresponding to him lived, it was a runaway adventurer, an upstart; through the legend he becomes the descendant and heir of the royal family of Alba Longa.

It is quite different in the case of Moses. Here is the first family, otherwise the distinguished one, humble enough. He is the child of Jewish Levites. The second, however, the low family, in which the hero usually grows up, has been replaced by the royal family of Egypt; the princess is raising him as her own son. This deviation from the type has seemed strange to many. Ed. Meyer, and others after him, assumed that the saga was originally different: the pharaoh had been warned by a prophetic dream[5] that a son would endanger his daughter and him and the rich man. He therefore has the child abandoned in the Nile after his birth.

But it is saved by Jewish people and raised as their child. As a result of "national motives", as Rank puts it,[6] the saga was reworked into the form we know.

But the next consideration teaches that such an original Mosque saga, which no longer differs from the others, cannot have existed. Because the legend is of either Egyptian or Jewish origin. The first case is mutually exclusive; Egyptians had no motive to glorify Moses, he was no hero for them. So the legend should be created in the Jewish people, i.e., in its known form, have been linked to the person of the leader. For this alone it was quite unsuitable,

---

5   Also mentioned in the report by Flavius Josephus.
6   *The Dawn of Conscience*, London 1934, p. 80.

IF MOSES WERE AN EGYPTIAN . . .

for what was the fruit of a legend that made his great man a stranger to the people?

In the legend of Moses in the form before us today, it notably falls short of its secret intentions. If Moses was not of royal birth, the legend cannot make him a hero; if he remains a Jewish child, she has done nothing to increase him. Only a small part of the whole myth remains effective, the assurance that the child has survived in spite of strong external forces, and this trait has also been repeated in the childhood story of Jesus, in which King Herod takes on the role of Pharaoh. It is then really up to us to assume that any later, [creator of the myth] found himself obliged to put something similar to the classic, heroic, saga of exposure to his hero Moses, which due to the special circumstances of the case could not suit him.

Our investigation should be content with this unsatisfactory and, moreover, uncertain result and would have done nothing to answer the question of whether Moses was an Egyptian. But there is another, perhaps more hopeful approach to the appreciation of the suspension saga.

We return to the two families of the myth. We know that they are identical at the level of analytical interpretation, at the mythical level they differ as the noble and the lower. If, however, it is a historical person to whom the myth is linked, there is a third level, that of reality. One family is the real one in which the person, the great man, was really born and grew up; the other is fictional, from the myth in pursuit of it. As a rule, the real family coincides with the low, the fictitious with the noble. In the case of Moses, something seemed to be different. And now perhaps the new point of view leads to the clarification that the first family, from which the child is abandoned, in all cases that can be exploited, is the invented one, but the later one, in which it is taken up and raised, is the real. we suddenly realize clearly that Moses is a - probably distinguished Egyptian, who is supposed to be made a Jew by the legend. And that would be our result! The water exposure was in its right place; In order to comply with the new tendency, its intention had to be changed, not without violence; from an abandonment it became a means of rescue.

The deviation of the Moses legend from all others of its kind could, however, be attributed to a special feature of the history of Moses. While otherwise a hero rises above his low beginnings in the course of his life, the heroic life of the man Moses began by descending from his height, lowering himself to the children of Israel.

We undertook this little study in the expectation that it would give us a second, new argument for the presumption that Moses was an Egyptian. We have heard that the first argument, which has made from the name, has not made a decisive impression on many.[7] You must be prepared for the new argument, from the analysis of the statement, not to be better fortunate. The objection will be that the conditions of the formation and transformation of legends are too opaque to justify a conclusion like ours, and that the traditions of Moses' hero form, in its puzzle, contradictions, with the unmistakable signs of centuries of tendentious transformation and superimposition, must frustrate all efforts, the core of historical truth to bring it to light. I myself do not share this negative attitude, but I am also unable to reject it.

If there was no more certainty, why did I have this investigation in the first place? I regret that my justification cannot go beyond what has been suggested. If we allow ourselves to continue with the two arguments put forward here and try to get serious with the assumption that Moses was an excellent Egyptian, we have very interesting and far-reaching prospects. With certain, not-far-reaching assumptions, one believes to understand the motives motivated by Moses in his unusual move, and in close connection with that, one captures the possible rationale of the many characters and peculiarities of legislation and religion that he has given to the people of Jews, and encourages even meaningful views about the emergence of monotheistic religions in general. Only such an important account cannot be based on psychological probabilities alone. If the If one accepts the fact that Moses was an Egyptian and to be regarded as one historical fixture, a second fixed point is needed at least to protect the abundance of possibilities that arise against criticism that they are the product of imagination and too far from reality. An objective demonstration of the time in which Moses' life, and thus the exodus from Egypt, falls would have been sufficient for the need. But it did not find one, so it is better to leave unmentioned any further implications of the discovery that Moses was an Egyptian.

---

7 So sagt z. B. Ed. Meyer: Die Mosessagen und die Leviten, Berliner Sitzber. 1905: „Der Name Moše ist wahrscheinlich, der Name Pinchas in dem Priestergeschlecht von Silo ... zweifellos ägyptisch. Das beweist natürlich nicht, daß diese Geschlechter ägyptischen Ursprungs waren, wohl aber, daß sie Beziehungen zu Ägypten hatten" (p. 651). Man kann freilich fragen, an welche Art von Beziehungen man dabei denken soll.

CHAPTER 4

The Dogma of Christ

Erich Fromm

Abstract

Fromm endeavored to analyze religion to achieve an emancipation from constraints imposed by external societal forms. His views were shaped by his considerations of the influence of social processes on the individual in which religion played an important role. [Editors]

1 Methodology and the Nature of the Problem

It is one of the essential accomplishments of psychoanalysis that it has done away with the false distinction between social psychology and individual psychology. On the one hand, Freud emphasized that there is no individual psychology of man isolated from his social environment, because an isolated man does not exist. Freud knew no *homo psychologicus*, no psychological Robinson Crusoe, like the economic man of classical economic theory. On the contrary, one of Freud's most important discoveries was the understanding of the psychological development of the individual's earliest social relations those with his parents, brothers, and sisters.

"It is true" Freud wrote,

> ...that individual psychology is concerned with the individual man and explores the paths by which he seeks to find satisfaction for his instinctual impulses; but only rarely and under certain exceptional conditions is individual psychology in a position to disregard the relations of this individual to others. In the individual's mental life someone else is invariably involved, as a model, as an object, as a helper, as an opponent; and so from the very first, individual psychology, in this ex-tended but entirely justifiable sense of the words, is at the same time social psychology as well.[1]

---

[1] Sigmund Freud, Group Psychology and the Analysis of the Ego (London: Hogarth Press), *Standard Edition, XVIII*, 69.

On the other hand, Freud broke radically with the illusion of a social psychology whose object was "the group." For him, "social instinct" was not the object of psychology any more than isolated man was, since it was not an "original and elemental" instinct; rather, he saw "the beginning of the psyche's formation in a narrower circle, such as the family." He has shown that the psychological phenomena operative in the group are to be understood on the basis of the psychic mechanisms operative in the individual, not on the basis of a "group mind" as such.[2]

The difference between individual and social psychology is revealed to be a quantitative and not a qualitative one. Individual psychology takes into account all determinants that have affected the lot of the individual, and in this way arrives at a maximally complete picture of the individual's psychic structure. The more we extend the sphere of psychological investigation that is, the greater the number of men whose common traits permit them to be grouped the more we must reduce the extent of our examination of the total psychic structure of the individual members of the group. The greater, therefore, the number of subjects of an investigation in social psychology, the narrower the insight into the total psychic structure of any individual within the group being studied. If this is not recognized, misunderstandings will easily arise in the evaluation of the results of such investigations. One expects to hear something about the psychic structure of the individual member of a group, but the social-psychological investigation can study only the character matrix common to all members of the group, and does not take into account the total character structure of a particular individual. The latter can never be the task of social psychology, and is possible only if an extensive knowledge of the individual's development is available. If, for example, in a social-psychological investigation it is asserted that a group changes from an aggressive-hostile attitude toward the father figure to a passive-submissive attitude, this assertion means something different from the same statement when made of an individual in an individual-psychological investigation. In the latter case, it means that this change is true of the individual's total attitude; in the former, it means that it represents an average characteristic common to all the members of the

---

2 Georg Simmel has strikingly indicated the fallacy of accepting the group as a "subject," as a psychological phenomenon. He says: "The unified external result of many subjective psychological processes is interpreted as a result of a unified psychological process i.e., of a process in the collective soul. The unity of the resulting phenomenon is reflected in the presupposed unity of its psychological cause! The fallacy of this conclusion, however, upon which the whole of collective psychology depends in its general distinction from individual psychology, is obvious: the unity of collective actions, which appears only on the side of the visible result, is transferred surreptitiously to the side of the inner cause, the subjective bearer." "Uber das Wesen der Sozialpsychologie," Archiv fur Sozialwissenschaft und Sozialpolitik, XXVI (1908).

THE DOGMA OF CHRIST

group, which does not necessarily play a central role in the character structure of each individual. The value of social-psychological investigation, therefore, cannot lie in the fact that we acquire from it a full insight into the psychic peculiarities of the individual members, but only in the fact that we can establish those common psychic tendencies that play a decisive role in their social development.

The overcoming of the theoretical opposition between individual and social psychology accomplished by psycho-analysis leads to the judgment that the method of a social-psychological investigation can be essentially the same as the method which psychoanalysis applies in the investigation of the individual psyche. It will, therefore, be wise to consider briefly the essential features of this method, since it is of significance in the present study.

Freud proceeds from the view that in the causes producing neuroses – and the same holds for the instinctual structure of the healthy – an inherited sexual constitution and the events that have been experienced form a complementary series:

> At one end of the series stand those extreme cases concerning which you may say with confidence: These people would have fallen ill whatever happened, whatever they experienced, how-ever merciful life had been to them because of their anomalous libido-development. At the other end stand cases which call forth the opposite verdict they would undoubtedly have escaped illness if life had not put such and such burdens upon them. In the intermediate cases in the series, more or less of the disposing factor (the sexual constitution) is combined with less or more of the injurious impositions of life. Their sexual constitution would not have brought about their neurosis if they had not gone through such and such experiences, and life's vicissitudes would not have worked traumatically "upon them if the libido had been otherwise constituted".[3]

For psychoanalysis, the constitutional element in the psychic structure of the healthy or of the ill person is a factor that must be observed in the psychological investigation of individuals, but it remains intangible. What psychoanalysis is concerned with is experience; the investigation of its influence on emotional development is its primary purpose. Psychoanalysis is aware, of course, that the emotional development of the individual is determined more or less by his constitution; this insight is a presupposition of psychoanalysis, but

---

3 Sigmund Freud, *A General Introduction to Psychoanalysis* (New York: Liveright Publishing Corp., 1943), p. 304. Freud says "the two factors" are "sexual constitution and events experienced, or if you wish, fixation of libido and frustration"; they "are represented in such a way that where one of them predominates the other is proportionately less pronounced."

psychoanalysis itself is concerned exclusively with the investigation of the influence of the individual's life-situation on his emotional development. In practice this means that for the psychoanalytic method a maximum knowledge of the individual's history mainly of his early childhood experiences but certainly not limited to them is an essential prerequisite. It studies the relation between a person's life pattern and the specific aspects of his emotional development. Without extensive information concerning the individual's life pattern, analysis is impossible. General observation reveals, of course, that certain typical expressions of behavior will indicate typical life patterns. One could surmise corresponding patterns by analogy, but all such inferences would contain an element of uncertainty and would have limited scientific validity. The method of individual psychoanalysis is therefore a delicately "historical" method: the understanding of emotional development on the basis of knowledge of the individual's life history.

The method of applying psychoanalysis to groups cannot be different. The common psychic attitudes of the group members are to be understood only on the basis of their common patterns. Just as individual psychoanalytic psychology seeks to understand the individual emotional constellation, so social psychology can acquire an insight into the emotional structure of a group only by an exact knowledge of its life pattern. Social psychology can make assertions only concerning the psychic attitudes common to all; it therefore requires the knowledge of life situations common to all and characteristic for all.

If the method of social psychology is basically no different from that of individual psychology, there is, nevertheless, a difference which must be pointed out.

Whereas psychoanalytic research is concerned primarily with neurotic individuals, social-psychological research is concerned with groups of normal people.

The neurotic person is characterized by the fact that he has not succeeded in adjusting himself psychically to his real environment. Through the fixation of certain emotional impulses, of certain psychic mechanisms which at one time were appropriate and adequate, he comes into conflict with reality. The psychic structure of the neurotic is therefore almost entirely unintelligible without the knowledge of his early childhood experiences, for, due to his neurosis an expression of his lack of adjustment or of the particular range of infantile fixations even his position as an adult is determined essentially by that childhood situation. Even for the normal person the experiences of early childhood are of decisive significance. His character, in the broadest sense, is determined by them and without them it is unintelligible in its totality. But because he has adjusted himself psychically to reality in a higher degree than the

THE DOGMA OF CHRIST   47

neurotic, a much greater part of his psychic structure is understandable than in the case of the neurotic. Social psychology is concerned with normal people, upon whose psychic situation reality has an incomparably greater influence than upon the neurotic. Thus it can forgo even the knowledge of the individual childhood experiences of the various members of the group under investigation; from the knowledge of the socially conditioned life pattern in which these people were situated after the early years of childhood, it can acquire an understanding of the psychic attitudes common to them.

Social psychology wishes to investigate how certain psychic attitudes common to members of a group are related to their common life experiences. It is no more an accident in the case of an individual whether this or that libido direction dominates, whether the Oedipus complex finds this or that outlet, than it is an accident if changes in psychic characteristics occur in the psychic situation of a group, either in the same class of people over a period of time or simultaneously among different classes. It is the task of social psychology to indicate why such changes occur and how they are to be understood on the basis of the experience common to the members of the group.

The present investigation is concerned with a narrowly limited problem of social psychology, namely, the question concerning the motives conditioning the evolution of concepts about the relation of God the Father to Jesus from the beginning of Christianity to the formulation of the Nicene Creed in the fourth century. In accordance with the theoretical principles just set forth, this investigation aims to determine the extent to which the change in certain religious ideas is an expression of the psychic change of the people involved and the extent to which these changes are conditioned by their conditions of life. It will attempt to understand the ideas in terms of men and their life pat-terns, and to show that the evolution of dogma can be understood only through knowledge of the unconscious, upon which external reality works and which determines the content of consciousness.

The method of this work necessitates that relatively large space be devoted to the presentation of the life situation of the people investigated, to their spiritual, economic, social, and political situation in short, to their "psychic surfaces." If this seems to involve a disproportionate emphasis, the reader should bear in mind that even in the psychoanalytic case study of an ill person, great space is given to the presentation of the external circumstances surrounding the person. In the present work the description of the total cultural situation of the masses of people being investigated and the presentation of their external environment are more decisive than the description of the actual situation in a case study. The reason for this is that in the nature of things the historical reconstruction, even though it is supposed to be offered only to a certain extent in detail, is incomparably more complicated and more extensive than the report of simple facts as they occur in the life of an individual. We believe, however, that this disadvantage must be tolerated, because only in this way can an analytical understanding of historical phenomena be achieved.

The present study is concerned with a subject that has been treated by one of the most prominent representatives of the analytic study of religion, Theodor Reik.[4] The difference in content, which necessarily results from the different methodology, will, like the methodological differences themselves, be considered briefly at the end of this essay.

Our purpose here is to understand the change in certain contents of consciousness as expressed in theological ideas as the result of a change in unconscious processes. Accordingly, just as we have done with regard to the methodological problem, we propose to deal briefly With the most important findings of psychoanalysis as they touch upon our question.

2 The Social-Psychological Function of Religion

Psychoanalysis is a psychology of drives or impulses. It sees human behavior as conditioned and defined by emotional drives, which it interprets as an outflow of certain physiologically rooted impulses, themselves not subject to immediate observation. Consistent with the popular classifications of hunger drives and love drives, from the beginning, Freud distinguished between the ego, or self-preservation, drives and the sexual drives. Because of the libidinous character of the ego drives of self-preservation, and because of the special significance of destructive tendencies in the psychic apparatus of man, Freud suggested a different grouping, taking into account a contrast between life-maintaining and destructive drives. This classification needs no further discussion here. What is important is the recognition of certain qualities of the sex drive that distinguish them from the ego drives. The sex drives are not imperative; that is, it is possible to leave their demands un-gratified without menacing life itself, which would not be the case with continued failure to satisfy hunger, thirst, and the need for sleep. Furthermore, the sex drives, up to a certain and not insignificant point, permit a gratification in fantasies and with one's own body. They are, therefore, much more independent of external reality than are

---

4   "Dogma und Zwangsidee," Imago, XII (1927). Cf. *Dogma and Compulsion* (New York: International Universities Press, Inc., 1951), and other works on psychology of religion by Reik; E. Jones, *Zur Psycho-analyse der christlichen Religion*; and A.J. Storfer, *Marias jungfrauliche Mutterschaft*.

THE DOGMA OF CHRIST 49

the ego drives. Closely connected with this are the easy transference and capacity for interchange among the component impulses of sexuality. The frustration of one libidinal impulse can be relatively easily offset by the substitution of another impulse that can be gratified. This flexibility and versatility within the sexual drives are the basis for the extraordinary variability of the psychic structure and therein lies also the basis for the possibility that individual experiences can so definitely and markedly affect the libido structure. Freud sees the pleasure principle modified by the reality principle as the regulator of the psychic apparatus. He says:

> We will therefore turn to the less ambitious question of what men themselves show by their behavior to be the purpose and intention of their lives. What do they demand of life and wish to achieve in it? The answer to this can hardly be in doubt. They strive after happiness; they want to become happy and remain so. This endeavor has two sides, a positive and a negative aim. It aims, on the one hand, at an absence of pain and unpleasure, and on the other, at the experiencing of strong feelings of pleasure. In its narrower sense the word "happiness" only relates to the last. In conformity with this dichotomy in his aims, man's activity develops in two directions, according as it seeks to realize in the main, or even exclusively the one or the other of these aims.[5]

The individual strives to experience under given circumstances a maximum of libido gratification and a minimum of pain; in order to avoid pain, changes or even frustrations of the different component sex impulses can be accepted. A corresponding renunciation of the ego impulses, however, is impossible.

The peculiarity of an individual's emotional structure depends upon his psychic constitution and primarily upon his experiences in infancy. External reality, which guarantees him the satisfaction of certain impulses, but which compels the renunciation of certain others, is defined by the existing social situation in which he lives. This social reality includes the wider reality which embraces all members of society and the narrow reality of distinct social classes.

Society has a double function for the psychic situation of the individual, both frustrating and satisfying. A person seldom renounces impulses because he sees the danger resulting from their satisfaction. Generally, society dictates such renunciations: first, those prohibitions established on the basis of social recognition of a real danger *for the individual himself,* a danger not readily

---

5 Sigmund Freud, *Civilization and Its Discontents* (Standard edition), XXI, 76.

sensed by him and connected with the gratification of impulse; second, repression and frustration of impulses whose satisfaction would involve harm not to the individual but to the group; and, finally, renunciations made not in the interest of the group but only in the interest of a controlling class.

The "gratifying" function of society is no less clear than its frustrating role. The individual accepts it only because through its help he can to a certain degree count on gaining pleasure and avoiding pain, primarily with regard to the satisfaction of the elementary needs of self-preservation and, secondarily, in relation to the satisfaction of libidinous needs.

What has been said has not taken into account a specific feature of all historically known societies. The members of a society do not indeed consult one another to determine what the society can permit and what it must prohibit. Rather, the situation is that so long as the productive forces of the economy do not suffice to afford to all an adequate satisfaction of their material and cultural needs (that is, beyond protection against external danger and the satisfaction of elementary ego needs), the most powerful social class will aspire to the maximum satisfaction of their own needs first. The degree of satisfaction they provide for those who are ruled by them depends on the level of economic possibilities available, and also on the fact that a minimum satisfaction must be granted to those who are ruled so that they may be able to continue to function as co-operating members of the society. Social stability de-pends relatively little upon the use of external force. It depends for the most part upon the fact that men find themselves in a psychic condition that roots them inwardly in an existing social situation. For that purpose, as we have noted, a minimum of satisfaction of the natural and cultural instinctual needs is necessary. But at this point we must observe that for the psychic submission of the masses, something else is important, something connected with the peculiar structural stratification of the society into classes.

In this connection Freud has pointed out that man's helplessness in the face of nature is a repetition of the situation in which the adult found himself as a child, when he could not do without help against unfamiliar superior forces, and when his life impulses, following their narcissistic inclinations, attached themselves first to the objects that afforded him protection and satisfaction, namely, his mother and his father. To the extent that society is help-less with respect to nature, the psychic situation of childhood must be repeated for the individual member of the society as an adult. He transfers from father or mother some of his childish love and fear and also some of his hostility to a fantasy figure, to God.

In addition, there is a hostility to certain real figures, in particular to representatives of the elite. In the social stratification, the infantile situation is

THE DOGMA OF CHRIST

repeated for the individual. He sees in the rulers the powerful ones, the strong and the wise persons to be revered. He believes that they wish him well; he also knows that resistance to them is always punished; he is content when by docility he can win their praise. These are the identical feelings which, as a child, he had for his father, and it is understandable that he is as disposed to believe uncritically what is presented to him by the rulers as just and true, as in childhood he used to believe without criticism every statement made by his father. The figure of God forms a supplement to this situation; God is always the ally of the rulers. When the latter, who are always real personalities, are exposed to criticism, they can rely on God, who, by virtue of his unreality, only scorns criticism and, by his authority, confirms the authority of the ruling class.

In this psychological situation of infantile bondage resides one of the principal guarantees of social stability. Many find themselves in the same situation they experienced as children, standing helplessly before their father; the same mechanisms operate now as then. This psychic situation becomes established through a great many significant and complicated measures taken by the elite, whose function it is to maintain and strengthen in the masses their infantile psychic dependence and to impose itself on their unconscious as a father figure.

One of the principal means of achieving this purpose is religion. It has the task of preventing any psychic independence on the part of the people, of intimidating them intellectually, of bringing them into the socially necessary infantile docility toward the authorities. At the same time it has another essential function: it offers the masses a certain measure of satisfaction that makes life sufficiently tolerable for them to prevent them from attempting to change their position from that of obedient son to that of rebellious son.

Of what sort are these satisfactions? Certainly not satisfactions of the ego drives of self-preservation, nor better food, nor other material pleasures. Such pleasures are to be obtained only in reality, and for that purpose one needs no religion; religion serves merely to make it easier for the masses to resign themselves to the many frustrations that reality presents. The satisfactions religion offers are of a libidinous nature; they are satisfactions that occur essentially in fantasy because, as we have pointed out before, libidinous impulses, in contrast to ego impulses, permit satisfaction in fantasies.

Here we confront a question concerning one of the psychic functions of religion, and we shall now indicate briefly the most important results of Freud's investigations in this area. In *Totem and Taboo*, Freud has shown that the animal god of totemism is the elevated father, that in the prohibition to kill and eat the totem animal and in the contrary festive custom of nevertheless violating the prohibition once a year, man repeats the ambivalent attitude which he had acquired as a child toward the father who is simultaneously a helping protector and an oppressive rival.

It has been shown, especially by Reik, that this transfer to God of the infantile attitude toward the father is found also in the great religions. The question posed by Freud and his students concerned the psychic quality of the religious attitude toward God; and the answer is that in the adult's attitude toward God, one sees repeated the infantile attitude of the child toward his father. This infantile psychic situation represents the pattern of the religious situation. In his *The Future of an Illusion*, Freud passes beyond this question to a broader one. He no longer asks only how religion is psychologically possible; he asks also why religion exists at all or why it has been necessary. To this question he gives an answer that takes into consideration psychic and social facts simultaneously. He attributes to religion the effect of a narcotic capable of bringing some consolation to man in his impotence and helplessness before the forces of nature:

> For this situation is nothing new. It has an infantile prototype, of which it is in fact only the continuation. For once before one has found oneself in a similar state of helplessness: as a small child, in relation to one's parents. One had reason to fear them, and especially one's father; and yet one was sure of his protection against the dangers one knew. Thus it was natural to assimilate the two situations. Here, too, wishing played its part, as it does in dream-life. The sleeper may be seized in a presentiment of death, which threatens to place him in the grave. But the dream-work knows how to select a condition that will turn even that dreaded event into a wish-fulfillment: the dreamer sees himself in an ancient Etruscan grave which he has climbed down into, happy to find his archaeological interests satisfied. In the same way, a man makes the forces of nature not simply into persons with whom he can associate as he would with his equals that would not do justice to the overpowering impression which those forces make on him but he gives them the character of a father. He turns them into gods, following in this, as I have tried to show, not only an infantile prototype but a phylogenetic one.

> In the course of time the first observations were made of regularity and conformity to law in natural phenomena, and with this the forces of nature lost their human traits. But man's helplessness remains and along with it his longing for his father, and the gods. The gods retain their threefold task: they must exorcize the terrors of nature, they must reconcile

THE DOGMA OF CHRIST

men to the cruelty of fate, particularly as it is shown in death, and they must compensate them for the sufferings and privations which a civilized life in common has imposed on them.[6]

Freud thus answers the question, "What constitutes the inner power of religious doctrines and to what circumstances do these doctrines owe their effectiveness independently of rational approval?"

These [religious ideas], which are given out as teachings, are not precipitates of experience or end results of thinking: they are illusions, fulfillments of the oldest, strangest, and most urgent wishes of mankind. The secret of their strength lies in the strength of those wishes. As we already know, the terrifying impression of helplessness in childhood aroused the need for protection protection through love which was provided by the father, and the recognition that this helplessness would last throughout life made it necessary to cling to the existence of a father, but this time a more powerful one. Thus the benevolent rule of divine Providence allays our fear of the dangers of life; the establishment of a moral world-order ensures the fulfillment of the demands of justice, which have so often remained unfulfilled in human civilization; and the prolongation of earthly existence in a future life provides the local and temporal frame-work in which these wish-fulfillments shall take place. Answers to the riddles that tempt the curiosity of man, such as how the universe began or what the relation is between the body and mind, are developed in conformity with the underlying assumptions of this system. It is an enormous relief to the individual psyche if the conflicts of its childhood arising from the father complex-conflicts which it has never wholly overcome are removed from it and brought to a solution that is universally accepted.[7]

Freud therefore sees the possibility of the religious attitude in the infantile situation; he sees its relative necessity in man's impotence and helplessness with respect to nature, and he draws the conclusion that with man's increasing control over nature, religion is to be viewed an an illusion that is becoming superfluous.

Let us summarize what has been said thus far. Man strives for a maximum of pleasure; social reality compels him to many renunciations of impulse, and

---

6 Sigmund Freud, *The Future of an Illusion* (Standard edition), XXI, 17–18.
7 Ibid., p. 30

society seeks to compensate the individual for these renunciations by other satisfactions harmless for the society – that is, for the dominant classes.

These satisfactions are such that in essence they can be realized in fantasies, especially in collective fantasies. They perform an important function in social reality. Insofar as society does not permit real satisfactions, fantasy satisfactions serve as a substitute and become a powerful support of social stability. The greater the renunciations men endure in reality, the stronger must be the concern for compensation. Fantasy satisfactions have the double function which is characteristic of every narcotic: they act both as an anodyne and as a deterrent to active change of reality. The common fantasy satisfactions have an essential advantage over individual daydreams: by virtue of their universality, the fantasies are perceived by the conscious mind as if they were real. An illusion shared by everyone becomes a reality. The oldest of these collective fantasy satisfactions is religion. With the progressive development of society, fantasies become more complicated and more rationalized. Religion itself becomes more differentiated, and beside it appear poetry, art, and philosophy as the expressions of collective fantasies.

To sum up, religion has a threefold function: for all mankind, consolation for the privations exacted by life; for the great majority of men, encouragement to accept emotionally their class situation; and for the dominant minority, relief from guilt feelings caused by the suffering of those whom they oppress.

The following investigation aims to test in detail what has been said, by examining a small segment of religious development. We shall attempt to show what influence social reality had in a specific situation upon a specific group of men, and how emotional trends found expression in certain dogmas, in collective fantasies, and to show further what psychic change was brought about by a change in the social situation. We shall try to see how this psychic change found expression in new religious fantasies that satisfied certain unconscious impulses. It will thereby become clear how closely a change in religious concepts is connected, on the one hand, with the experiencing of various possible infantile relationships to the father or mother, and on the other hand, with changes in the social and economic situation.

The course of the investigation is determined by the methodological presuppositions mentioned earlier. The aim will be to understand dogma on the basis of a study of people, not people on the basis of a study of dogma. We shall attempt, therefore, first to describe the total situation of the social class from which the early Christian faith originated, and to understand the psychological meaning of this faith in terms of the total psychic situation of these people. We shall then show how different the mentality of the people was at a later

THE DOGMA OF CHRIST   55

period. Eventually, we shall try to understand the unconscious meaning of the Christology which crystallized as the end product of a three-hundred-year development. We shall treat mainly the early Christian faith and the Nicene dogma.

3   Early Christianity and Its Idea of Jesus

Every attempt to understand the origin of Christianity must begin with an investigation of the economic, social, cultural, and psychic situation of its earliest believers.[8]

Palestine was a part of the Roman Empire and succumbed to the conditions of its economic and social development. The Augustan principate had meant the end of domination by a feudal oligarchy, and helped bring about the triumph of urban citizenry. Increasing international commerce meant no improvement for the great masses, no greater satisfaction of their everyday needs; only the thin stratum of the owning class was interested in it. An unemployed and hungry proletariat of unprecedented size filled the cities. Next to Rome, Jerusalem was the city with relatively the largest proletariat of this kind. The artisans, who usually worked only at home and belonged largely to the proletariat, easily made common cause with beggars, unskilled workers, and peasants. Indeed, the Jerusalem proletariat was in a worse situation than the Roman. It did not enjoy Roman civil rights, nor were its urgent needs of stomach and heart provided for by the emperors through great distributions of grain and elaborate games and spectacles.

The rural population was exhausted by an extraordinarily heavy tax burden, and either fell into debt slavery, or, among the small farmers, the means of production or the small landholdings were all taken away. Some of these farmers swelled the ranks of the large-city proletariat of Jerusalem; others resorted to desperate remedies, such as violent political uprising and plundering. Above this impoverished and despairing proletariat, there arose in Jerusalem, as throughout the Roman Empire, a middle economic class which, though suffering under Roman pressure, was nevertheless economically stable. Above this group was the small but powerful and influential class of the feudal, priestly,

---

8   For the economic development, see especially M. Rostovtzeff, *Social and Economic History of the Roman Empire* (Oxford: 1926); Max Weber, "Die sozialen Griinde des Untergangs der antiken Kultur," in *Gesammelte Aufsdtze zur Sozial-und Wirtschaftsgeschichte*, 1924; E. Meyer, "Sklaverei im Altertum," Kleine Schriften, ad ed., Vol. I; K. Kautsky, *Foundations of Christianity* (Russell, 1953).

and moneyed aristocracy. Corresponding to the severe economic cleavage within the Palestinian population, there was social differentiation. Pharisees, Sadducees, and Am Ha-aretz were the political and religious groups representing these differences. The Sadducees represented the rich upper class: "[their] doctrine is received by but a few, yet those of the greatest dignity."[9] Although they have the rich on their side, Josephus does not find their manners aristocratic: "The behavior of the Sadducees one towards another is in some degree wild, and their conversation is as barbarous as if they were strangers to them."[10]

Below this small feudal upper class were the Pharisees, representing the middle and smaller urban citizenry, "who are friendly to one another, and are for the exercise of concord and regard for the public."[11]

> Now, for the Pharisees, they live meanly, and despise delicacies in diet; and they follow the conduct of reason, and what that prescribes to them as good for them, they do; and they think they ought earnestly to strive to observe reason's dictates for practice. They also pay respect to such as are in years; nor are they so bold as to contradict them in anything they have introduced; and, when they determine that all things are done by fate, they do not take away from men the freedom of acting as they think fit; since their notion is, that it hath pleased God that events should be decided in part by the council of fate, in part by such men as will accede thereunto acting therein virtuously or viciously. They also believe that souls have an immortal vigour in them, and that under the earth there will be rewards or punishments, according as they have lived virtuously or viciously in this life; and the latter are to be detained in an everlasting prison, but that the former shall have power to revive and live again; on account of which doctrines, they are able greatly to persuade the body of the people, and whatsoever they do about divine worship, prayers, and sacrifices, they perform them according to their direction.[12]

Josephus' description of the middle class of the Pharisees makes it appear more unified than it was in reality. Among the following of the Pharisees were elements that stemmed from the lowest proletarian strata that continued their relationship with them in their way of life (for example, Rabbi Akiba). At the

---

9   *The Life and Works of Flavius Josephus, The Antiquities of the Jews*, XVIII, i, 4, translated by William Whiston (New York: Holt, Rinehart and Winston, Inc., 1957).

10 *The Life and Works of Flavius Josephus, The Wars of the Jews*, II, 8,14.

11 Ibid.

12 Josephus, *The Wars of the Jews*, XVIII, i, 3.

THE DOGMA OF CHRIST   57

same time, however, there were members of the well-to-do urban citizenry. This social difference found expression in different ways, most clearly in the political contradictions within Pharisaism, with regard to their attitude toward Roman rule and revolutionary movements.

The lowest stratum of the urban *Lumpenproletariat* and of the oppressed peasants, the so-called "Am Ha-aretz" (literally, land folk), stood in sharp opposition to the Pharisees and their wider following. In fact, they were a class that had been completely uprooted by the economic development; they had nothing to lose and perhaps something to gain. They stood economically and socially outside the Jewish society integrated into the whole of the Roman Empire. They did not follow the Pharisees and did not revere them; they hated them and in turn were despised by them. Entirely characteristic of this attitude is the statement of Akiba, one of the most important Pharisees, who himself stemmed from the proletariat: "When I was still a common [ignorant] man of the Am Ha-aretz, I used to say: If I could lay my hands on a scholar I would bite him like an ass.'"[13] The Talmud goes on: "Rabbi, say 'like a dog,' an ass does not bite," and he replied: "When an ass bites he generally breaks the bones of his victim, while a dog bites only the flesh." We find in the same passage in the Talmud a series of statements describing the relations between the Pharisees and the Am Ha-aretz.

> A man should sell all his possessions and secure the daughter of a scholar for a wife, and if he cannot secure the daughter of a scholar, he should try to obtain a daughter of a prominent man. If he cannot succeed in that, he should endeavor to obtain a daughter of a synagogue director, and if he cannot succeed in that, he should try to obtain a daughter of an alms collector, and if he cannot succeed even in this, he should try and obtain the daughter of an elementary-school teacher. He should avoid wedding the daughter of a common person [a member of the Am Ha-aretz], for she is an abomination, their women are an abhorrence, and concerning their daughters it is said, "Accursed be any who sleepeth with a cow." (Deut. 27)

Or, again, R. Jochanan says:

> One may tear a common person to pieces like a fish.... One who gives his daughter to a common person in marriage virtually shackles her before a lion, for just as a lion tears and devours his victim without shame, so does a common person who sleeps brutally and shamelessly with her.

---

13   *Talmud*, Pesachim 49b.

R. Eliezer says:

> If the common people did not need us for economic reasons, they would long ago have slain us... The enmity of a common person toward a scholar is even more intense than that of the heathens toward the Israelites... Six things are true of the common person: One may depend upon no common person as a witness and may accept no evidence from him, one may not let him share a secret, nor be a ward for an orphan, nor a trustee of funds for charitable funds, one may not go on a journey in his company and one should not tell him if he has lost something.[14]

The views here cited (which could be multiplied considerably) stem from Pharisaic circles and show with what hatred they opposed the Am Ha-aretz, but also with what bitterness the common man may have hated the scholars and their following.[15]

It has been necessary to describe the opposition within Palestinian Judaism between the aristocracy, the middle classes and their intellectual leaders on the one hand, and the urban and rural proletariat on the other, in order to make clear the underlying causes of such political and religious revolutionary movements as early Christianity. A more extensive presentation of the differentiation among the extraordinarily variegated Pharisees is not necessary for the purpose of the present study and would lead us too far afield. The conflict between the middle class and the proletariat within the Pharisaic group increased, as Roman oppression became heavier and the lowest classes more economically crushed and uprooted. To the same extent the lowest classes of society became the supporters of the national, social, and religious revolutionary movements.

These revolutionary aspirations of the masses found expression in two directions: political attempts at revolt and emancipation directed against their own aristocracy and the Romans, and in all sorts of religious-messianic movements. But there is by no means a sharp separation be-tween these two streams moving toward liberation and salvation; often they flow into each other. The messianic movements themselves assumed partly practical and partly merely literary forms.

The most important movements of this sort may be briefly mentioned here.

---

14   These three passages just cited are in the *Talmud*, Pesachim 4gb.

15   Cf. Friedlander, *Die religiosen Bewegungen innerhalb des Judentums im Zeitalter Jesu* (Berlin, 1905).

THE DOGMA OF CHRIST

Shortly before Herod's death, that is, at a time when, in addition to Roman domination, the people suffered oppression at the hands of Jewish deputies serving under the Romans, there took place in Jerusalem, under the leadership of two Pharisaic scholars, a popular revolt, during which the Roman eagle at the entrance to the Temple was destroyed. The instigators were executed, and the chief plotters were burned alive. After Herod's death a mob demonstrated before his successor, Archelaus, demanding the release of the political prisoners, the abolition of the market tax, and a reduction in the annual tribute. These demands were not satisfied. A great popular demonstration in connection with these events in the year 4 B.C. was suppressed with bloodshed, thousands of demonstrators being killed by the soldiers. Nevertheless, the movement became stronger. Popular revolt progressed. Seven weeks later, in Jerusalem, it mounted to new bloody revolts against Rome. In addition, the rural population was aroused. In the old revolutionary center, Galilee, there were many struggles with the Romans, and in Trans-Jordan there was riot-ing. A former shepherd assembled volunteer troops and led a guerrilla war against the Romans.

This was the situation in the year 4 B.C. The Romans did not find it altogether easy to cope with the revolting masses. They crowned their victory by crucifying two thousand revolutionary prisoners.

For some years the country remained quiet. But shortly after the introduction in A.D. 6 of a direct Roman administration in the country, which began its activity with a popular census for tax purposes, there was a new revolutionary movement. Now began a separation between the lower and the middle classes. Although ten years earlier the Pharisees had joined the revolt, there developed now a new split between the urban and the rural revolutionary groups on the one side and the Pharisees on the other. The urban and rural lower classes united in a new party, namely, the Zealots, while the middle class, under the leadership of the Pharisees, was prepared for reconciliation with the Romans. The more oppressive the Roman and the aristocratic Jewish yoke became, the greater the despair of the masses, and Zealotism won new followers. Up to the outbreak of the great revolt against the Romans there were constant clashes between the people and the administration. The occasions for revolutionary outbreaks were the frequent attempts of the Romans to put up a statue of Caesar or the Roman eagle in the Temple of Jerusalem. The indignation against these measures, which were rationalized on religious grounds, stemmed in reality from the hatred of the masses for the emperor as leader and head of the ruling class oppressing them. The peculiar character of this hatred for the emperor becomes clearer if we remember that this was an epoch in which reverence for the Roman emperor was spreading widely throughout the empire and in which the emperor cult was about to become the dominant religion.

The more hopeless the struggle against Rome became on the political level, and the more the middle class withdrew and became disposed to compromise with Rome, the more radical the lower classes became; but the more revolutionary tendencies lost their political character and were transferred to the level of religious fantasies and messianic ideas. Thus a pseudo-messiah, Theudas, promised the people he would lead them to the Jordan and repeat the miracle of Moses. The Jews would pass through the river with dry feet, but the pursuing Romans would drown. The Romans saw in these fantasies the expression of a dangerous revolutionary ferment; they killed the followers of this messiah and beheaded Theudas. Theudas had successors. Josephus provides an account of an uprising under the provincial governor Felix (52–60). Its leaders

> ... deceived and deluded the people under pretense of divine inspiration, but were for procuring innovations and changes of the government; and these prevailed with the multitude to act like madmen, and went before them into the wilderness, as pretending that God would there show them the signals of liberty; but Felix thought this procedure was to be the beginning of a revolt; so he sent some horsemen, and footmen both armed, who destroyed a great number of them. But there was an Egyptian false prophet that did the Jews more mischief than the former; for he was a cheat, and pre-tended to be a prophet also, and got together thirty thousand men that were deluded by him: these he led round about from the wilderness to the mount which was called the Mount of Olives, and was ready to break into Jerusalem by force from that place.[16]

The Roman military made short shrift of the revolutionary hordes. Most of them were killed or put in prison, the rest destroyed themselves; all tried to remain hiding at home. Nevertheless, the uprisings continued:

> Now, when there were quieted, it happened, as it does in a diseased body, that another part was subject to an inflammation; for a company of deceivers and robbers [that is, the messianists and more politically-minded revolutionaries] got together, and persuaded the Jews to revolt, and exhorted then to assert their liberty, inflicting death on those that continued

---

16   Josephus, *The War of the Jews*, II, 13, 4, 5.

THE DOGMA OF CHRIST

in obedience to the Roman government, and saying, that such as willingly chose slavery, ought to be forced from their desired inclinations; for they parted themselves into different bodies, and lay in wait up and down the country, and plundered the house of the great men, and slew the men themselves, and set the villages on fire; and this all Judea was filled with the effects of their madness. And thus the flame was everyday more and more blown up, till it came in to a direct war.[17]

The growing oppression of the lower classes of the nation brought about a sharpening of the conflict between them and the less oppressed middle class, and in this process the masses became more and more radical. The left wing of the Zealots formed a secret faction of the "Sicarii" (dagger carriers), who began, through attacks and plots, to exert a terrorist pressure on the well-to-do citizens. Without mercy they persecute the moderates in the higher and middle classes of Jerusalem; at the same time they invaded, plundered, and reduced to ashes the villages whose inhabitants refused to join their revolutionary bands. The prophets and the pseudo-messiahs, similarly, did not cease their agitation among the common folk.

Finally, in the year 66 the great popular revolt against Rome broke out. It was supported first by the middle and lower classes of the nation, who, in bitter struggles, overcame the Roman troops. At first the war was led by the property owners and the educated, but they acted with little energy and with tendency to arrive at a compromise. The first year, therefore ended in failure despite several victories, and the masses attributed the unhappy outcome to the weak and indifferent early direction of war. Their leaders attempted by every means to seize power and to put themselves in the place of the existing leaders. Since the latter did not leave their positions voluntarily, in the winter of 67–68 there developed: a bloody civil war and abominable scenes, such as only the French Revolution may boast."[18] The more hopeless the war became, the more the middle classes tried their luck in a compromise with the Romans; as a result, the civil war grew more fierce, together with the struggle against the foreign enemy.[19]

While Rabbi Jochanan ben Sakkai, one of the leading Pharisees, went over to the enemy and made peace with him, the small tradesmen, artisans, and peasants defended the city against the Romans with great heroism for five

---

17   Ibid, II, 13,6. It is important to note that Josephus, who himself belonged to the aristo-
      cratic elite, is describing the revolutionaries in terms of his own bias.
18   E. Schurer, *Geschichte des judischen Volkes in Zeitalter Jesu Christi* (3rd ed,; 1901), I 617.
19   Cf. T. Mommsen, *History of Rome*, Vol. v.

months. They had nothing to lose, but also nothing more to gain, for the struggle against the Roman power was hopeless and had to end in collapse.

Many of the well-to-do were able to save themselves by going over the Romans, and although Titus was extremely embittered against the remaining Jews, he nevertheless admitted those who were in flight. At the same time the embattled masses of Jerusalem stormed the king's palace, into which many of the well-to-do Jews had brought their treasures, took the money, and killed the owners, the roman war and the civil war ended with victory of the Romans. This was accompanied by the victory of the ruling Jewish group and the collapse of a hundred thousand Jewish peasants and the urban lower classes.[20]

Alongside the political and social struggles and the mesianically colored revolutionary attempts are the popular writings originating at that time and inspired by the same tendencies: namely, the apocalyptic literature. Despite its variety, the vision of the future in this apocalyptic literature is comparatively uniform. First there are the "Woes of the Messiah" (Macc. 13:7,8), which refer to events that will not trouble "the elect" – famine, earthquakes, epidemics, and wars then comes the "great affliction" prophesied in Daniel 12:1, such as had not occurred since the creation of the world, a frightening time of suffering and distress. Throughout apocalyptic literature in general there runs the belief that the elect will also be protected from this affliction,. The horror of desolation prophesied in Daniel 9:27, 11:31, and 12:11 represents the final sign of the end the picture of the end bears old prophetic features. The climax will be the appearance of the Son of Man on the clouds in great splendor and glory.[21]

Just as in the struggle against the Romans the different classes of people participated in different ways, so apocalyptic literature, too, originated in different classes. Despite a certain uniformity, this is clearly expressed by the difference in emphasis on individual elements within the various apocalyptic writing despite the impossibility of detailed analysis here, we may cite as an expression of the same revolutionary tendencies that inspired the left wing of the defenders of Jerusalem, the concluding exhortation of the book of Enoch:

> Woe to those that build their homes with sand; for they will be overthrown from they foundation and will fall by the sword. But those who acquire gold and silver will perish in the judgment suddenly. Woe to you rich, for ye have trusted on your riches and from your riches ye shall be torn away, because you have not remembered the most High in the days of judgment... Woes to you who requite your neighbor with evil, for you

---

20   Josephus, *The Wars of the Jews, Vol. VI*.

21   Cf. Johannes Weiss, *Das Urchristentum* (Gottingen, 1917).

THE DOGMA OF CHRIST 63

will be requited according to your works. Woes to you lying witnesses...
Fear not, ye that suffer, for healing will be your portion: A bright light will
shine and you will hear the voices of rest from heaven (Enoch 94–96).

Besides theses religious-messianic, sociopolitical, and literary movements
characteristic of the time of the rise of Christianity, another movement must
be mentioned, in which political goals played no role and which led directly
to Christianity, namely, the movement of John the Baptist. He enkindled a
popular movement. The upper class. regardless of its persuasion, would have
nothing to do with him. His most attentive listeners came from the ranks of the
despised masses.[22] He preached that the kingdom of heaven and judgment day
were at hand, bringing deliverance for the good, destruction for the evil. "Re-
pent ye, for the kingdom of heaven is at hand" was the burden of his preaching.

To understand the psychological meaning of the first Christians' faith in
Christ and this is the primary purpose of the present study-it was necessary for
us to visualize what kind if people supported early Christianity. They were the
masses of the uneducated poor, the proletariat of Jerusalem, and the peasants
in the country who, because of social restriction and content, increasingly felt
the urge to change existing conditions. They longed for a happy time for themselves, and also harbored hate and revenge against both their own rules and
the Romans. We have observed how varied were the forms of these tendencies,
ranging from the political struggle against Rome to the class struggle in Jerusalem, from Theudas' movement and the apocalyptic literature. From political
activity to messianic dreams there were all sorts of different phenomena; yet
behind all these different forms was the same motivating force: the hatred and
the hope of the suffering masses, caused by their distress and the inescapabil-
ity of their socioeconomic situation. Whether these eschatological expectation had more social, more political, or more religious content, it became
stronger with the increasing oppression, and more active "the deeper we de-
scend into the literature masses, to the so-called Am Ha-aretz, the circle of
those who experienced the present as oppression and therefore had to look to
the future for the fulfillment of all their wishes."[23]

The bleaker the hope for real improvement became, the more this hope had
to find expressions in fantasies. The Zealots' desperate final struggle against
the Romans and John Baptists' movement were the two extremes, and were
rooted in the same soil: the despair of the lowest classes. This stratum was psychologically characterized by the presence of hope for a change in their

---

22 Cf. M. Dibelius, *Die urchristliche Ueberlieferung von Johannes des Taufer* (Stuttgart, 1911).
23 Ibid., p.130.

condition (analytically interpreted, for a good father who would help them), and at the same time, a fierce hatred of oppressors, which found expression in feelings directed against the Roman emperor, the Pharisees, the rich in general, and in the fantasies of punishment of the Day of Judgment. We see here an ambivalent attitude: these people loved in fantasy good father who would help and deliver them, and they hated the evil father who oppressed, tormented, and despised them.

From this stratum of the poor, uneducated, revolutionary masses, Christianity arose as a significant historical messianic-revolutionary movement. Like John the Baptist, early Christian doctrine addressed itself not to the educated and the property owners, but the poor, the oppressed, and the suffering.[24] Celsus, an opponent of the Christians, gives a good picture of the social composition of the Christian community as he saw it almost two centuries later:

He asserts:

> In private houses also we see wool-workers, cobblers, laundry-workers, and the most illiterate and bucolic yokels, who would not dare to say anything at all in front of their elders and more intelligent masters. But whenever they get hold of children in private and some stupid woman with the, they let out some astounding statements as, for examples, that they must not pay any attention to their father and school-teachers, but must obey them; they say that these talk nonsense and have no understanding, and that in reality they neither know nor are able to do anything good, but are taken up with mere empty chatter, but they alone, they say, know the right way to live, and if they children would believe them, they would become happy and make their home happy as well. And if just as they are speaking they see one of the school-teachers coming, or some intelligent person, or even the father himself, the more cautious if them flee in all directions; but the more reckless urge the children on to rebel. They whisper to them that in the presence of their father and their schoolmaster they do not feel able to explain anything to the children, since they do not want to have anything to do with the silly and obtuse teachers who are totally corrupted and far gone in wickedness and who inflict punishment on the children. But, if they like, they should

---

24   C.F for the social structure of primitive Christianity, R. Kopf, *Das nachapostolische Zeitalter* (Tubingen, 1905); Adolph Harnack, *Die Mission und Ausbreitung des Christentums* (4th ed.; 123), Vol. I; Adolph Harnack, "Kirche und Staat bis zur Grundung der Staatskirche," *Kultur des Gegenwart,* 2d ed.; Adolph Harnack, "Das Urchistentum und die soziale Frage," *Preussusche Jahrbucher*, 1908, vol.131; K. Kautsky, *Foundations of Christianity* (Russell, 1953).

THE DOGMA OF CHRIST

65

leave father and their schoolmasters, and go along with the women and little children who are they playfellows to the wooldresser's shop, or to the cobbler's or the washerwoman's shop, that they may learn perfection. And by saying this they persuade them.[25]

The picture Celsus gives here of the supporters if Christianity is characteristic not only of their social bit also of their psychic situation, their struggle and hatred against paternal authority.

What was the content of the primitive Christian message?[26]

In the foreground stands the eschatological expectation. Jesus preached the nearness of the kingdom of God. He taught the people to see in his activities the beginning of this new kingdom. Nevertheless,

> The competition of the kingdom will only appear when he returns in glory in the clouds of heaven to judgment. Jesus seems to have announced this speedy return a short time before his death, and to have comforted his disciplines at his departure with the assurance that he would immediately enter into a super mundane position with God.

> The instructions of Jesus to his disciplines are accordingly dominated by the thought that the end-the day and hour of which the exhortation to renounce all earthly goods takes prominent place.[27]

The conditions of entrance to the kingdom are, in the first place, a complete change of mind, in which a man renounces the pleasure of this world, denies himself, and is ready to surrender all that he has in order to save his soul, then, a believing trust in God's grace which he grants to the humble and the poor, and therefore hearty confidence in Jesus and the Messiah chosen and called by God to realize his kingdom on the earth. The announcement is therefore directed to the poor, the suffering whose hungering and thirsting for righteousness... to those who wish to be healed and redeemed, and finds them prepared for entrance into... the kingdom of God, while it brings down upon the

---

25 Origen, *Contra Celsum*, translated by Henry Chadwick (London: Cambridge University Press, 1953), III, 55.

26 The problem of the historical Jesus need not concern us in this connection. The social effect of the primitive Christian message is to be understood only on the basis of the classes to which it was directed and by which it was accepted; and only the understanding of their psychic situation is important for us here.

27 Adolf Harnack, *History of Dogma* (New York: Dover Publications, Inc., 1961) I, 66–67.

self-satisfied, the rich and those proud of their righteousness, the judgment of obduracy and the damnation of Hell.[28]

The proclamation that the kingdom of heaven was at hand (Matt. 10:7) was the germ of the oldest preaching. It was this that aroused in the suffering and oppressed masses an enthusiastic hope. The feeling of the people was that everything was coming to an end. They believed that there would not be time to spread Christianity among all the heathen before the new era arrived. If the hopes of the other groups of the same oppressed masses were directed to bringing about political and social revolution by their own energy and effort, the eyes of the early Christian community were focused solely on the great event, the miraculous beginning of a new age. The content of the primitive Christian message was not an economic nor a social-reform program but the blessed promise of a not-distant future in which the poor would be rich, the hungry would be satisfied, and the oppressed would attain authority.[29]

The mood of these first enthusiastic Christians is clearly seen in Luke 6:20 ff.:

> Blessed are you poor, for yours is the kingdom of God.
> Blessed are you the hunger now, for you shall be satisfied.
> Blessed are you the weep now, for you shall laugh.
> Blessed are you when men hate you, and when they exclude you and revile you, and cast out your name as evil, on account of the Son of man! Rejoice in that day, and leap for joy, for behold, your reward is great in heaven; for so their fathers did to the prophets.
> But woe to you that are rich, for you have received your consolation.
> Woe to you that are full now, for you shall hunger.
> Woe to you that laugh now, for you shall mourn and weep.

These statements express not only the longing and expectation of the poor and oppressed for a new and better world, also their complete hatred of the authorities – the rich, the learned, and the powerful. The same mood is found in the story of the poor man Lazarous, "who desired to be fed with what fell from rich man's table" (Luke 16:21), and in the famous words of Jesus: "How hard it is for those who have riches to enter the kingdom of God!" (Luke 18:24) The hatred of the Pharisees and the tax collectors runs like a red thread through the gospels, with the result that for almost two thousand years, opinion of the Pharisees throughout Christendom has been determined by thus hatred.

---

28   Ibid., pp. 62–63.

29   Cf. Weiss, *Das Urchristentum*, p. 55.

THE DOGMA OF CHRIST

We hear thus hatred of the rich again in the Epistle of James, in the middle of the second century:

> Come now, you rich, weep and howl for the miseries that are coming upon you. Your riches have rotted and your garments are moth-eaten. Your gold and silver have rusted, and their rust will be evidence against you and will eat your flesh like fire. You have laid up treasure for the last days. Behold, the wages of the labors who mowed your fields, which you kept back by fraud, cry out; and the cries of the harvesters have reached the ears of the Lord of host. You have lived on the earth in luxury and on pleasure; you have fattened your hearts in a day of slaughterer.

> You have condemned, you have killed the righteous man; he does not resist you.
> Be patient, therefore, brethren, until the coming of the Lord.
> ... behold, the judge is standing at the doors. (James 5:1 ff.)

Speaking of this hatred, Kautsky rightly says: "Rarely has the class hatred of the modern proletariat attained such forms as that of the Christian proletariat."[30] It is the hatred of the Am Ha-aretz for the Pharisees, of the Zealots and the Sicarii for the well to do and the middle class, of the suffering and harassed people of town and country for those in authority and in high places, as it had been expressed in the pre-Christian political rebellions and in messianic fantasies.

Intimately connected with this hatred for the spiritual and social authorities is an essential feature of the social and psych structure of early Christianity, namely, its democratic, brotherly character. If the Jewish society of the time was characterized by an extreme caste spirit pervading all social relationships, the early Christian community was free brotherhood of the poor, unconcerned with institutions and formulas.

> We find ourselves by an impossible task if we wish to sketch a picture of the organization during the first hundred years... The whole community is held together only by the common bond of faith and hope and love, the office does not support the person, but always the person the office... Since the first Christians felt they were pilgrims and strangers on the earth, what need was there for permanent institutions?[31]

---

30   K. Kautsky, *Der Ursprung de Chrisrtentums*, p. 345.
31   H. von Schubert, *Grundzuge der Kitchengeschichte* (Tübingen, 1904).

In this early Christian brotherhood, mutual economic assistance and support, "love-communism," as Harnack calls it, played a special role.

We see, therefore, that the early Christians were men and women, the poor, uneducated, oppressed masses of the Jewish people, and later, of other peoples. In place of the increasing impossibility of altering their hopeless situation through realistic means, there developed the expectation that a change would occur in a very short time, at a moment's notice, and that these people would then find the happiness previously missed, bit that the rich and the nobility would be punished, in accordance with justice and the desires of the Christian masses, the fist Christians were brotherhood of socially and economically oppressed enthusiasts held together by hope and hatred.

What distinguished the early Christians from the peasants and proletarians struggling against Rome was not the basis psychic attitude. The first Christians were no more "humble" and resigned to the will of God, no more convinced of the necessary and immutability of their lot, no more inspired by the wish to be loved by their rules than were the political and military fighters. The two groups hated the ruling fathers in the same way, hoping with equal vigor to see the latter's downfall and the beginning of their own rule and of a satisfactory future, the difference between them lay neither in the presuppositions nor in the goal and direction of their wishes, but only in the sphere in which they tried to fulfill them. While the Zealots and Sicarii endeavored to realize their wishes in the sphere of political reality, the complete hopelessness of realization led the early Christians to formulate the same wishes in fantasy. The expression of this was the early Christian faith, especially the early Christian idea concerning Jesus and his relationship to the Father-God.

What were the ideas of these first Christians?

> The contents of faith of the disciples, and the common proclamation which united them, may be comprised in the following propositions. Jesus of Nazareth is the Messiah promised by the prophets. Jesus after his death is by the Divine awakening raised to the right hand of God, and will soon return to set up his kingdom visibly upon the earth. He who believes in Jesus, and has been received into community of the disciplines of Jesus, who, in virtue of a sincere change of mind, calls on God as Father, and lives accordingly to the commandments of Jesus, is a saint of God, and as such can be certain of the sin-forgiving grace of God, and of a share in the future glory, that is, of redemption.[32]

---

32   Adolph Harnack, *History of Dogma*, I, 78.

THE DOGMA OF CHRIST

"God has made him both Lord and Christ" (Acts 2:36). This is the oldest doctrine of Christ that we have, and is therefore of great interest, especially, since it was later supplanted by other, more extensive, doctrines. It is called the "adoptionist" theory because here an act of adoption is assumed. Adoption is here used in contrast to the natural sonship which exists from birth. Accordingly, the thought present here is that Jesus was not the messiah from the beginning; in other words, he was not from the beginning the Son of God but became so only by a definite, very distinct act of God's will. This is expressed particularly in the fact that the statement in Psalms 2:7, "You are my son, today I have begotten you," is interpreted as referring to the moment of the exaltation of Jesus (Acts 13:33).

According to an ancient Semitic idea, the king is a son of God, whether by descent or, as here, by adoption, on the day he mounts the throne. It is therefore in keeping with the oriental spirit to sat that Jesus, as he was exalted to the right hand of God, became the Son of God. This idea is echoed even by Paul, although for him the concept "Son of God" had already acquired another meaning. Romans 1:4 says of the Son of God that he was "designated son of God in power ... by his resurrection from the dead." Here the different forms of the concept conflict: the Son of God who was Son from the very beginning (Paul's idea); and Jesus, who, after the resurrection, was exalted to Son of God in power, that is, to kingly ruler of the world (the concept of the early community). The difficult combination of the two ideas shows very clearly that here two different though patterns encountered each other. The older, stemming from the early Christian community, is consistent, in that the early community characterizes Jesus, before the exaltation, as a man: "a man attested to you by God with mighty works and wonders and signs which God did through him in your midst" (Acts 2:22). One should observe here that Jesus has not performed the miracle, but God through him. Jesus was the voice of God. This idea prevails to some extent in the Gospel tradition, where, for example, after the healing of the lame, the people praise God (Mark 2:12). In particular, Jesus is characterized as the prophet whom Moses promised: "The lords God will raise up for you a prophet from your brethren" (Acts 3:22; 7:37; Deut 18:15).[33]

We see thus that the concept of Jesus held by the early community was that he was a man chosen by God and elevated by him as a "messiah," and later as "Son of God." This Christology of the early community resembles in many respects the concept of the messiah chosen by God to introduce a kingdom of righteousness and love, a concept which had been familiar among the Jewish masses for a long time. In only two ideas of the new faith do we find elements

---

33   Weiss, *op. cit.,* p. 85.

that signify something specifically new: in the fact of his exaltation as Son of God to sit at the right hand of the Almighty, and in the fact that this messiah is no longer the powerful, victorious hero, but his significance and dignity reside just in his suffering, in his death on the cross. To be sure, the idea of a dying messiah or even of a dying God was not entirely new in the popular consciousness. Isaiah 53 speaks of this suffering servant of God. The Fourth Book of Ezra also mentions dying messiah, although of course in an essentially different form, for he dies after four hundred years and after his victory.[34] The idea of a dying God may have become familiar to the people from an entirely different source, namely, the Near Eastern cults and myths (Osiris, Attis, and Adonis).

> The fate of man finds its prototype in the passion of a God who suffered on earth, dies, and rises again. This God will permit all those to share in that blessed immortality who join him in the mysteries or even identify themselves with him.[35]

Perhaps those who were also Jewish esoteric traditions of a dying God or a dying messiah, but all those precursors cannot explain the enormous influence which the teaching about the crucified and suffering savior immediately had upon the Jewish masses, and soon upon the pagan masses as well.

In the early to community of enthusiasts, Jesus was thus a man exalted after his death into a God who would soon return in order to execute judgment, to make happy those who suffer, and to punish the rulers.

We have now gained insight into the psychic surfaces of the followers of early Christianity sufficiently to attempt our interpretation of these first christological statements. Those intoxicated by this idea were people who were tormented and despairing, full of hatred for their Jewish and pagan oppressors, with no prospect of effecting a better future. A message which would allow them to project into fantasy all that reality had denied them must have been extremely fascinating.

If there was nothing left for the Zealots but to die in hopeless battle, the followers of Christ could dream of their goal without reality immediately showing them the hopelessness of their wishes. By substituting fantasy for reality, the Christian message satisfied the longings for hope and revenge, and although

---

34 Cf. Psalm 22 and Hosea 6.

35 F. Cumont, "Die orientalischen Religionen in ihrem Einfluss auf die europaischen Religionen des Altertums," *Kultur der Gegenwart* (2nd Ed,; 1923), Vol. I, Pt. III, p. 1; cf. also Weiss, *op. cit.,* p. 70.

THE DOGMA OF CHRIST   71

it failed to relieve hunger, it brought a fantasy satisfaction of no little significance for the oppressed.[36]

The psychoanalytic investigation of the christological faith of the early
Christian community must now raise the following questions: What was the
significance for the first Christians of the fantasy of the dying man elevated to
a God? Why did this fantasy win the hearts of so many thousands in a short
time? What were its unconscious sources, and what emotional needs were satisfied by it?

First, the most important question: a man is raised to a God; he is adopted
by God. As Reik has correctly observed, we have here the old mythology the
rebellion of the son, an expression of hostile impulse toward the father-God.
We now understand what significance this myth must have had for the followers of Christianity. These people hated intensely the authorities that confront-
ed them with "fatherly" power. The priests, scholars, aristocrats, in short, all the
rulers who excluded them from the enjoyment of life and who in their emotional worlds played the role of the severe, forbidding, threatening, tormenting
father-they also had to hate this God who was ally of their oppressors, who
permitted them to suffer and to be oppressed. They themselves wanted to rule,
even to be masters, but it seemed to them hopeless to try to achieve this in reality and to overthrow and destroy their present masters by force. So they satisfied their wishes in fantasy. Consciously they did not dare to slander the fatherly God. Conscious hatred was reserved for the authorities, not for the
elevated father figure, the divine being himself. But the unconscious hostility
to the divine father found expression in the Christ fantasy. The out a man at
God's side and made him co-regent with God the father. This man who became

---

36   A remark must be inserted here about one problem which has been the object of severe
      polemics, the question as to how far Christianity can be understood as a revolutionary
      class movement. Kautsky, in *Vorlaufer Des never Sozialismus* (Stuttgart, 1895), and later in
      Foundations of Christianity, has set forth the view that Christianuty is a proletarian class
      movement, that in essence, however, its significance lay in its practical activity, that is, in
      its charitable work and nit its "pious fanaticisms." Kautsky overlooks the fact that a
      movement may have a class origin without the existence of social and economic motives
      in the consciousness of its instigators. His contempt for the historical significance of reli-
      gious ideas demonstrates only his complete lack of understanding of the meaning of fan-
      tasy satisfaction within the social process. His interpretation of historical materialism is
      so banal that it is easy for Troeltsch and Harnack to give an appearance of refuting histori-
      cal materialism, They, like Kautsky, do not put at the center of the inquiry the problem of
      the class relationships played in the consciousness and ideology of the first Christians.
      Although Kautsky misses the real problem, the class foundations of early Christianity are
      nevertheless so clear that the tortuous attempt, especially of Troeltsch (in his *Social
      Teaching of the Christian Churches*), to explain them away, betrays all to plainly the politi-
      cal tendencies of the author.

a God, and with whom as humans they could identify, represented their Oedipus wishes; he was a symbol of their unconscious hostility to God the father, for if a man could become God, the latter was deprived of his privileged fatherly position of being unique and unreadable. The belief in the legation of a man to God was thus the explores soon of unconscious wish for the removal of the divine father.

Here lies the significance of the fact that the early Christians community held the adoptionist doctrine, the theory of the elevation of man to God. In this doctrine the hostility to God found its expression, while in the doctrine that later increased in popularity and became dominant-the doctrine about the Jesus who was always a God-was expressed the elimination of these hostile wishes toward God (to be discussed in greater detail later). The faithful identified with this son; they could identify with him because he was a suffering human like themselves. This is the basis of the fascinating power and effect upon the masses of the idea of the suffering man elevated to a God; only with a suffering being could they identify. Thousands of men before had been crucified, tormented, and humiliated. If they thought of this crucified one as elevated to God, this meant that in their unconscious, this crucified God was themselves.

The pre-Christian apocalypse mentioned a victorious, strong messiah. He was the representative of the wishes and fantasies of a class of people who were oppresses, but who in many ways suffered less, and still harbor end the hope of victory. The class from which the early Christian community grew, and in which the Christianity of the first one hundred to one hundred fifty years had a great success, could not identify with such a strong, powerful messiah; their messiah could only be a suffering, crucified one. The figure of the suffering savior was determined in a threefold way: First in the sense just mentioned; secondly by the fact that some of the death wishes against the father-god were shifted to the son. In the myth of the dying god (Adonis, Attis, Osiris), god himself was the who death was fantasied. In the early Christian myth the father is killed in the son.

But, finally, the fantasy of the crucified son had still a third function: Since the believing enthusiasts were imbued with hatred and death wishes-consciously against against their rulers, unconsciously against God the father-they identified with the crucified; they themselves suffered death on the cross and atoned in this way for their death wishes against the father. Through his death Jesus expiated the guilt of all, and the first Christians greatly needed such an atonement. Because of their total situation, aggression and death wishes against the father were particularly active in them.

The focus of the early Christian fantasy, however in contrast with the later Catholic faith, to be dealt with presently – seems to lie, not in a masochistic

THE DOGMA OF CHRIST

expiation through self-annihilation, but in the displacement of the father by identification with the suffering Jesus.

For a full understanding of the psychic background of the belief in Christ, we must consider the fact that at that time the Roman Empire was increasingly devoted to the emperor cult, Mohicans transcended all national boundaries. Psychologically it was closely related to monotheism, he belief in a righteous, good father. If the pagans of eye. Referred to Christianity as atheism, in a de-personalize psychological sense they were right, for this faith in the suffering man elevated to a God was the fantasy of a suffering, oppressed class that wanted to displace the ruling powers-God, emperor, and father-and put them-selves in their places. If the main accusations of the pagans against Christians included the charge that they committed Oedipus crimes, this accusation was actually senseless slander; but the unconscious of the slanderers hand under-stood well the unconscious meaning of the Christ myth, its Oedipus wishes, and its concealed hostility to God the father, the emperor, and authority.[37]

To sum up: In order to understand the later development of dogma, one must understand first the distinctive feature of early Christology, its adoption-ist character. The belief that a man is elevated to a God was an expression of the unconscious impulse of hostility to the father that was present in the mass-es. It presented the possibility of an identification and corresponding expecta-tion that the new age would soon begin when those who were suffering and oppressed would be rulers and thus become happy. Since one could, and did, identify with Jesus because he was the suffering man, the possibility was of-fered of a community organization without authorities, statutes, and bureau-cracy, United by the common identification with the suffering Jesus raised to a God. The early Christian adoptionist belief was born of the masses; it was an expression of their revolutionary tendencies, and offered a satisfaction for their strongest longing. This explains why in such an extraordinarily rapid time it became the religion also of the oppressed pagan masses (although soon not theirs exclusively).

4   The Transformation of Christianity and the Homoousian Dogma

The early beliefs concerning Jesus underwent a change. The man raised to God became the Son of Man who was always God and existed before all creation, one with God and yet to be distinguished from Him. Has this change of ideas

---

37   The accusations of ritual murder and of sexual licentiousness can be understood in a similar way.

about Jesus also a sociopsychological meaning such as we were able to demonstrate for the early adoptionist belief? We shall find an answer to this question but subduing the people who, two or three hundred years later, created this dogma and believe in it. In this way we may be able to understand their real life situation and its psychic aspects.

The most important questions are these: Who were the Christians in the early centuries after Christ? Does Christianity remain the religion of the suffering Jewish enthusiasts of Palestine, or who takes their place and joins them?

The first great change in the composition of believers occurred when Christian propaganda turned toward the pagans, and, in a great victorious campaign, won followers among them in almost the entire Roman Empire. The significance of change of nationalizing the followers of Christianity should not be underestimated, but it played no decisive role as pig as the social composition of the Christian community did not change essentially, as long, that is, as it was made up of poor, oppressed, uneducated people feeling common suffering, common hatred, and common hope.

> The familiar judgement of Paul concerning the Corinthian community holds without doubt for the second and third generations of most Christian communities as well as for the apostolic period:

> "For consider your call, brethren; not many of you were wise according to worldly standards, not many were powerful, not many were noble of birth; but God chose what is foolish in the world to shame the wise, God chose what is weak in the world to shame the strong, God chose what is low and despised in the world, even things that are not, to bring to nothing things that are." (I Corinthians 1:26–28)[38]

But although the great majority of the followers Paul won for Christianity in the first century were still people of the lowest class-artisans, slaves, and emancipated slaves-gradually another social element, the educated and the well-to-do, began to infiltrate the communities. Paul was indeed one of the first Christian leaders that did not stem from the lower classes. He was the son of a well-to-do Roman citizen, had been Pharisee and therefore one of the intellectuals that scorned Christians and was hated by them.

> He was not a proletarian unfamiliar with and hatefully opposed to the police order, no one who had no interest in its continuance and who

---

38   Knopf, *Das nachapostolische Zeitalter*, p. 64.

THE DOGMA OF CHRIST

hoped for its destruction. He had from the beginning been too close to the power of government, had too much experience of the blessings of the sacred order not to be of a quite different mind concerning the ethical worth of the state, than, say, a member of the native Zealot party, or even than his Pharisaic colleagues who saw in the Roman domination at most the lesser evil compared with the half Jewish Herodians.[39]

With his propaganda, Paul appealed primarily to the lowest social strata, but certainly also to some of the well-to-do and of the educated people, especially merchants who through their wandering and travels became decidedly significant to the spread of Christianity.[40] But until well into the second century, a substantial element in the communities belonged to the lower classes. This is shown by certain passages from the original literature, which, like the Epistle of James or the Book of Revelation, breathe flaming hatred for the powerful and the rich. The artless form of such pieces of literature and the general tenor of eschatology show that "the members of the [Christian] communions of the post-apostolic period were still drawn mainly from the ranks of the poor and the unfree.[41]

---

39   Weiss, *op. cit.,* p. 132.

40   Cf. Knopf, *op. cit.,* p. 70.

41   Knopf, *op. cit.,* pp. 69 ff. The admonition a of St. Hippolytus still reveal the ethical rigorism and the hostility to middle-class life, as is seen in chapter 41 (cited by Harnack, *Die Mission and Ausbreitung des Christentums,* I, 300): "Inquiry shall likewise be made about the professionals and trades of those who are brought to be admitted to the faith. If a man in pander, he must desist or be rejected. If the man is a sculptor or painter, he must be charged not to make idols; if he does not desist, he must be rejected. A teacher of young children had best desist, but if he has no other occupation, he may be permitted to continue. A charioteer, likewise, who races or frequents races, must desist or be rejected. A gladiator or a trainer of gladiators, or a huntsman (in the wild beast shows), or anyone connected with these shows, or a public official in charge of gladiatorial exhibitions must desist or be rejected. A soldier of the civil authority must be taught not to kill men and to refuse to do so if he is commanded, and to refuse to take an oath; if he is unwilling to comply, he must be rejected. A military commander or civic magistrate that wears purple must resign or be rejected. If a catechumen or a believer seeks to become a soldier, they must be rejected, for they have despised God. A harlot or licentious man or one who has emasculated himself, or any other who does things not to be named must be rejected, for they are defiled. An enchanter, a diviner, a soothsayer, a user of magic verses, a juggler, a mountebank, an amulet maker must desist or be rejected. A concubine, who is a slave and has reared her children and has been faithful to her master alone, may become a hearer; but if she failed in these matters she must be rejected. If a man has a concubine, he must desist and marry legally; if he is unwilling, he must be rejected. If, now, we have omitted anything, the facts will instruct your mind; for we all have the spirit of God."

76 FROMM

About the middle of the second century, Christianity began to win followers among the middle and higher classes of the Roman Empire. Above all, it was women of prominent position, and merchants, who took charge of the propaganda; Christianity spread in their circles and then gradually penetrated the circles of the ruling aristocracy. By the end of the second century, Christianity had already ceased to be the religion of the poor artisans and slaves. And when under Constantine it became the state religion, it had already become the religion of larger circles of the ruling class in the Roman Empire.[42]

---

42 As an example of the character of the community in Rome, Knopf gives a picture of the development of the social composition of the Christian church in the first three centuries. Paul, in the Epistle of the Philippians (4:22), asks that his greeting be conveyed "especially to those of Caesar's household." The fact that the death sentences impose by Nero upon the Christians (m national by Tacitus, *Annales,* xv, 44), such as being sewed up in hides, dog-baiting, crucifixion, being made into living torches, might be used against only *humiliores* and not against *honestiores* (the more prominent), shows that the Christians of this period belonged mainly to the lower ranks, even though some rich and prominent people may already have joined them. How greatly the composition of the post-apostolic had changed is shown by a passage cited by Knopf from *I Clement,* 38:2: "The rich should offer help to the poor and the poor man should thanks God that He has given him someone through whom his need can be helped." One does not observe here any trace of that animosity against the rich which pervades other documents. This is the way in which one can speak in a church where richer and more prominent people are not so very rare and also where they perform their duties to the poor (Knopf, *op. cit.,* p. 65). From the fact that in A.D. 96, eight months before his death, Domition had his cousin, Consul Titus Flavius, executed, and sent the cousin's first wife into exile (punishing him probably and the woman certainly on account of their adherence to Christianity), shows that already at the end of the first century, Christians in Rome had penetrated into the emperors household. The growing number of rich and prominent Christians naturally created tensions and differences in the churches. One of these differences arose early, as to whether Christian masters should free their Christian slaves. This is shown by Pauls exhortation that slaves should not seek emancipation. But since in the course of its development, Christianity became more and more the faith of the ruling groups, these tensions were bound to grow. "The rich did not fraternize any to well with the slaves, the emancipated and proletarians, especially in public. The poor for their part see the rich as belonging half to the devil" (Knopf, *op. cit.,* p. 81) Kermas gives a good picture of the changed social composition: "Those who do much business also sin much, being engrossed in their business, and serving their Lord in nothing" (*Sim* VIII, 9). "These are they who were faithful, but became rich and in honor among the heathen; then they put on great haughtiness and be some high-minded, and abandoned the truth, and did cleave to the righteous, but lived together with the heathen, and this way pleased them better" (*Sim.* XX, 2). It would appear that only in times after the Antonines did the rich and prominent, the people of blood and means, join the Christian church, as is rightly understood by Eusebius in a familiar passage where he says that " during the reign of Commodus the affairs [of the Christians] took an easier turn, and, thanks to the define grace, peace embraced the churches throughout the world...insomuch that already large numbers even of those at Rome,

THE DOGMA OF CHRIST   77

Two hundred and fifty to three hundred and fifty years after the birth of Christianity, the adherents of this faith were quite different from the first Christians. They were no Jews with the belief, held more passionately than by any other people, in a messianic time soon to come. They were, rather, Greeks, Romans, Syrians, and Gauls-in short, members of all the nations of the Roman Empire. more important than this shift in nationality was the social difference. Indeed, slaves, artisans, and the "shabby proletariat," that is, the masses of the lower classes, still constituted the bulk of the Christian communion, but Christianity simultaneously become the religion also of the prominent and ruling classes of the Roman Empire.

In connection with this charge in the social structure of the Christian churches we must glance at the general economic and political situation of the Roman Empire, which had undergone a fundamental change during the same period. The national differences within the world empire had been steadily disappearing. Even an alien could become a Roman citizen. At the same time, the emperor cult functioned as a unifying bond, leveling national differences. The economic development was characterized by a process of gradual progressive feudalization:

> The new relationships, as they were consolidated after the end of the third century, no longer knew any free work, but only compulsory work in the status groups (or estates) that had become hereditary, in the rural population and the colonies, as well as with the artisans and the guilds, and also (as is well known) with the patricians who had become the principal bearers of the tax burden. Thus the circle was completed. The development comes back to the point from which it has started. The medieval order is being established.[43]

The political expression of this declining economy, which was regressing into a new estate-bound "natural economy," was absolute monarchy as it was shaped by Diocletian and Constantine. A hierarchical system was developed with infinite dependencies, at the apex of which was the person of the divine emperor, to whom the masses were to render reverence and love. In a relatively short time the Roman Empire became a feudal class state with a rigidly

---

highly distinguished for wealth and birth, were advancing toward their own salvation with all their households and kindred" (Eusebius, *Ecclesiastical History,* Book V, 21, 1). This in the main metropolis of the world, Christianity has ceased to be a religion primarily of poor people and slaves. From then on its power of attraction appeared in the different ranks of property and education.

43   Eduard Meyer, "Sklaverei im Altertum," *Kleine Schriften* (2nd Ed.; 1924), I, 81.

established order in which the lowest ranks could not expect to rise because the stagnation due to the recession of productive powers mass a profession development impossible. The social system was stabilized and was regulated from the top, and it was imperative to make it easier for the individual who stood at the bottom to be content with his situation.

In the main this was the social situation in the Roman Empire from the beginning of the third century in. The transformation which Christianity, especially the concept of Christ and of his relation to God the Father, underwent from its early days down to this era, must be understood primarily in the light of this social change and of the psychic change conditioned by it, and of the new sociological function which Christianity had to assume. The vital element in this situation is simply not understood if we think that "the" Christian religion spread and won over to its thinking the great majority of the population of the Roman Empire. The truth is, rather, that the original religion was transformed into another one, but the Catholic religion had good reason for concealing this transformation. We shall no point out what transformation Christianity underwent during the first three centuries, and show how the new religion contrasted with the old.

The most important point is that the eschatological expectations which had constituted the center of the faith and hope of the early community gradually disappeared. The core of the missionary preaching of the early communion was, "The kingdom of God is at hand." People had prepared for the kingdom, they had even expected the o experience it themselves, and they doubted whether in the short time available before the coming of the new kingdom, it would be possible to proclaim the Christian message to the majority of the heathen world. Paul's faith is still imbued with eschatological hopes, but with him the expected time of the kingdom's coming already began to be postponed further into the future. For him the final consummation was assured by the elevation of the messiah, and the last struggle, which was still to come, lost its significance in view of what had already happened. But in the subsequent development, belief in the immediate establishment of the kingdom tended more and more to disappear: "What we perceive is, rather, the gradual disappearance of an original element, the Enthusiastic and Apocalyptic, that is, of the sure consciousness of an immediate possession of the Divine Spirit, and the hope of the future conquering the present."[44]

---

44 Harnack, *History of Dogma,* I, 49. Harnack emphasizes that originally, two interrelated views prevailed regarding the purpose of the coming of Christ or the nature and means of salvation: Salvation was conceived, on the one hand, as sharing in the glorious kingdom of Christ soon to appear, and everything else was regarded as preparatory to this sure

THE DOGMA OF CHRIST

If the two conceptions, the eschatological and the spiritual, were closely bound together at the beginning, with the main stress on the eschatological conception, they slowly became separated. The eschatological hope gradually receded, the nucleus of the Christian faith drew away from the second advent of Christ, and "it would then necessarily be found in the first advent, in virtue of which salvation was already prepared for man and man for salvation."[45]

The process of propagating the early Christian enthusiasm quickly died out. to be sure, throughout the later history of Christianity (from the Montanists to the Anabaptists), there were continual attempts to revive the old Christian enthusiasm with its eschatological expectation-attempts that emanated from those groups who, in their economic, social, and psychic situation, because they were oppressed and striving for freedom, resembled the first Christians. But the church was through its these revolution at attempts, ever since she had, in the course of the second century won the first decisive victory. From that time on, the burden of the message was not in the cry, "The kingdom is at hand," in the expectation that judgment day and the return of Jesus would come soon; the Christians no longer looked to the future or to history, but, rather, they looked backward. The decisive event had already taken place. The appearance of Jesus had already represented the miracle.

The real, historical world no longer needed to change; outwardly everything could remain as it was-state, society, law, economy-for salvation had become inward, spiritual, unhistorical, individual matter guaranteed by faith in Jesus. The hope for real, historical deliverance was replaced by faith in the already complete spiritual deliverance. The historical interest was supplanted but the cosmological interest. Hand in hand with it, ethical demands faded away. The first century of Christianity was characterized by rigorous ethical postulates, in the belief that the Christian community was primarily a fellowship of holy living. This practical, ethical rigorism is replaced by the means of grace dispensed by the Church. Very closely connected with the renunciation of the original rigorous ethical practice was the growing reconciliation of Christians with the state. "The second century of the existence of the Christian church already exhibits along all lines a development which moves toward a reconciliation

---

prospect; on the other hand, however, attention was turned to the conditions and provisions of God wrought by Christ, which first made men capable of becoming sure of it. Forgiveness of sin, righteousness, faith, knowledge, etc., are the things which come into consideration here, and these blessing themselves, so far as they have as their sure result life in the kingdom of Christ, or, more accurately, eternal life, may be regarded as salvation. (*Ibid.,* pp. 129–130).

45   Ibid., p. 130

with the state and society."[46] Even the occasional persecutions of the Christians by the state did not affect in the least this development. Although there were attempts here and there to maintain the old rigorist ethic hostile to the state and middle-class life,

> ...the great majority of Christians, especially the leading bishops, decided differently. It now sufficed to have God in one's heart and to confess faith in Him when a public confession before the authorities became unavoidable. It was enough to flee the actual worship of idols, otherwise the Christian could remain in every honorable calling; there he was allowed to come into external contact with the worship of idols, and he should conduct himself prudently and cautiously so that he neither contaminated himself nor even ran the risk of contaminating himself or others. The church adopted this attitude everywhere after the beginning of the third century. The state hereby gained numerous quiet, dutiful, and conscientious citizens who, far from causing it any difficulty, supported order and peace in society....Since the church had abandoned her rigid, negative attitude toward the world, she developed into a state-supporting and state-reforming power. If we may introduce a modern phenomenon for comparison, we may say that the world-fleeing fanatics who awaited the heavenly state of the future became revisionists of the existing order of life.[47]

This fundamental transformation of Christianity from the religion of the oppressed to the religion of the rulers and the masses manipulated by them, from the expectation of the imminent approach of judgement day and the new age to a faith in the already consummated redemption; from the postulate of a pure, moral life to satisfaction of conscience through ecclesiastical means of grace; from hostility to the state to cordial agreement with it-all this is closely connected with the final great change about to be described. Christianity, which had been the religion of a community of equal brothers, without hierarchy or bureaucracy, became "the Church," the reflected image of the absolute monarchy of the Roman Empire.

In the first century there was not even a clearly defined external authority in the Christian communities, which were accordingly built upon the independence and freedom of the individual Christian with respect to matters of faith.

---

46 Harnack, "Kirche und Staat bis zur Grundung der Staatskirche," *Kultur der Gegenwart,* Vol. I, Pt. 4, p. 1; 2nd ed., p. 239

47 Harnack, *op.cit.,* p. 143.

THE DOGMA OF CHRIST

The second century was characterized by the gradual development of an ecclesiastical union with authoritative leaders and thus, also, by the establishment of a systematic doctrine of faith to which the individual Christian has to submit. Originally it was not the Church but God alone who could forgive sins. Later, *Extra ecclesiam nulla salus;* the Church alone offers protection. Against any loss of grace. As an institution, the Church became holy by virtue of her endowment, the moral establishment that educates for salvation. This function is restricted to the priests, specially to the episcopate, "which in its unity guarantees the legitimacy of the church and has received the jurisdiction of forgiveness of sins."[48] This transformation of the free brotherly fellowship into a hierarchical organization clearly indicates the psychic change that had occurred.[49] As the first Christians were imbued with hatred and contempt for the educated rich and rulers, in short, for all authority, so the Christians from the third century on we're imbued with reverence, live, and fidelity to the new clerical authorities.

Just as Christianity was transformed in every respect the first three centuries of its existence and became a new religion as compared with the original one, this was true also with respect to Jesus. In early Christianity the adoptionist doctrine prevailed, that is, the belief that the man Jesus had been elevated to a God. With the continued development of the Church, the concept of the nature of Jesus leaned more toward the pneumatic viewpoint: A man was not elevated to a God, but a God descended to become man. This was the basis of the new concept of Christ, until it culminated in the doctrine of Athanasius, which was adopted by the Nicene Council: Jesus, the Son of God, begotten of the Father before all time, of one nature with the Father. The Arian view that Jesus and God the Father were indeed of similar but not identical nature is rejected in favor of the logically contradictory thesis that two natures, God and his Son, are only one nature; this is the assertion of a duality that is simultaneously a unity. What is the meaning of this change in the concept of Jesus and his relation to God the Father, and what relation does the change in dogma bear to the change in the whole religion?

Early Christianity was hostile to authority and to the state. It's satisfied in fantasy the revolutionary wishes of the lower classes, hostile to the father. The Christianity that was elevated to the official religion of the Roman Empire three hundred years later had a completely different social function. It was intended to be, at the same time, a religion for both the leaders and the led; the rulers and the ruled. Christianity fulfilled the function which the emperor and

---

48   Cyprian, *Epistle* 69, 11.

49   Cf. Harnack, *History of Dogma,* II, 67–94.

the Mithras cult could not nearly as well fulfill, namely the integration of the masses into the absolutist system of the Roman Empire. The revolutionary which had prevailed until the second century had disappeared. Economic regression had supervened; the Middle Ages began to develop. The economic situation led to a system of social ties and dependencies that came to their peak politically in the Roman-Byzantine absolutism. The new Christianity came under leadership of the ruling class. The new dogma of Jesus was created and formulated by this ruling group and its intellectual representatives, not the masses. *The decisive element was the change from the idea of man becoming God to that of God become man.*

Since the new concept of the Son, who was indeed a second person beside God yet one with him, changed the tension between God and his Son into harmony, and since it avoided the concept that a man could become God, it eliminated from the formula the revolutionary character of the older doctrine, namely hostility to the father. Th Oedipus crime contained in the old formula, the displacement of the father by the son, was eliminated in the new Christianity. The father remained in his position. Now, however, it was not a man, but his only begotten Son, existing before all creation, who was beside him. Jesus himself became God without dethroning God because he had always been a component of God.

Thus far we have understood only the negative point: why Jesus could no longer be the man raised to a God, the man set at the right hand of the father. The need for recognition of the father, or passive subordination to him, could have been satisfied by the great competitor of Christianity, the emperor cult. Why did Christianity and not the emperor cult succeed in becoming the established state religion of the Roman Empire? Because Christianity had a quality that made it superior for the social function it was intended to fulfill, namely, faith in the crucified Son of God. The suffering and the oppressed masses could identify with him to a greater degree. But the fantasy satisfaction changed. The masse no longer identified with the crucified man in order to dethrone the father in fantasy, but, rather, in order to enjoy his love and grace. The idea that a man became a God was a symbol of aggressive, active, hostile-to-the-father tendencies. The idea that God became a man was transformed into a symbol of the tender, passive tie to the father. The masses found their satisfaction in the fact that their representative, the crucified Jesus, was elevated in status, becoming himself a pre-existent God. People no longer expected an imminent historical change but believed, rather, that deliverance had already taken place, that deliverance they opted for had already happened. They rejected the fantasy which represented hostility to the father, and accepted another in its

THE DOGMA OF CHRIST

place, the harmonizing one of the sons placed beside the father by the latter's free will.

The theological change is the expression of a sociological one, that is, the change in the social function of Christianity. Far from being a religion of Rebels and revolutionaries, this religion of the ruling class was now determined to keep the masses in obedience and lead them. Since the old revolutionary representative was retained, however, the emotional need of the masses as satisfied in a new way. The formula of passive submission replaced the active hostility to the father. It was not necessary to displace the father, since the son had indeed been equal to God for the beginning, precisely because God himself had "emitted" him. The actual possibility of identifying with a God who had suffered yet had from the beginning been in heaven, and at the same time eliminating tendencies hostile to the father, is the basis for the victory of Christianity over the emperor cult. Moreover, the change in the attitude toward the real, existing father figures-the priests, the emperor, and especially the rulers-corresponded to this changed attitude toward the father-god.

The psychic situation of the Catholic masses of the fourth century was unlike that of any early Christians in that the hatred for the authorities, including the father-God was no longer conscious, or was only relatively so; the people had given up their revolutionary attitude. The reason for this lies in the change of the social reality. Every hope for the overthrow of the rulers and for the victory of their own class was so hopeless that, from the psychic viewpoint, it would have been futile and uneconomical to persist in the attitude of hatred. If it was hopeless to overthrow the father, then the better psychic escape was to submit to him, to love him, and to receive love for him. This change of psychic attitude when the inevitable result of the final defeat of the oppressed class.

But the aggressive impulses could not have disappeared. Nor could they even have dismissed, for their real cause, the oppression by the rulers, was neither removed or reduced. Where were the aggressive impulses now? They were turned away from the earlier objects-the fathers-and directed back toward the individual self. The identification with the suffering crucified Jesus offered a magnificent opportunity for this. In Catholic dogma the stress was no longer, as in the early Christian doctrine, on the overthrow of the father but on the self-annihilation of the son. The original aggression directed against the father was turned against the self, it thereby provided an outlet that was harmless for social stability.

But this was possible only in connection with another change. For the first Christians, the authorities and the rich were evil people who would reap the deserved reward for their wickedness. Certainly the early Christians were not without guilt feelings on account of their hostility to the father; and the identification with the suffering Jesus had also served the expiate their aggression; but without doubt the emphasis for them was not in the guilt feelings and the masochistic, atoning reaction. For the Catholic masses later on the situation changed. For them no longer were the rulers to blame for their wretchedness and suffering; rather, the sufferers themselves were guilty. They must reproach themselves if they are unhappy. Only through constant expiation, only through personal suffering could they atone for their guilt and win the love and pardon of God and his earthly representatives. By suffering and castrating oneself, one finds escape from the oppressive guilt fling and has a chance to receive pardon and love.[50]

The Catholic Church understood how to accelerate and strengthen in a masterful way this process of changing the reproaches against God and the rulers into reproach of the self. It increased the guilt feeling of the masses to a point where it was almost unbearable; and in doing so it achieved a double purpose: first, it helped turn reproaches and aggression away from the authorities and toward the suffering masses: and second, it offered itself to these suffering masses as a good and loving father, since the priests granted pardon and expiation for the guilt feeling which they themselves had engendered. It ingeniously cultivated the psychic conditions from which it, the upper class, derived a double advantage: the diversion of the aggression of the masses and the assurance of their dependency, gratitude, and love.

For the rulers, however, the fantasy of the suffering Jesus not only had this social function but also an important psychic function. It relieved them of the guilt feelings they experienced because of the distress and suffering of the masses whom they had oppressed and exploited. By identifying with the suffering Jesus, the exploiting groups could themselves do penance. They could comfort themselves with the idea that, since God's only-begotten Son had suffered voluntarily, suffering, for the masses was a grace of God, and therefore they had no reason to reproach themselves for causing such suffering.

The transformation of christological dogma, as well as that of the whole Christian religion, merely corresponded to the sociological function of religion in general, the maintenance of social stability by preserving the interests of the governing classes. For the first Christians it was a blessed and satisfying dream to create the fantasy that the hated authorities would soon be overthrown and that they themselves, now poor and suffering, would achieve mastery and happiness. After their final defeat, and after all their expectations had proven futile, the masses became satisfied with a fantasy in which they accepted

---

50   Cf. Freud's remarks in *Civilization and Its Discontents* (Standard edition), XXI, 123 ff.

THE DOGMA OF CHRIST

responsibility for all suffering; they could, however, atone for their winds through their own suffering and then hope to be loved by a good father. He had proved himself a loving father when, in the form of the son, he became a suffering man. Their other wishes for happiness, and, not merely forgiveness, were satisfied in the fantasy of a blissful hereafter, a hereafter which was supposed to replace the historically happy condition in this world for which early Christians had hoped.

In our interpretation of the Homoousion formula, however, we have not yet found its unique and ultimate unconscious meaning. Analytic experience leads us to expect that behind the logical contradiction of the formula, namely, the two are equal to one, must be hidden a specific unconscious meaning to which the dogma owes it significance and its fascination. This deepest, unconscious, waning of the Homoousian doctrine becomes clear when we recall a simple fact: There is one actual situation in which the formula makes sense, the situation of the child in its mother's womb. Mother and child are then two beings and at the same time are one.

We have now arrived at the central problem of the change in the idea of the relation of Jesus to God the Father. Not only the son had changed but the father as well. The strong, powerful father has become the sheltering and protecting mother; the once rebellious, then suffering and passive son has become the small child. Under the guise of the fatherly God of the Jews, who in the struggle with the Near Eastern motherly divinities had gained dominance, the divine figure of the Great Mother emerges again, and becomes the dominating figure of medieval Christianity.

The significance that the motherly divinity had for Catholic Christianity, from the fourth century on, becomes clear, first, in the role that the Church, as such, begins to play; and second, in the cult of Mary.[51] It has been shown that for early Christians the idea of a *church* was still quite alien. Only in the course of historical development does the Church gradually assume a hierarchical organization; the Church itself becomes a holy institution and more than merely the sum of its member. The Church mediates salvation, the believers are her children, she is the Great Mother through whom alone man can achieve security and blessedness.

Equally revealing is the revival of the figure of the motherly divinity in the cult of Mary. Mary represents the divinity grown independent by separating itself from the father-god. In her, the motherly qualities, which had always unconsciously been a part of God the Father, we're now consciously and clearly experienced and symbolically represented.

---

51 Cf. A. J Storfer, *Marias fungfrauliche Mutterschaft* (Berlin, 1913).

In the New Testament account, Mary was in no way elevated beyond the sphere of ordinary men. With the development of Christology, ideas about Mary assumed an ever increasing prominence. The more the figure of the historical human Jesus receded in favor of the pre-existent Son of God, the more Mary was defiled. Although, according to the New Testament, Mary in her marriage with Joseph continued to bear children, Epiphanius disputed that view as heretical frivolous. In the Nestorian controversy a decision against Nestorius was reached in 431 that Mary was not only the mother of Christ but also the mother of God, and at the end of the fourth century there arose a cult of Mary, and men addressed prayers to her. About the same time the representation of Mary in the plastic arts began to play a great and ever increasing role. The succeeding centuries attached more and more significance to the mother of God, and her worship became more exuberant and more general. Altars were erected to her, and her pictures were shown everywhere. From a recipient of grace she became the dispenser of grace.[52] Mary with the infant Jesus became the symbol of the Catholic Middle Ages.

The full significance of the collective fantasy of the nursing Madonna becomes clear only through the results of psychoanalytic clinical investigations. Sandor Rado has pointed out the extraordinary significance which the fear of starvation, on the one hand, and the happiness of oral satisfaction, on the other, play in the psychic life of the individual:

> The torments of hunger become a psychic foretaste of later "punishments," and though the school of punishment they become the primitive mechanism of a self-punishment which finally in melancholia achieves so fateful a significance. Behind the boundless fear of pauperization felt by the melancholy is hidden nothing other than the fear of starvation; this fear is the reaction of the vitality of the normal ego-residue to the life-threatening, melancholic act of expiation or penance imposed by the Church. Drinking from the breast, however, remains the shining example of the unfailing, pardoning proffer of love. It is certainly no accident that the nursing Madonna with the child has become the symbol of a whole epoch of our Western culture. In my opinion, the derivation of the

---

52   The connection of the worship of Mary with the worship of the pagan mother divinities has been dealt with a number of times. A particularly clear example is found in the Collyridians, who, as priestesses of Mary, carry cakes about in solemn procession on a day consecrated to her, similar to the cult of the Canaanite queen of heaven mentioned by Jeremiah. Cf. Rosch (Th. St. K., 1888, p. 278 f), who interprets the cake as a phallic symbol and views the Mary worshiped by the Collyridians as identical with the Oriemntal-Phoenician Astarte [see *Realenzyklopadie fur protestantische Theologie und Kirche*, Vol. XII (Leipzig 1915)].

THE DOGMA OF CHRIST

meaning-complex of guilt atonement and pardon from the early infantile experience of rage, hunger, and drinking from the breast solves our riddle as to why the hope for absolution and love is perhaps the most powerful configuration we encounter in the higher levels of human psychic life.[53]

Rado's study makes entirely intelligible the connection between the fantasy of the suffering Jesus and that of the child Jesus on the mother's breast. Both fantasies are an expression of the wish for pardon and expiation. In the fantasy of the crucified Jesus, pardon is obtained by a passive, self-castrating submission to the father. In the fantasy of the child Jesus on the breast of the Madonna, the masochistic element is lacking; in place of the father one finds the mother who, while she pacifies the child, grants pardon and expiation. The same happy feeling constitutes the unconscious meaning of the Homoousian dogma, the fantasy of the child sheltered in the womb.

This fantasy of the great pardoning mother is the optimal gratification which the Catholic Christianity had to offer. The more the masses suffered, the more their real situation resembled that of the suffering Jesus, and the more the figure of the happy, suckling babe, could, and must, appear alongside the suffering Jesus. But this meant also that men had to regress to a passive, infantile attitude. This position precluded active revolt; it was the psychic attitude corresponding to the man of hierarchically structure medieval society, a human being who found himself dependent on the rulers, who expected to secure from them his minimum sustenance, and for whom hunger was proof of his sins.

5   The Development of the Dogma Until the Nicene Council

Thus far we have followed the changes in the concepts of Christ and his relation to God the Father from their beginning in the early Christian faith to the Nicene dogma, and have tried to point out the motives for the changes. The development had several immediate stages, however, which are characterized by the different formulations that appeared up to the time of the Nicene Council. This development proceeds by contradiction, and this can be understood dialectically only together with the gradual evolution of Christianity from a revolutionary into a state-supporting religion. To demonstrate that the different formulations of the dogma correspond at each time to a particular class and its needs constitutes a special study. Nevertheless, the basic feature should be indicated here.

---

53   *Internationale Zeitschrift fur Psychoanalyse*, XII, 445.

Second-century Christianity, which had already begun its "revisionism," was characterized by a battle on two fronts: On the one hand, the revolutionary tendencies which still flared up with some force in widely different places had to suppressed; on the other hand, tendencies which were inclined to develop too quickly in the direction of social conformity, indeed more quickly than the social development permitted, also had to be suppressed. The masses could take only a slow, gradual course from the hope in a revolutionary Jesus to faith in a state-supporting Jesus.

The strongest expression of early Christian tendencies was Montanism. Originally the powerful effort of a Phrygian prophet, Montanus, in the second half of the second century, Montanism was a reaction against the conforming tendencies of Christianity, a reaction that sought to restore the early Christian enthusiasm. Montanus wished to withdraw the Christians from their social relationships and to establish through his followers a new community apart from the world, a community that was to prepare itself for the descent of the "upper Jerusalem." Montanism was a flare-up of the early Christian mood, but the transformation process of Christianity had already gone so far that this revolutionary tendency was fought as heresy by the Church authorities, who acted like bailiffs of the Roman state. (The behavior of Luther toward the revolting peasants and the Anabaptists was similar in many respects.)

The Gnostics, on the other hand, were the intellectual representatives of the well-to-do Hellenistic middle class. According to Harnack, Gnosticism represented the "acute secularizing" of Christianity, and anticipates a development which was to continue for another one hundred and fifty years. At that moment it was attacked by the official Church, along with Montanism, but only an undialectical interpretation can overlook the fact that the struggle of the Church against Montanism was very different in character from that against Gnosticism. Montanism was resisted because it was the resurgence of a movement which had already been subdued and which was dangerous for the present leaders of Christianity. Gnosticism was resisted because it wanted to accomplish too quickly and too suddenly what it wished, since it announced the secret of the coming Christian development before the consciousness of the masses could accept it.

The Gnostic ideas of faith, especially their christological and eschatological conceptions, correspond exactly with the expectations which we must have on the basis of our study of the social-psychological background of dogmatic development. It is not surprising that Gnosticism denies entirely the early Christian eschatology, especially the second coming of Christ and the resurrection of the flesh, and expects of the future only the freeing of the spirit from its material covering. This thorough rejection of eschatology, which was achieved

THE DOGMA OF CHRIST   89

in Catholicism a hundred and fifty years later, was at that time premature; eschatological concepts were still ideologically retained by the apologists, who had in other respects had already become widely separated from the early Christian conception. Such a remnant was judged "archaic" by Harnack, but necessary at that time for the satisfaction of the masses.

Another doctrine of Gnosticism closely connected with this rejection of eschatology should be noted: that is, the Gnostic stress on the discrepancy between the supreme God and the creator of the world, and the assertion that "the present world sprang from a fall of man, or from an undertaking hostile to God, and is, therefore, the product of an evil or intermediate being."[54] The meaning of this thesis is clear: If creation, that is, the historical world, as it finds its expression in social and political life, is evil from the beginning, if it is the work of an intermediary, indifferent, or feeble God, then indeed it cannot be redeemed, and all the early Christian eschatological hopes must be false and unfounded. Gnosticism rejected the real collective change and redemption of humanity, and substituted and individual ideal of knowledge, dividing men along religious and spiritual lines in definite classes and castes; social and economic divisions were regarded as good and God-given. Men were divided into pneumatics, who enjoyed the highest blessedness; psychics, who shared somewhat lesser blessedness; and hylics, who had fallen completely into decline. It was a rejection of collective redemption and an assertion of the class stratification of society like that which Catholicism established later in the separation of laity from clergy, and the life of the common people from that of the monks.

What then was the concept of the Gnostics concerning Jesus and his relation to God the Father? They taught that

> ...the heavenly Aeon, Christ, and the human appearance of that Aeon must be clearly distinguished. Some, like Basilides, who acknowledged no real union between Christ and the man Jesus, whom they regarded as an earthly man. Others, e.g., part of the Valentinians...taught that the body of Jesus was a heavenly psychical formation, and sprang from the womb of Mary only in appearance. Finally, a third party, such as Saturinus, declared that the whole visible appearance of Christ was a phantom, and therefore denied the birth of Christ.[55]

---

54   Harnack, *History of Dogma*, I, 258.

55   Ibid., pp. 259–260.

What is the meaning of these conceptions? The decisive feature is that the original Christian idea that a real man (whose character as a revolutionary and one hostile to the father we have already set forth) become a God is eliminated. The different Gnostic tendencies are only expressions of the different possibilities of this elimination. All of them deny that Christ was a real man, thus maintaining the inviolability of the father-God. The connection with the concept of redemption is also clear. It is just as unlikely that this world, which is by nature evil, can become good, as it is that a real man can become a God; this means that it is equally unlikely that there is anything in the existing social situation that can be changed. It is a misunderstanding to believe that the Gnostics thesis-that God the Creator of the Old Testament is not the highest God, but an inferior God-is an expression of especially hostile tendencies to the father. The Gnostics had to assert the inferiority of God the Creator in order to demonstrate the thesis of immutability of the world and of human society, and fir them this assertion was therefore not an expression of hostility to the father. Their thesis, in contrast to the first Christians, dealt with a God alien to them, the Jewish Yahweh, whom these Greeks had no reason to respect. For them, to dethrone this Jewish deity entailed nor presupposed any special hostile emotions toward the father.

The Catholic Church, which fought Montanism as a dangerous remnant and Gnosticism as a premature anticipation of what was to come, moved gradually but steadily toward the final achievement of her goal in the fourth century. The apologists were first to provide the theory for this development. They created dogmas-they were the first to use this term in the technical sense-in which the changed attitude toward God and society found expression. To be sure, they were not so radical as the Gnostics: It has been pointed out that they retained the eschatological ideas and thus served as a link with early Christianity. Their doctrine of Jesus and his relation to God the father, however, was closely related to the Gnostic position, and contained the seed of the Nicene dogma. They attempted to present Christianity as the highest philosophy; they "formulated the content of the Gospel in a manner which appealed to the common sense of all serious thinkers and intelligent men of the age."[56]

Though the apologists did not teach that matter is evil, they did not, however, make God the direct originator of the world, but personified divine intelligence and inserted it between God and the world. One thesis, though less radical than the corresponding Gnostic one, has the same opposition to historical redemption. The Logos, ejected by God out of himself for the purpose of creation, and produced by a voluntary act, was for them the Son of

---

56 Harnack, *op. cit.,* II, 110.

THE DOGMA OF CHRIST   91

God. On the other hand, he was not separated from God but was rather the result of God's own unfolding, he was God and Lord, his personality had a beginning, he was creature in relation to God; yet this subordination lay not in his nature but rather in his origin.

This Logos christology of the apologists was in essence identical with Nicene dogma. The adoptionist, anti-authoritarian theory concerning the man who became God was discarded, and Jesus became pre-existent only-begotten Son of God, of one nature with him and yet a second person inside him. Our interpretation of this source of the Nicene doctrine therefore holds in essence, for the Logos christology, which was the decisive precursor for the new Catholic Christianity.

> The assimilation of the Logos Christology into the faith of the Church... involved a transformation of faith into doctrine with Greek-philosophical featured; it pushed back the old eschatological ideas; indeed, it suppressed them; it substituted for the Christ of history a conceptual Christ, a principle, and transformed the historical Christ into phenomena. It led Christians to "Nature" and to naturalistic greatness, instead of to the personal and the moral; it gave to the faith of the Christians definitely the direction toward the contemplation of ideas and dogmas, thus preparing the way, on the one hand, for the monastic life, and, on the other, for a tutored Christianity of imperfect, working laymen. It legitimized hundreds of questions of cosmology and of the nature of the world as religious questions, and it demanded a definite answer on pain of losing salvation. This led to a situation where, instead of preaching faith, people preached a situation where, instead of preaching faith, people preached faith in the faith and stunted religion while ostensibly enlarging it. But since it perfected the alliance with science, it shaped Christianity into a world religion, and indeed into a cosmopolitan religion, and prepared the way for the Act of Constantine.[57]

Thus in the Logos christology the seed if the definitive Christian-Catholic dogma was created. Its recognition and adoption did not proceed, however, without a severe struggle against ideas which contradicted it, behind which were hidden remnants of early Christian views and the early Christian mood. The concept has been called *monoarchianism* (first by Tertullian). Within monarchianism, two tendencies can be distinguished; the adoptionist and the modalist. Adoptionist monarchianism started with Jesus as a human who

---

57   Harnack, *Lehrbuch der Dogmengeschichte* (6th ed., 1922), p. 155.

became God. The modalist view held that Jesus was only a manifestation of God the Father, not a God alongside him. Both tendencies, therefore, asserted the monarchy of God: one, that a man was inspired by the divine spirit, while God remained inviolable as a unique being; the other, that the Son was only a manifestation of the Father, again preserving the monarchy of God. Although two branches of monarchianism appeared to contradict each other, the contrast was actually much less sharp. Harnack points out that the two views, apparently so opposed, in many ways coincide, and psychoanalytic interpretation makes fully intelligible the affinity of the two monarchian movements. It has already been indicated that the unconscious meaning of the adoptionist conception is the wish to displace the father-God; if a man can become God and be enthroned at the right hand of God, then God is dethroned. However, the same tendency is clear in the modalist dogma; if Jesus were only a manifestation of God, then certainly God the Father himself was crucified, suffered, and died-a view that has been called *Patripassianism*. In this modalistic conception we recognize a clear affinity with the old New Eastern myths of the dying God (Attis, Adonis, Osiris), which imply an unconscious hostility to the father-God.

It is precisely the reverse of what an interpretation which disregarded the psychic situation of the people supporting the dogma might believe. Monarchianism, adoptionist as well as modalist, signifies not an increased reverence for God but the opposite – the wish for his displacement, which is expressed in the deification of a man or the crucifixion of God himself. From what has already been said, it is fully understandable that Harnack emphasizes, as one of the essential points on which the two monarchian movement agree, the fact that they represented the eschatological as opposed to the naturalistic conception of the person of Christ. We have seen that the former idea, that Jesus will return to establish the new kingdom, was an essential part if the primitive Christian belief, which was revolutionary and hostile to the father. We are therefore not surprised to find this conception also in the two monarchian movements, whose relationship to early Christian doctrine has been demonstrated. Nor are we surprised that Tertullian and Origen testified that the bulk of the Christian people thought it monarchian terms, and we understand that the struggle against both types of monarchianism was essentially an expression of the struggle against tendencies, still rooted in the masses, of hostility to the father-God and to the state.

We pass over individual nuances within dogmatic development and turn to the great disagreement which found a preliminary settlement in the Nicene Council, namely, the controversy between Arius and Anthanasius. Arius taught

THE DOGMA OF CHRIST

that God is One, beside whom there is no other, and that his Son was an independent being different in essence from the Father. He was not true God and he had divine qualities only as acquired ones, and only in part. Because he was not eternal, his knowledge was not perfect, therefore, he was not entitled to the same honor as the Father. But he was created before the world, as an instrument for the creation of other creatures, having been created by the will of God as an independent being. Athanasius contrasted the Son, who belonged to God, with the world: he produced from the essence of God, shared completely the whole nature of the Father, had one and the same essence with the Father, and forms with God a strict unity.

We can easily recognize behind the opposition between Arius and Athanasius the old controversy between the monarchian conception and the Logos christology of the apologists (even though Anthanasius made minor changes in the old Logos doctrine through new formulations), the struggle between the revolutionary tendencies hostile to the father-God and the conformist movement supporting father and state, and renouncing a collective and historical liberation. The latter finally triumphed in the fourth century, when Christianity became the official religion of the Roman Empire. Arius, a pupil of Lucien, who was in proponents of adoptionism, represented adoptionism no longer in its pure, original form but already mixed with elements of the Logos christology. That could not be otherwise, for the development of Christianity away from the early enthusiasm and toward the Catholic Church had already progressed so far that the old conflict could be fought out only in the language and in the climate of ecclesiastical views. If the controversy between Athanasius and Arius seemed to revolve around a small difference (whether God and the Son are of the same nature or of equal nature, *Homoousian* or *Homoiousian*), the smallness of this difference was precisely the consequence of the victory, now nearly complete, over the early Christian tendencies. But behind this debate lay nothing less than the conflict between revolutionary and reactionary tendencies. The Arian dogma was one of the final convulsions of the early Christian movement; the victory of Athanasius sealed the defeat of the religion and the hopes of the small peasants, artisans, and proletarians in Palestine.

We have tried to show with broad stroked how the various stages in the dogmatic development were in character with the general trend of this development from the early Christian faith to the Nicen dogma, It would be an attractive task, which we must forgo in this study, to show also the social situation of the groups that were involved at each stage. It would also be worth while to study the reason why nine-tenths of the Orient and the Germans adhered to Arianism. We believe, however, that we have shown sufficiently that the various

94 FROMM

stages of dogma development and both its beginning and end can be understood only on the basis of changes in the actual social situation and function of Christianity.

6   Another Attempt at Interpretation

What are the differences in method and in content be-tween the present study and that of Theodor Reik dealing with the same material?

Reik proceeds methodologically in the following manner. The special object of his investigation is dogma, particularly christological dogma. Since he is "concerned with pursuing the parallels between religion and compulsion-neurosis and showing the connection between the two phenomena in single examples," he tries to show, "especially in this representative example, that religious dogma in the evolutionary history of humanity corresponds to neurotic obsessional thought, that it is the most significant expression of irrational compulsive thinking." The psychic processes that lead to the construction and development of dogma follow throughout the psychic mechanism of obsessional thinking, and the same motives predominate in both. "In the shaping of dogma the same defense mechanisms are involved as in the compulsive processes in the individual."

How does Reik proceed to develop his thesis concerning the fundamental analogy between dogma and compulsion?

First, on the basis of his idea of the analogy between religion and the compulsion-neurosis, he expects to find this agreement in all individual aspects of both phenomena, and therefore also between religious thinking and compulsive thinking. He then turns to the evolution of dogma and sees how it is carried out along the lines of a continued struggle over small differences; it does not seem to him farfetched to interpret this striking similarity between dogmatic development and obsessional thinking as proof of the identity of the two phenomena. Thus the unknown is to be explained by the known; the shaping of dogma is to be understood as following the same laws that govern compulsive-neurotic processes. The hypothesis of an inner relationship between the two phenomena is strengthened by the fact that in the christological dogma in particular, the relation to God the Father, with its basic ambivalence, plays a striking and special role. In Reik's methodological attitude there are certain assumptions which are not explicitly mentioned, but whose exposition is necessary for the criticism of his method. The most important is the following: Because a religion, in this case Christianity, is conceived and presented as

THE DOGMA OF CHRIST   95

one entity, the followers of this religion are assumed to be a unified subject, and the masses are thus treated as if they were one man, an individual. Like organicistic sociology, which has conceived of society as a living entity and has understood the different groups within society as different parts of an organism, thus referring to the eyes, the skin, the head, and so on, of society, Reik adopts an organicistic concept – not in the anatomic but in the psychological sense. Furthermore, he does not attempt to investigate the masses, whose unity he assumes, in their real life situation. He assumes the masses are identical, and deals only with the ideas and ideologies produced by the masses, not concerning himself concretely with living men and their psychic situation. He does not interpret die ideologies as produced by men; he reconstructs the men from the ideologies. Consequently his method is relevant for the his-tory of dogma and not as a method for the study of religious and social history. Thus it is quite similar not only to organicistic sociology but also to a method of religious re-search oriented exclusively to the history of ideas, which has already been abandoned, even by many historians of religion, for example, Harnack. By his method Reik implicitly supports the theological approach, which the content of his work consciously and explicitly rejects. This theological viewpoint emphasizes the unity of Christian religion indeed, Catholicism claims immutability; and if we adopt as method the analysis of Christianity as if it were a living individual, we will, logically, be brought to the orthodox Catholic position.

The methodology just discussed is of great significance in the investigation of Christian dogma because it is decisive for the concept of ambivalence, which is central for Reik's work. Whether the assumption of a unified subject is acceptable or not is a matter that can be decided only after an investigation lacking in Reik of the psychic, social, and economic situation, of the "psychic surfaces" of the group. The term ambivalence applies only when there is a conflict of impulses within one individual, or perhaps within a group of relatively homogeneous individuals. If a man simultaneously loves and hates another person, we can speak of ambivalence. But if, when there are two men, one loves and the other hates a third man, the two men are opponents. We can analyze why one loves and the other hates, but it would be rather confusing to speak of an ambivalence. When within a group we confront the simultaneous presence of contradictory impulses, only an investigation of the realistic situation of this group can show whether behind their apparent unity we might not find different subgroups, each with different desires, and fighting with each other. The apparent ambivalence might, indeed, turn out to be a conflict between different subgroups.

An example may illustrate this point. Let us imagine that in several hundred or a thousand years, a psychoanalyst, using Reik's method, made a study of the political history of Germany after the revolution of 1918, and particularly the dispute over the colors of the German flag. He would establish that there were in the German nation some, the monarchists, who favored a black-white-red flag; others, the republicans, who insisted on a black-red-gold flag; and others again who wanted a red flag and then an agreement was reached whereby it was decided to make the main flag black-red-gold, and the trade flag on ships black-white-red with a black-red-gold corner. Our imaginary analyst would first examine the rationalizations and find that one group claimed it wanted to keep the black-white-red flag because these colors are more visible on the ocean than black-red-gold. He would indicate what significance the attitude toward the father had in this battle (monarchy or republic), and he would go on to discover an analogy to the thinking of a compulsive neurotic. He would then cite examples where the doubt as to which color was the right one (Reik's example of the patient who cudgeled his brains over the white or black necktie serves excellently here) is rooted in the conflict of ambivalent impulses, and would see in the fuss over the colors of the flag and in the final flag compromise a phenomenon analogous to obsessional thinking conditioned by the same causes.

No one who understands the real circumstances will doubt that the inference from analogy would be false. It is clear that there were different groups whose different realistic and affective interests are in conflict with one another, that the struggle over the flag was a struggle between groups differently oriented both psychically and economically, and that one is concerned here with anything but an "ambivalence conflict." The flag compromise was not the result of an ambivalence conflict, but rather the compromise between different claims of social groups fighting with each other.

What substantial differences result from the methodological difference? Both in the interpretation of the content of christological dogma and in the psychological evaluation of dogma as such, a different method leads to different results.

There is a common point of departure, the interpretation of early Christian faith as an expression of hostility to the father. In the interpretation of the further dogmatic development, however, we come to a conclusion precisely the opposite of Reik's. Reik considers Gnosticism a movement in which rebellious impulses, supported by the son-religion of Christianity, have predominated to the extreme, to the downgrading of the father-god. We have tried to show that, on the contrary, Gnosticism eliminated the early Christian revolutionary tendencies. Reik's error seems to us to grow out of the fact that, according to his

THE DOGMA OF CHRIST   97

method, he notices only the Gnostic formula of the removal of the Jewish father-god, instead of looking at Gnosticism as a whole, in which a quite different significance can be attributed to the formula of hostility to Yahweh. The interpretation of further dogmatic development leads to other equally contrary results. Reik sees in the doctrine of the pre-existence of Jesus the survival and conquest of the original Christian hostility to the father. In direct opposition to this idea, I have tried to show that in the idea of the pre-existence of Jesus, the original hostility to the father is replaced by an opposite harmonizing tendency. We see that the psychoanalytic interpretation leads here to two opposite conceptions of the unconscious meaning of different dogma formulations. This opposition certainly does not depend upon any difference in the psychoanalytic presuppositions as such. It rests only upon the difference in the method of applying psychoanalysis to social-psychological phenomena. The conclusions to which we come seem to us to be correct because, unlike Reik's, they stem not from the interpretation of an isolated religious formula but rather from the examination of this formula in its connection with the real life situation of the men holding it.

No less important is our disagreement, resulting from the same methodological difference, with respect to the interpretation of the psychological significance of dogma as such. Reik sees in dogma the most significant expression of popular compulsive thought, and tries to show "that the psychic processes which lead to the establishment and development of dogma consistently follow the psychic mechanisms of compulsive thinking, that the same motives predominate in the one area as in the other." He finds the development of dogma conditioned by an ambivalent attitude toward the father. For Reik, the hostility to the father finds its first high point in Gnosticism. The apologists then develop a Logos christology, where the unconscious purpose of replacing God the Father by Christ is clearly symbolized, although the victory of unconscious impulses is prevented by strong defense forces. Just as in a compulsive neurosis, and where two opposite tendencies alternately win the upper hand, according to Reik the same conflicting tendencies appear in the development of dogma, which follows the same laws as the neurosis. We have just shown in detail the source of Reik's error. He overlooks the fact that the psychological subject here is not a man and is not even a group possessing a relatively unified and unchanging psychic structure, but, rather, is made up of different groups with different social and psychic interests. The different dogmas are an expression of just those conflicting interests, and the victory of a dogma is not the result of an inner psychic conflict analogous to that in an individual, but is the result, rather, of a historical development which, in consequence of quite different external circumstances (such as the stagnation and retrogression of the economy and of the social and political forces connected with it), leads to the victory of one movement and the defeat of another.

Reik views dogma as an expression of compulsive thinking, and ritual as an expression of collective compulsive action. Certainly it is correct that in Christian dogma, as well as in many other dogmas, ambivalence toward the father plays a great role, but this in no way demonstrates that dogma is compulsive thinking. We have tried to show precisely how the variations in the development of dogma, which at first suggest compulsive thinking, require, in fact, a different explanation. Dogma is to a large extent conditioned by realistic political and social motives. It serves as a sort of banner, and the recognition of the banner is the avowal of membership in a particular group. On this basis it is understandable that religions which are sufficiently consolidated by extra-religious elements (such as Judaism is by the ethnic element) are able to dispense al-most completely with a system of dogmas in the Catholic sense.

But it is obvious that this organizing function of dogma is not its only function; and the present study has at-tempted to show what social significance is to be attributed to dogma by the fact that in fantasy it gratifies the demands of the people, and functions in place of real gratification. Given die fact that symbolic gratifications are condensed into the form of a dogma which the masses are required to believe on the authority of priests and rulers, it seems to us that dogma may be compared with a powerful suggestion, which is experienced subjectively as reality because of the consensus among the believers. For the dogma to reach the unconscious, those contents which are not capable of being consciously perceived must be eliminated and presented in rationalized and acceptable forms.

7   Conclusion

Let us summarize what our study has shown concerning the meaning of the changes occurring in the evolution of the dogma of Christ.

The early Christian faith in the suffering man who be-came God had its central significance in the implied wish to overthrow the father-god or his earthly representatives. The figure of the suffering Jesus originated primarily from the need for identification on the part of the suffering masses, and it was only secondarily determined by the need for expiation for the crime of aggression against the father. The followers of this faith were men who, because of their life situation, were imbued with hatred for their rulers and with hope for their own happiness. The change in the economic situation and in the social

THE DOGMA OF CHRIST 99

composition of the Christian community altered the psychic attitude of the believers. Dogma developed; the idea of a man becoming a god changes into the idea of a god becoming a man. No longer should the father be overthrown; it is not the rulers who are guilty but the suffering masses. Aggression is no longer directed against the authorities but against the persons of the sufferers themselves. The satisfaction lies in pardon and love, which the father offers his submissive sons, and simultaneously in the regal, fatherly position which the suffering Jesus assumes while remaining the representative of the suffering masses. Jesus eventually became God without overthrowing God because he was always God.

Behind this there lies a still deeper regression which finds expression in the Homoousian dogma: the fatherly God, whose pardon is to be obtained only through one's own suffering, is transformed into the mother full of grace who nourishes the child, shelters it in her womb, and thus provides pardon. Described psychologically, the change taking place here is the change from an attitude hostile to the father, to an attitude passively and masochistically docile, and finally to that of the infant loved by its mother. If this development took place in an individual, it would indicate a psychic illness. It takes place over a period of centuries, however, and affects not the entire psychic structure of individuals but only a segment common to all; it is an expression not of pathological disturbance but, rather, of adjustment to the given social situation. For the masses who retained a remnant of hope for the overthrow of the rulers, the early Christian fantasy was suitable and satisfying, as was Catholic dogma for the masses of the Middle Ages. The cause for the development lies in the change in the socioeconomic situation or in the retrogression of economic forces and their social consequences. The ideologists of the dominant classes strengthened and accelerated this development by suggesting symbolic satisfactions to the masses, guiding their aggression into socially harmless channels.

Catholicism signified the disguised return to the religion of the Great Mother who had been defeated by Yahweh. Only Protestantism turned back to the father-god.[58] It stands at the beginning of a social epoch that permits an active attitude on the part of the masses in contrast to the passively infantile attitude of the Middle Ages.[59]

---

58   Luther personally was characterized by his ambivalent attitude to the father; the partly loving, partly hostile encounter between him and the father-figures constituted the central point of his psychic situation.

59   Cf. Frazer, *The Golden Bough*; and also the conception, related to ours, in Storfer, *op. cit.*

This essay was translated from the German by James Luther Adams. This chapter was originally published in Fromm, E. (1955). The dogma of Christ. In *The dogma of Christ and other essays on religion, psychology, and culture* (pp. 3–91). New York: Holt, Rinehart and Winston.

CHAPTER 5

Two Traditions from Pascal's Childhood

Imre Hermann

Abstract

This article is a worthy example of Hermann's emphasis on the primacy of the urge toward relationships in human development. Hermann terms this urge "clinging" and conceives it as equally powerful to the internal dynamics of the Oedipus Complex. These parallel anecdotes from the childhood of Blaise Pascal both revolve around distortions in his relationship with his father. In the first episode, the father's relationship with Pascal is disrupted by a curse placed on the boy by a witch. In the second episode the father's relationship with Pascal by a distorted belief of the father that prevents his sharing coveted ideas with the boy. In both stories Pascal carries remnants of these disruptions in adulthood. [Editors]

The uncritical communication of collected materials is a scholarly method not always to be despised; in this way data can be preserved which would be discarded in an anthology constrained by one theory or point of view. In older biographies one can find traditions told in detail which a newer biography may not be able to work with, since these older tales describe no hard-and-fast data. Analytically, such traditions can be utilized from a different standpoint, for here [with analysis] the sole question is not whether something is true or false. If one has only fantasies with which to work, the meaning of the fantasies may also have something to say. Reuchlin begins the biography of Pascal with the following fantastically charming story. This piece will be reproduced word for word: the expert will not need many elucidations with it.

"In their myths the ancients had their gods, their heroes, their great men threatened in the cradle by hostile, envious gods and forces, by snakes and monsters. Pascal is also endangered in the cradle by a spell of hell; only it takes on, be it a fable or a story, the color and form of the time. Blaise Pascal lived from 1623 until 1662. We shall have Margarethe Perier (the daughter of his older sister) tell us the adventure (H. Reuchlin: Pascals Leben und der Geist seiner Schriften, 1840).

"When my uncle was a year old he encountered something extraordinary. Throughout her younger days my grandmother was very pious and charitable. She had a large number of poor families to whom she gave a small sum each month. Among the poor women to whom she gave alms was one who was considered a witch; the whole world knew it of her. But my grandmother, who had a lot of common sense and did not listen to these gullible people, laughed at the warnings and continued to give her the alms. Now at this time it happened that the little Pascal came down with consumption, which in Paris is called *tomber en chartre*; but it was accompanied by two unusual circumstances. The first was that he could not see water without becoming greatly agitated; the second, however, was even much more astonishing, for he could not bear to see his father and mother near each other. He would be particularly delighted if either of the two hugged him, but as soon as they came to him together, he screamed and struggled against them with all his might. All this lasted over a year, during which the malady grew and he fell into such a desperate situation that he was thought to be very near death.

Everyone told my grandparents it was certainly a spell which this witch had put on the child (*sort qu'elle avait jeté*). Both scoffed at this and considered such talk to be fancies which one makes up upon seeing extraordinary things. So they took no precautionary measures, but rather gave the woman free access to the house to receive her alms. Finally one day my grandfather, angry about everything he was being told about her, called this woman into his chambers. He believed he would speak to her in a way which would give him a chance to silence all this chatter; but he was quite shocked when at his very first word she answered very discreetly that it was not so, and that it was said of her merely out of envy of the alms she received. Now he wanted to frighten her, so he pretended to be certain she had cast a spell on his child and threatened her with the gallows unless she confessed the truth to him. This alarmed her greatly and she threw herself on her knees before him and swore she would tell everything if he would promise to spare her life. My grandfather, very surprised by this, asked her what she had done and what had moved her to do it. Now she told him that she had once asked him to try a case for her, but he turned her down because he believed she was not in the right. To get revenge for it, she cast a spell on his child because she saw that he was so dear to him. She was sorry to tell him, but the spell was to the death. My grandfather cried out: How is it that my son must die? There is still a way, she replied. Someone must die for him upon whom the spell could be transferred. But as my grandfather said he would sooner his son [die] than have someone die for him, she responded that one could also transfer the spell onto an animal. My grandfather offered her a horse, but she said one need not pay so great a cost; a cat would suffice. So she threw the cat out the window and even though it fell only six feet, it still died. The woman asked for another cat, which my grandfather also gave her. Great love for his child made him forget that to transfer the spell,

TWO TRADITIONS FROM PASCAL'S CHILDHOOD

one would have to call forth the devil anew. The thought came to him only much later, and he regretted having given occasion for it. Now, the next day the old woman made a covering for the child's abdomen from three herbs which a child not yet seven years old gathered for her. When my grandfather came home from the palace of justice about noon, he found the whole house and his wife in tears. He was told that the child was dead, and lay even now in his cradle. He met the old woman on the stairs and gave her such a blow that she fell down them. She stood up again and said she had forgotten to predict that the next day the child would appear dead until midnight, but then he would regain consciousness. Now, even though he [the child] had all the signs of death, he [the father] instructed everyone to ignore it. They laughed at his gullibility, for it was not his custom to believe these people. So then my grandmother and grandfather remained at the child's side, since they trusted no one else. They listened as one hour after another struck, finally even midnight, without the child having given one sign of life. Finally, between midnight and one o'clock, indeed it was closer to one, the child began to yawn. With astonishment they picked him up and warmed him, and he was given wine and sugar, which he swallowed. Then he took the breast of his wet-nurse, still without giving any signs of consciousness, without opening his eyes. This lasted until six o'clock in the morning, but upon seeing his father and mother together he began, as was his custom, to scream. From this they could see that he had not yet been completely healed, but were comforted by the fact that he was not dead. About six or seven days later he began to endure the sight of water; when my grandfather came home from high mass one day he found him playing in his mother's arms, pouring water from one glass to another. He wanted to come near, but the child could not yet stand him. This happened only after a few days, and in three weeks he [the child] was completely healed and regained his earlier healthy stoutness."

So much for the story! Now we will make some remarks on interpretation. The whole story is, so to speak, set up around the father; he arranges the scene with the witch, he has the woman seized, he has the cat sacrificed (after offering a horse), he boxes the witch's ears, he comes close to the mother when the child still reacts with screaming. This story appears to be, so one could view the whole thing, a story of the father, not of the son. It appears that the father is guilty of something, it appears that his conscience is not clear, he appears to wish something bad and yields to better judgment only slowly. What can this evil thing have been? It is precisely that which almost happens and which he must, so to speak, buy his way out of the death of his son. First the witch fulfills his unconscious intentions, then comes the conversation with his unconscious impulses (with the witch). In his initial reaction he wants to sacrifice himself (the horse), but then only the female genitalia are sacrificed[1] – he renounced his paternal right, sexual intercourse (*nota bene*, Blaise was two years old when his younger sister was born). Are we justified in drawing this conclusion from the symbol of the cat? To justify our position, let us now consider the story from the standpoint of the son. Against what is he protesting? He can see no water and cannot bear his parents being close together. As if the child – in consequence of this phobia – actually would watch his parents (like the parents watch the child during the night) and would want to prevent their sexual intercourse. When the child showed signs of life but gave no signs of consciousness, the happy parents attempted intercourse – but they were disturbed again by the child around six o'clock in the morning. Given the central issues, we may perceive in the story an Oedipal fantasy, projected back by the relatives into the son's infancy. (The projection back into such an early age serves the tendency to render the offense harmless.) The hydrophobia, too, is to be placed in this category. It can be connected with an infantile coitus fantasy (urination), then, projected back, it would signify the protest against begetting children (amniotic fluid, baptism).[2]

We must now admit something. Pascal was a Jansenist, and, as such, as an adult he had particular thoughts about the baptism of children – it should not take place before some education; and about the family – it should not come between the individual person and humanity, the state, the church. But then our interpretation of the story above indeed would not be wrong, but – go one could think – pointless, for [then it is simply a matter of] the state of mind of the older Blaise Pascal being projected back into this story.

Some data from the life of the two Pascals – of the father and of the son – suggest a particularly intense Oedipal relation.

Here, seeming to leave our train of thought in the lurch, we will insert the second tradition from Pascal's youth. It runs: Blaise was educated by his father.

---

1 Perhaps the story intends to indicate the sacrifice of the mother through the giving of the second cat – she died when Blaise was three (at the most five) years old. There is also a formal duel step at work here. The sister Jacqueline is "to be considered as the spiritual twin sister of Blaise," (p. 2) and in Blaise' pathological ideation – seeing an abyss at his left side – we perhaps can perceive the loss of this intimate relationship – Jacqueline became a nun – as one of the certainly very few causes. To ease this phobia Blaise placed a chair [there].

2 Further motivation of the fear of water (in the back projection): Around the age of eighteen Blaise was suffering, he could only swallow lukewarm liquids and only drop by drop (p. 21) – a condition which I lack understanding of (but precisely this condition makes a similar childlike one very probable); furthermore: the doctors stated that the cause of his headache before his death was the water which they had prescribed for him (p. 216).

TWO TRADITIONS FROM PASCAL'S CHILDHOOD

The father spoke with the child of everything possible, [everything] of which he seemed capable... "Blaise wanted to know the cause of everything." (p. 6) The father himself was a man of great learning in mathematics. He even wrote an essay *de maximis et minimis* in response to the objections of Descartes. The sister (Gilberte) recounting: "My father was very educated in mathematics and was in correspondence with all the educated men in this science, who also visited with him often. But since it was his intention to instruct my brother in languages for the time being, and knew well that mathematics is a science which very much fulfills and satisfies the spirit, he desired that my brother would know nothing of it until he had attained a certain level of accomplishment in the languages. So he shut away all his mathematics books and refrained from speaking with his friends of it in his son's presence. Blaise begged in vain repeatedly for his father to give him lessons therein. He refused every time, and promised it to him as a reward as soon as he understood Latin and Greek. My brother (he was twelve years old) asked him one day what science was about; the father answered him only in generalities that it was the science of making precise, correct (*juste*) figures, of finding the relationships between them; but at the same time forbade him to speak of it again or even to think of it."

But the boy reflected on the father's answer during the rest period; when he was alone in his playroom he took coals, drew figures on the floor and sought, for example, how one could make a perfectly round circle, a triangle whose sides and angles were absolutely equal, and other such things. He found this on his own and immediately sought the relationships of the shapes to each other. But as my father kept all this such a strict secret, the boy did not even know the names of them, and felt compelled to make them up, like the definitions, himself. So, for example, he named a circle "round thing," a line "staff." According to the definitions, he made up axioms and finally complete proofs. In this way he pursued it through the inner correlation to the 32nd theorem of the first book of Euclid.

From the history of science we know several stages where the gifted, respected father instructed the likewise gifted son. While with J. St. Mill[3] this relationship led to an intense hatred toward his father, mutual hostility, mistrust and jealousy. with Pascal, according to the tradition, there was a reason that his relationship with his father took shape differently; here the father allegedly forbade the gifted son the pursuit of his favorite thing, mathematics. Strikingly, the likely wish of the son to have found everything by himself, not to have obtained

---

3   Siehe Imago IX, Heft 4, 1923.

it from the father, corresponded to the content of the tradition. We consider it hardly believable that the old Pascal could keep everything mathematical from the son. How would it be if in this tradition we would perceive a wish fulfillment (the wish of the sister would correspond to the (unconscious) wish of the brother), and in addition a displacement as well: the secretiveness refers to the sexual arena ("round thing," "staff") and not to mathematics.

Then, after the reversal of the content of this tradition, we can assume the same intense Oedipal attitude for Blaise Pascal as was present with J. St. Mill. Analogous to the comments on J. St. Mill, we also find in Blaise Pascal a struggle for Realism (p. 252), and a struggle against certain authorities: "Jansen particularly had attacked and shaken the respect for Aristotle in theology. Pascal attacked it in the area of natural science and theology at the same authority thus caused him to join the Jansenists, who also accommodated his inner tendencies in their view of the family.

Both traditions can be explained, then, by the assumption of an intense Oedipal attitude. Certain of Pascal's ways of thinking also fit our explanation. Now separate life events point to the effect of these factors. The younger sister wanted to become a nun. Blaise supported her desire, but the father opposed her and would not allow the betrothal of the daughter with heaven. He was even so mistrustful of son and daughter (the mother indeed had been dead for a long time) he watched both closely. Significantly, after the death of the father, Blaise, would not tolerate his sister taking the veil. (p. 43.)

The death of the father at first left the son cold, he wrote a long study on death; in the fifth line of this study it says: "we know that death is laid upon man for Sin and is necessary" (p. 32). And a striking transformation was soon the reaction to the father's death: for a considerable time, Pascal immersed himself completely in "vanity, idleness, pleasure, and the love of pleasure." Yet in three years he had become an ascetic.[4]

---

4 I feel called upon in this connection to also say something about the utilization of the readiness to suffer, the asceticism in Pascal. He "made good use of his illness" – since his eighteenth year he was not without pain for a single day (p. 21) – and his tradition from his thirties informs us: "This redoubling of his ailment began with a strong toothache which completely robbed him of sleep. In one of his long, sleepless nights there came to him involuntarily some thoughts on the problem of the roulette, or cycloid, which was raised by Father Mersema. He sought something which would cause him to forget his pain through strong stimulation, and [he] pursued the matter until he finally solved the problem. When he came to the end of it he felt healed of his ailment ... Pascal said he considered it (the device) only as a remedy which indeed reached his goals." (p. 179.) Cf. with this my articles on the psychology of the gifted in Imago and International Zeithechrift für Psychoanalyse.

Background

Imre Hermann (1889–1984) was a Hungarian neurologist and psychoanalyst who lived almost all of his life in Budapest. Early in his career he became interested in animal behavior and observed the almost universal tendency toward "clinging" – relating toward others quite apart from alimentary needs. Anthropoid apes, for example, cling to the fur of their mothers several of their early months of life. Hermann generalized this impulse to humans and is widely thought to have anticipated "attachment needs" – concepts that have become central to much contemporary theorizing. He definitely is noted as preparing the way for John Bowlby and Rene Spitz. He was a prolific writer whose man works have not receive the significance they deserve because they were all in Hungarian. He wrote on a wide range of subjects (e.g., obsessional neurosis) in which he related psychoanalysis.

CHAPTER 6

A Psychoanalytic Study of the Holy Spirit

Ernest Jones

Abstract

Ernest Jones was an enthusiastic proponent of Freud and the applications of psycho-analysis. In this essay, Jones interpolates the unconscious meanings of the "Holy Spirit" through the lens of psychoanalysis and the Oedipus myth.

In the Christian myth, the Holy Spirit is seen as the *over* development of the feminine component in this drama. Genesis conceives God as "hovering" (a feminine act) over the abyss prior to creation. Adam gives into the feminine impulse of Eve to feed him and God is pictured as taking a walk in the cool of the day in His garden – as a female might do.

Further, continuing the evidence that the Holy Spirit is seen as embodiment of female ideas in the story, Mary is impregnated by a spirit and blesses Jesus's baptism (water itself is feminine) is blessed by the appearance of a dove. It is significant that Mary the mother, not Joseph the father, is enmeshed in the crucifixion narrative from beginning to the end. The ritual of the Mass codifies this narrative. It is a concrete embodiment of the place of the Holy Spirit in the psychic resolution of ego development as seen in psychoanalytic theory.

Here the psychic problem of patricide of the father and incest with the mother is resolved by embodiment of the mother and identification with the father. Jones perceives the Holy Spirit as the incorporation of this resolution within public religious practice but that similar issues can be identified in a number of mythological stories. It is worth noting that this theory implies that ego-development can be understood for both genders through a masculine dynamic. It would be of interest to understand the ways further that psychoanalytic development has dealt with this issue. Jones advises that this essay is an extension of an article he had written earlier on The Madonna that was unavailable for comparison. [Editors]

Whatever the time may reveal about the historical personality of the founder of Christianity, there is no doubt among those who have conducted comparative religious research that many of the faiths that surround themselves are attached to the original foundation and to foreign pagan sources: The name of

A PSYCHOANALYTIC STUDY OF THE HOLY SPIRIT

Christian mythology may be ascribed to these deviations. As Frazer[1] puts it, "Nothing is more certain than the saying of a weed about the Great historical figures of the past."

Some of the more important elements that say circle are already using the psychoanalytic method from Freud[2] have been explored. According to him, the main dogma of the Christian religion – the belief that humanity is to be saved from its sins by the sacrificial death of Jesus Christ on the cross – represents the elaboration of the primitive totemic system. He sees the essence of this system in the attempt to alleviate it The sense of guilt which comes from the Oedipus complex, namely that satisfied in primordial times; Impulse of the father's death and mother's test. There is good reason to suppose that this complex is the last source of the "original sin" described by the theologians. This was the first great sin of humanity and the one from which our moral conscience and our guilt was born. The early history of mankind, the tendency towards this great sin, and the moral reaction to it, is repeated in every child who comes into the world, and the history of religion is a never-ending attempt to overcome the Oedipus complex and the peace of the soul Through reconciliation with the father. Freud has emphasized that the most striking characteristic of the Christian problem-solving is, in comparison with others, for example, the Mithra, the way in which this reconciliation comes about, by submission to the father rather than by open rebellion and overcoming. This submission, whose prototype is the crucifixion, is repeated from time to time in the ceremony of the Holy Mass or Communion, which is psychologically equivalent to the totem meal. In this way the father's wrath is avoided and the son takes his place at his side, as a peer. In the meal, the original act of the killing and eating of the father is experienced again, and also the repentant piety, the reunion and identification with him wishes. We will see that, according to this view, Christian reconciliation with the father is achieved at the expense of an overdevelopment of the feminine component. I hope, that the present communication will confirm Freud's conclusions by studying the same lines. About 10 years ago I published an essay on the conception of the Madonna in the "Yearbook of Psychoanalysis" and what I have here to present is largely based on a recently written extended edition of this work, which will be published in English shortly.[3]

Thus, it is not surprising to learn that the Christian myth, like so many religious myths, is dealing with the centuries old fight between father and son.

---

1   Frazer: *Adonis, Attis, Osiris*, Third ed., 1914, p.160.
2   Freud: *Totem and Taboo*, 1913. p. 142.
3   Chapter 7 of my "Essays in Applied Psycho-Analysis", 1923.

As it is remembered, the conception of Jesus happened in the most extraordinary way. Usually, when a god wants to fertilize an earthly woman, he appears on earth either in a human form or as an animal with particularly pronounced phallic symbols, (as a bull, a snake etc.) and fertilizes her in an act of sexual union. However, in the Madonna myth, God the Father does not appear at all, unless we regard the Archangel Gabriel to be his embodiment, the fertilization itself happens by the Angel's salute and the dove's breath, which at the same time enters Madonna's ear. The dove itself, which should embody the Holy Spirit, originates from the Father's mouth. Therefore, the Holy Spirit and its breath play the role of a sexual tool here, and they appear where we would usually expect the phallus or the semen. I quote St Zeno, "Maria's womb swells by the word, not by the semen", or St Eleutherius: "O hallowed virgin... Who has become a mother without the involvement of a man. For here, the ear has been the wife, and the word of the angel has been the husband".

We will see that our problems will instantly complicate. It only means adding a second mystery to the first one when we find that the mysterious figure replacing the mother is a male being symbolizing the genital organs of the father. But before we address this, it is necessary to consider the details of the fertilization itself more precisely.

Here, a comparative analysis leads us to an unexpected conclusion. When we seek to discover why the concept of breath is connected to the fertilization in primitive, i.e. unconscious imaginations, we will find this to happen very indirectly. As I have extensively shown in the paper cited above, in the primitive psyche, the breath does not have the strictly defined meaning we give it now. Studies of the psychological philosophy, particular in the Greek and in Hindu culture, shows that the breath had a much larger idea connection, the so-called pneuma-conception, so most likely the larger part of this conception, or at least its sexual side, is derived from another gaseous excretion, namely the one originating at the lower end of the digestive tract. It is this downward moving breath, as it is called in Vedic Literature, which is the fertilizing element by word or breath in the various beliefs of creation. In a similar way, and analysis of the idea that the ear is a female organ of conception leads us to the conclusion that this is a symbolic replacement, a "shift from the bottom to the top" of parallel thoughts referring to the lower end of the digestive tract.

When we correlate these two conclusions, we can hardly avoid the implication that the mystic legend in question is a highly refined and transformed collaboration of the infantile sexual theory, which I already called attention to before[4] according to which fertilization should happen by the passing of wind

---

4 *Jahrbuch der Psychoanalyse.* Band IV. P. 586 ff.

A PSYCHOANALYTIC STUDY OF THE HOLY SPIRIT

from the father to the mother. I have also emphasized why this most disgusting of all sexual phantasies is more suitable than all the others to express the most exalted and witty ideas the human intellect can imagine.

This infantile theory is accompanied by certain characteristics traits which we can both discover by the means of individual psychoanalysis and by studying related comparing material. From a superficial observation, one might assume that it hints to a denial of fatherly fertility and represents a kind of desire of castration, and without any doubt, this is partly correct. But on the other hand, one might be surprised to see that all the numerous associations regarding the idea of creation in connection with wind almost always include the opposing concept of a specific powerful phallus emitting the wind. So, in most of the religions all over the world, a kind of thunder weapon belongs to the divine pro-creating thunder; the most well-known and most popular one is the Bull Roarer. Yes, further, the idea of fertilization but the wind itself often seems to be a sign of great fertility by the Primitives, like the power to create by a mere sound, a word or even by thought would be a final proof of enormous masculinity. This reaches its climax and reference to the procreation without a sound, only by silent thought, like in the belief of various nuns in the middle ages of being fertilized only because "Jesus has thought of them".

A great example of this complex of ideas, interesting from various points of view, is given by certain Egyptian beliefs regarding the crocodile. They are also directly connected to the present topic as the crocodile has been regarded as the symbol of Logos or the Holy Spirit by the first Christians, and additionally they believed that the crocodile fertilizes his female through the ear, like the virgin had been fertilized. Now on the one hand, the crocodile has been peculiar to the ancient Egyptians, as it had no external sexual organs, no tongue and no voice (symbols of impotence), and yet, on the other hand, despite these purely negative characteristics, or maybe exactly because of them, it was regarded the highest type of masculinity, and a number of aphrodisiac practices were based on this belief. The crocodile has been an emblem of wisdom, like the snake or other phallic items, and as such flaunts on Minerva's breast, so the Old seem to have concluded that the most powerful tool of procreation is the silence of the Wiseman, that the omnipotence of thoughts is even more impressive then the omnipotence of the word.

We know that this over emphasizing of the fatherly fertility is not a main phenomenon, but it is the transfer of the individual person's narcissism, caused by the fear of castration as a punishment for the desires of castration. So, we reach a conclusion that has been widely verified by individual psychoanalyses, that a belief in a gaseous fertilization is a reaction to an unusually intense castration phantasy, and that it is only present when did the attitude towards the father is particularly ambivalent, when hostile denial of fertility alternates with the confirmation and submission to the higher power. Both attitudes are implied in the Christian myth. The fertilization through *action à distance*, by mere heralds, and the choice of the gaseous way unveil an idea of a tremendous power, which the son is certainly subject to. On the other hand, the tool chosen for fertilization is by no means especially masculine.

Although the dove is obviously a phallic symbol – Zeus seduced Phteia in the incarnation of a dove, and does have been that Cupidesque emblems of all major goddesses of love, Asart, Semiramis, Aphrodite and the others – its connection to love is mainly due to its tender ans caressing nature of wooing. So, we can say that it is one of the most feminine phallic symbols.

This makes it obvious that the power of the father can only be expressed at the expense of a connection with significant femininity. The same topic is expressed even more obvious with the sun. He reaches a greatness including the eventual possession of the mother and reconciliation with the father, but only after undergoing the greatest humiliation, including a symbolic castration and death. Each of Jesus' followers has to follow a similar path; salvation can only be reached by gentleness, humility and submission to the will of the father. This way has logically led to cases of actual self-castration in extreme cases, and it still points towards this way, although, of course, this has been replaced by various actions serving as a symbol for this in reality. The profit by this is double: introjection of the mother is replaced by regression towards the initial identification with her, so incest is avoided and the father is soothed; furthermore, there is an opportunity to win the love of the father by adopting a feminine attitude towards him. Peace of mind is reached by transformation of affection in the direction of a transformation of gender.

At this point, let us return to the problem stated above: The psychological meaning of the Holy Spirit. We have seen that it compromises of the original mother goddess and of the fertile being (sexual organs) of the father. From this point of view one can approach a comprehension of the special fertility of a blasphemy against the Holy Spirit, the so-called "unforgivable sin", as such an insult would be symbolically synonymous with a staining the Holy Mother and an attempt of castration on the father. It would be a repetition of the original sin.

In Christian mythology we encounter a surprising fact. It is the only mythology in which the original figures do not survive, in which the three-worship to be venerated is no longer the mother-father-son. Father and son still appear, but the mother, the cause of the whole conflict, has been replaced by the mysterious figure of the Holy Spirit.

It seems impossible to arrive at any result other than that which has just been said. The mother must not only logically form the third member of every

A PSYCHOANALYTIC STUDY OF THE HOLY SPIRIT

triad whose two other members are father and son; this is not only so in all the other numerous trinities known to us, but there is also a considerable number of direct proofs in the Christian myth. Frazer[5] has collected some evidence for this purpose, and makes this conclusion on a historical basis seem highly probable. The original mother, recognized, for example, by the Ophite sect as the third member of the triad, was apparently of Babylonian and Egyptian origin, although there is no lack of evidence, That a foggy mother-shape also floats in the background of Hebrew theology. Thus the passage in Genesis, "And the Spirit of God hovered over the waters," was actually meant: "The mother of the gods brooded (or fluttered) over the abyss and brought forth new life," a bird-like conception of the mother (The Holy Spirit replacing the mother), but also the legend that Isis received Horus while she fluttered over the dead body of Osiris in the form of a hawk.

While the strictly patriarchal theology of the Hebrew exiled the mother to a subordinate role and the Son of Messiah into a distant future, she retained nothing more normal than the relationship between the three persons. It is therefore probable that any enlightenment of the transformation of the mother into the Holy Spirit will cast a light on the inner nature of the psychological revolution, which is reflected in the development from Judaism to Christianity.

The path pursued here consists in the consideration of the circumstances accompanying the conception of the Messiah. This path appears justified for two reasons. It is well known, first, that the figure of the Holy Spirit appears in myth only as the tool of fertilization at the conception of the Son, and later as an ambrosial blessing which is cast upon the Son when he submits himself to the introductory rites of baptism Relationship with the followers of the son). Second, Otto Rank[6] has shown a long time ago that the tendency of a myth is already revealed in its first stages; He calls this the myth of the birth of the hero. The consideration of the Christian myth.

Background

Ernest Jones is known as the preeminent publisher of Freud's writings. He became Freud's official biographer. His three volumes *The Life and Work of Sigmund Freud* was considered "a masterpiece of contemporary biography" by Time magazine.

---

5   Frazer: The Dying God. 1911, p. 5.
6   [not included in document]

Jones introduced Psychoanalysis to the English speaking world. He grew up in Wales and became a neurologist in several hospitals in London where his close friend Wilfred Trotter introduced him to Freud's writings in a German psychiatric journal about a new form of therapy. Using Freud's writing as a stimulus he used the "repressed memory" approach in treating a young girl's arm paralysis. He became intrigued with Freud's ideas. He began to actually listen to every word his patients spoke – a novel idea among other physicians.

CHAPTER 7

Is the Mark of Cain Circumcision? A Critical Contribution to Biblical Exegesis

Ludwig Levy

Abstract

In this essay, Levy draws upon a phylogenetic understanding of the Mark of Cain in which prehistory figures in the construction of biblical texts. [Editors]

Dr. Theodor Reik recently published in Volume V, Issue 1 (1917) of this journal, A Psychoanalytic Contribution to Biblical Interpretation: The Mark of Cain. Reik defends the thesis that the mark of Cain was circumcision and is to be placed in the same category as incisions which the primitives made in their bodies in mourning the dead. To the question, against whom did the mark protect – Cain? Reik answered: against himself, from the self-punishing tendencies which live unconsciously within him. Cain's crime consisted not only of fratricide, but also of gratifying incestuous impulses. The mark was a self-mutilation of the penis according to the lex talionis, which in its motive would be equivalent to castration. Thus, it is to be understood as circumcision and signifies a punishment for the incestuous wishes which had driven Cain to fratricide. Reik finds the incestuous wishes indicated in the plowing of the field, which is known to be a sexual symbol for the woman. He cites a legend from the later Judeo-Christian tradition which explains Cain's fratricide from the elder brother's jealousy over his big sister whom the parents intended for Abel.

I consider this hypothesis to be an error, as it appears to me impossible that the mark of Cain can be circumcision. Above all, the interpretation deviates too far from the report of the Bible and brings in elements for which no basis is given.

There is no basis for seeing a mourning mutilation in the mark of Cain over against the text of the Bible which expressly speaks of a protective mark. Tattoos were made in part on esthetic grounds, in part they were tribal markings. The tribal marking was a protective mark "against anyone who meets someone," because the attacker would risk bringing upon himself the blood revenge of the entire tribe. Now, could this tribal mark on Cain be circumcision?

The most important arguments speak against it. First, the Bible, as it actually did in the passages which refer to the origin of circumcision, would have

© KONINKLIJKE BRILL NV, LEIDEN, 2021 | DOI:10.1163/9789004429222_008

clearly named a mark that later would play such a role. Second, it is out of the question that a mark of religious and national sanctity, such as circumcision, would be traced back to a murder. Finally, however, it would contradict completely the structure of Genesis if in this passage the discourse were to be of circumcision.

Prehistory explains phenomena which touch upon all the peoples of the world. The milieu is depicted in which Israel appears. All prehistory intends this. The history of Israel begins with Abraham and that is the place to speak of circumcision first. In fact, it is introduced there with solemn words in chap. 17, verse 10, as a mark of the covenant between God and Israel. Besides, circumcision is not a mark that anyone sees, that has an affect on someone. Not even savages were at such a primitive level of dress [as would display the genitals], and by no means did the mark of Cain arise in such an inferior society. This shows indeed the grandiose view of sin.

Now as concerns the incestuous wishes, the one support that Cain plowed a field for the first time, that is, committed incest is not applicable. Not Cain, but Adam first tilled. Adam's tilling is actually to be understood in terms of sexual symbolism, as I demonstrated in the same installment of this journal in the article "Sexual symbolik in der biblischen Paradieegeschichte" ["Sexual symbolism in the biblical story of paradise"].

The story of paradise answers the question: How did sexual intercourse come into the world? With Cain, the field plays, as we will see, a different role. That later Judeo—Christian tradition which speaks of a sister of Cain arose from a dilemma in the biblical tale. With whom did Cain beget children if Adam and Eve had only two sons? The later writing answered that he had another sister whom he married.

Because the author was already fantasizing, and for him the rejected sacrifice was not adequate and interesting enough to explain the fratricide, the romance of the brothers' jealousy was written in.

Scholarship explains the difficulty in a completely different way: The story of Cain [originally] stood on its own and only later was connected with the story of paradise. And with that the romance of the sister is dropped. Later fantasy which grow up around the Bible like rank weeds may be drawn upon for explanation of the Genesis narratives only with greatest caution and after critical examination.

Now, how is the Cain story to be understood? What was the mark of Cain? Many myths and legends of the Bible are of an etiological nature; that is, they give answers to specific questions, their intent is to explain phenomena. Man and woman long for sexual union, so the legend asks: Whence comes this impulse? And it answers: The woman is created out of the body of the man; originally they were one and therefore they want to be one again. The myth of Gen.

IS THE MARK OF CAIN CIRCUMCISION?

6 raises the question: Why do people now live to a much lower age than the person of early times? And it answers: Because their daughters once engaged in incest with the sons of gods, their highest age was set at 120 years. The myth of paradise answers the question: How did sexual intercourse come into the world?

But also [asks] the question: Why does the earth yield its gifts so reluctantly? Why must a person wrench them from it with such tiring, such hard work? The answer rung: The field was cursed, humanity had eaten from the tree of knowledge against the divine command, that is, sowed seed with his wife, thus he must now work the land by the sweat of his brow.

A similar question underlying the Cain legend and so this legend was immediately connected with the paradise narrative. The question was: Why does the earth yield no fruit to the Bedouins, the Cainites? ... why do they not farm? And the answer runs: The earth once drank blood through the sin of Cain, the tribal father of the Kainites, the blood of fratricide stained it. "The blood of your brother cries to me from the ground. So then be cursed, away from the ground which had to open its mouth to receive your brother's blood from your hand! When you wish to till the land it will no longer yield to you its strength."

Here and there in the Bible the earth, echoing old myths, is perceived as a living being, as with the Egyptians or with the Greek *GE* and the Indian *Prithvi*. It is stained by blood, profaned by unchastity; it spews out the unchaste Canaanites, and in Leviticus 18 Israel is warned against sexual error so that it will not pollute the earth, that it may not spew Israel out – as it did with earlier occupants. In Ezekiel, Palestine is called the navel of the earth.

This is the one question which the Cain legend answers. The second question runs: How did the tribal mark of the Cainites arise? And it gives the answer: In those days their tribal father Cain received it from God when he slew his brother Abel. The alien tribe is ridiculed with this tracing of their tribal mark back to a murder by their tribal father. Indeed, so far as we know, Israel lived amicably with the Cainites, but they were also described later as bloodthirsty.

The Kenite woman Jael, killed the fleeing general Sisera whom she had hospitably invited into her tent and who trustfully stayed with her.

We encounter such disparagements yet today between the inhabitants of different villages and territories, and they were certainly customary in early times. In the Bible we encounter the explanation of the names Moab and Amon: The daughters of Lot had intercourse with their father, and the one named her son begotten of the incestuous communion water or seed of my father, the other named her Mongolian peon of my (closest) relative. Just as there, the tribal name is made an object of contempt, so here the tribal mark of the Cainites, and at the same time the thievish Bedouin tribe, is represented as condemned to its nomadic desert life from the very beginning because of a murder. "Once," one said, "the tribal father of these wild fellows also tilled the land, but then he killed his brother, the God-pleasing sheep farmer (the legend undoubtedly arose in this group), was cursed and made to be a wanderer and a fugitive because the stained earth no longer would yield its fruits to him. As he repented God made him a mark which the Cainites bear yet today."

Such tribal markings are: certain kinds of haircuts, shaving one's head, incisions and tattoos. Thug Kedar had shaved hair around the edges, Ishmael golden earrings, Israel circumcision. These tribal markings are originally of a religious nature and indicate that their bearer belongs to his god who protects him. That the custom continued to express this affiliation through scratches in the skin is shown by Isaiah 44:5: "The one will say: I am JHWH's [the Lord's] and he calls me by the name of Jacob." and that one writes on his hand: "'JHWH's the Lord and received the adopted name of 'Israel.'" Also in Ezekiel 9:4 the angel marks the foreheads of the men who lament the abominations in Jerusalem with a mark that was a protective mark for them. The head tephillin very probably appeared in lieu of a mark on the forehead between the eyes, as incisions in the body were forbidden as customs of a pagan cultus.

According to the tradition, the mark of Cain, too, would have been a tattoo. There is much that says this tradition is right. A tribal marking of that sort could also serve as a protective mark as the Cain legend conceives it. The bearer stood under the protection of his god, but also of his tribe, which would avenge the death of any member "sevenfold" in blood revenge.

This explains in addition why JHWH rejected Cain's sacrifice, but accepted that of Abel with pleasure. I believe that the reason lies in this, that Cain offered whatever fruit of the field he had, not the first fruits, but Abel brought the first born of his flock. JHWH is due, so the legend suggests, the firstborn. He accepts only this with pleasure.

The legend is significant in the history of religion through its portrayal of a bad conscience, of the voice of God, and through the phenomenal power of its representation of how God warned Cain against sin. The myth makes a deep impression in its lapidary brevity. The resource of psychoanalysis, particularly of sexual symbolism and, in this I agree with Reik, can still shed light on many difficult passages of the Bible.

We recommend, however, greater caution in its use.[1]

---

1 Reik also cites Zeydner, who in the *Zeitschrift für die alttestamentliche Wiesenschaft*, Jahrgang 1898, S. 120, expresses the same hypothesis that the mark of Cain was circumcision. Zeydner did not furnish, however, one single solid bit of evidence for his idea, so that an investigation of his remarks is pointless. In the same journal, 1894, p. 308, in *Beiträge zur Pentateuchkritik, Das Kainszeichen*, Stade had already spoken briefly against the identification [of the mark of Cain] with circumcision.

CHAPTER 8

The Illusion of the Future: A Friendly Dispute with Professor Sigmund Freud

Oskar Pfister

Abstract

This is the article written by Oskar Pfister, the Swiss Reform Church pastor and psychoanalyst who was a close friend of Sigmund Freud. A selection of their letters are discussed in another chapter of this volume. This article is Pfister's review of Freud's book, *The Future of an Illusion,* that was printed in the journal *Imago* under the title "The Illusion of the Future." Freud's book declares religion a neurosis that had no future; Pfister declares that religion is an illusion that had a future. He wrote that Freud's faith in science was erroneous and that Freud put too much faith in its future. He defends religion on the basis of Jesus' teaching and the fact that many scholars supported his viewpoint. Freud gave Pfister permission to write this review. [Editors]

Dear Professor,

You have declared it as your wish in the kind manner that I have gotten used to during nineteen years of common work with you that I present my objections against your little book *The Future of an Illusion* to the public, and you have offered me with a liberality. which is self-evident in your thinking, for this purpose a journal that you yourself are editing. I would like to thank you heartily for this new proof of your friendship which in no way surprised me. From readily willing to have me sit at your feet, showered with the riches and the blessing from the fullness of your mind.

Your book was for you an inner necessity, an act of your life work would have been impossible without smashing of idols, whether they stood in universities or church halls. Everybody knows how much you serve science with a reverence and devotion that elevate your study to a temple, all that know you know this. To say it in new words: I have the particular suspicion that you fight religion – out of religion. Schiller gives you his brotherly hand; will you refuse it?

And from the standpoint of faith even more I do not see any reason to join the screaming of some who want to watch over Zion. Whoever fought with such greatness for truth as you do and so courageously argued for the liberation of love, is after all, whether he wants to say this or not, according to the Protestant norm a faithful servant of God, and whoever created through the development of psychoanalysis the instrument through which the fetters of suffering souls are cut through and prison doors are opened so that they may hurry to the sunny land of a life- giving faith, is not far from the Kingdom of God. Jesus tells us a beautiful parable of two sons, in which one of them faithfully promises to go to the vineyard of his father without keeping his word, while the other obstinately rejects the father's suggestion, the beginning you have never kept secret your affirmed unbelief before me and the rest of the world, so that your present prophecy of a religionless future is nothing new to· me. And you will smile a little if I affirm that I see in that psychoanalytic method that has been created by ou an excellent means for purifying and furthering religion, the way you smiled during that time of famine in which we walked in the middle of a snowstorm on Beethoven' s trail on Vienna' s hills and once again we were not able to convince each other, as already had been the case in earlier years, in this particular point, even though at other times I was so but nevertheless carries out the order.

MATT 21: 28ff.

You do know how friendly the founder of the Christian religion preferred the latter. Do you want to be angry with me that in spite of your proposed unbelief I see you, who caught such beautiful rays of the eternal light and were so consumed by the search for truth and the love of humanity., closer to the throne of God – to say it in an image – than a many church people that murmur their prayers and carry out their ceremonies, but never were put on fire in their hearts for knowledge and the well-being of humanity, and since for the Christian who is oriented to the Gospel everything depends on the doing of the divine will rather than the saying of "Lord, Lord.", do you understand that I too would like to envy you,

> Nevertheless, with every determination I oppose your evaluation of religion. I do this with the humbleness that is appropriate to the one who is inferior, but also with the joy in which one defends a sacred and much beloved matter, and with the seriousness of truth that your rigorous school has furthered so much. But I also do this with the hope to bring many·who through your rejection of a religious faith were scared away from psychoanalysis back again to it as a method and summary of understandings of an empirical science.
>
> Therefore, rather than writing against you I would like to write for you, since whoever stands up for psychoanalysis is fighting for it. But I also fight on your side, since nothing else is so crucial to you as it is to me than

THE ILLUSION OF THE FUTURE   121

the overcoming of illusion through the truth. Whether you with your *The Future of an Illusion* or I with my "The Illusion of a Future" come closer to this ideal will be decided by a higher tribunal. We both do not take on the coat of the prophet, but are content with the humble role of the meteorologist; but even meteorologists can miscalculate.

Cordially, your OSKAR PFISTER

1   Freud's Critique of Religion

1.1   *The Charges*

Freud *in* his little book *The Future of an Illusion* presents religion as an illusion, however defines the term illusion in a different way than it *is* usually the case. Normally it implies the characteristic of deception and invalidity. But Freud emphasizes: "An illusion is not necessarily an error."(p. 48) "We call a faith an illusion if *in* its motivation wishful thinking prevails, and thereby we do not consider its relationship to reality, as much as an illusion itself does without its confirmations"(p. 49ff.). In a different context Freud rejects the idea to take a position in his essay on the truth value of the religious teachings (p. 52).

It therefore appears as a possibility that religion is still given some validity. Freud's example of the illusion of Columbus to have found a new seaway to India (p. 48) shows this since even though the discoverer of America did not reach India, others did it on the way that had been opened by him. The same Genoese also reminds us of the fact that in an illusion a great amount of excellent reality thinking can be invested; without the observation of the curbed surface of the ocean and the thus inferred form of the globe of the earth the courageous journey to the West would not have been undertaken.

I already now would like to draw the attention to the intimate connection between wishful and reality thinking and see the question raised whether here in religion, as in a major part of science as such, a pure decomposition is possible, or whether not reality thinking in both fields to a great extent tries in vain to peel off a pure objectivity beyond the wishing or out of the result of those wishes. Yet let me stop for a moment. I do not intend to blab here and also do not already want to commit myself here for what follows.

The hope that religion would disappear cannot be sustained very long. Because very soon we hear that religion is comparable to the neurosis of the child and that psychology is optimistic enough to assume that this neurotic phase will be overcome. It is said that, of course, this is not sure, but the hope is clearly expressed. (p. 86) More precisely, the neurosis which religion represents is described as the "universal human compulsive neurosis" and like the one of the child derived from the oedipal complex, the relationship to the father. (p. 70) With this Freud connects the prognosis: "According to this understanding it could be foreseen that the moving away from religion has to happen with the fateful inexorability of a growth process, and that right now we are in the middle of this developmental phase"

The climax of the critique is to be found in the sentence: "While on the one hand it (religion) brings with itself compulsive limitations, as only an individual compulsive neurosis does, on the other hand it contains a system of wishful illusions with a denial of reality, as we only find it isolated in an amentia, a joyful, hallucinatory confusion." (p. 71)

Finally, religion is honored as a protection of culture (p. 60), however it is rejected as unsatisfactory in this regard, inasmuch as humans also do not find the desired happiness and moral constraint through it.

Let us look at these charges more closely!

1.2   *Religion as a Neurotic Compulsion*

We start with an examination of the neurotic – compulsive character that religion is supposed to carry. Without question Freud is fully correct – and through this discovery Freud has earned for himself immeasurably great merit in the field of the psychology of religion – so far as many expressions of religious life are affected by it. These compulsions are mistakes in many primitive religions which are not aware yet of any actual church formation, as well as in all the orthodoxies. We also know that this fatality is already inherent in the beginnings of these religions as the effects of the suppressions of instincts which developed out of the biological ethical progression of mankind as a necessary obligation. It is, after all, the unfortunate fate of our species that the simple and useful most often is only found on the detour through enormously bizarre ways. The history of languages and moral attitudes shows this so clearly, as does the development of the religions.

But even if this burden of compulsion can hardly be denied already in the first stage of religion, it can nevertheless be asked whether it belongs to the essence of religion. Could not this collective-neurotic aspect very well fall away without any loss, and even to the advantage of the whole thing, just as the tadpoles sacrifice their tails in order to hop around more comfortably in the world as frogs?

The renunciation of instincts precedes religion. However, is this not the case with every culture? Whoever gives himself over totally to primal instincts, does not have enough energy left for cultural achievements. If we just imagine such a purely instinctual existence, which by the way almost always is already denied through the wise scarcity of nature, often also through the Ash Wednesday

THE ILLUSION OF THE FUTURE

protest of our human nature, then we can hardly doubt that this may be true for most animals, but certain: not for definition of nature is understood one-sidedly and in a totally insufficient way if only understood "naturalistically." Nothing justifies the contention that an animalistic vegetating corresponds better to the nature of mankind than a culturally adequate growing up and acting. It is also the surrounding natural environment itself which makes the spiritual ascent a necessity. Culture is always the product of two natures: an outer-human and human nature. Culture itself is only developed human nature, as much as those needs and renunciations that lure it are the results of nature. The one who frees the term nature from its false narrowing definition recognizes in the development of culture the same mutual correspondence between mankind and the rest of the world, as we find in epistemology for the process of knowing

I do not agree with Freud's earlier assertion that the formation of religion is based on the renunciation of acting on egoistic instincts, while neurosis pre-supposes the suppression of sexual function. Precisely the history of the oedi-pal attitude shows that sexuality is an integrating element of the Ego-instincts, and the other way around. (with the exception of their most primitive forms) as truly separate, we fall into an error. This "organic perspective," as I like to call the right perspective, is essential for the understanding of the development of religion. I do not think that today there is still a disagreement on this point between Freud and me. As he now presents the negative father relation as the most important factor for religion, he also pays attention to the libido drives. I think that we have to the singling out of particular instincts can only be done as an abstraction; as soon as we look for the renunciations of instincts that lead to religion in a very broad area, as much as we find, on the other hand, an ex-traordinary variety in the ways in which religion is formed. The determinative aggregate of the totem cult is very different, for instance, from the socio-ethical monotheism of the classical prophets in Israel, as the basis of the esthetic and pacifist faith of Echnaton is very different from the piety of the Spanish con-quistadors. But renunciations of instincts, which cause more or less compre-hensive and deep suppressions, obviously play a role in every formation of religion.

But do compulsive formation really always have to be inherent in religion? I believe, on the contrary, that the highest formations of religion precisely super-sede the element of compulsion. One just ought to think of genuine Christian-ity! Against that compulsive-neurotic nomism that burdened the people with a faith, of the letter and an embarrassing ceremonialism, Jesus put his "com-mandment" of love. "You know that the ancients were told – but I say to you" (Matth 5) – here we find the enormous act of liberation. And – this does not happen to be based on a new demand of allegiance, but rather is based on the authority of that freedom that was gained because of the victorious recognition of love and truth. Jesus overcame, according to the best rule of psychoanalysis, the collective neurosis of his people in putting love, although ethically perfected love, at the center of life. In his father concept, which however is thoroughly cleansed from all the dross of an oedipal relation, we can see all the heteronomy and all the embarrassment of being bound fully overcome. What is expected of mankind is nothing else than what corresponds to its essence and to its true destiny, what furthers the general well-being of mankind and creates – in order also to include the biological aspect an optimal health of the individual and the totality. It is a grave misunderstanding to interpret Jesus' basic commandment: "You shall love your God with all your heart and your neighbor as yourself" (Matth 22: 37ff.) as a law in the spirit of the Mosaic religion. The form of the imperative is kept, but who could not feel the subtle irony with which the content, namely our act of love as only something freely to be accomplished, supersedes the character of law. How beautifully Jesus had practiced psychoanalysis 1900 years before Freud – however, one ought not press the term too strictly in this regard – I already showed elsewhere (*Analytische Seelsorge*, Gttingen 1927, pp. 20–24). I may want to point out the fact that he does not just suggest away the symptom of the lame, but enters into his underlying ethical-religious conflict, reconciles it and thus overcomes his paralysis from inside. His belief in demons may estrange us as metaphysics, but as neurology we can accept it. The historio-psychological direction in which Jesus examines the biblicist compulsive authority finds the fullest approval from the analyst (for instance Matt 19: 8: The Mosaic law of a letter of divorce was instituted because of the hardness of heart of mankind). The treatment of transference, which is accepted as love, but at the same time directed further to absolute, ideal achievements so that there will not be a new form of binding, deserves the admiration of all disciples of Freud, as well as the termination of that parent fixation that causes this compulsion through the commitment to the absolute father who is love. Far be it from me, however, to suggest, as some nosy greenhorns might want to suggest, that Jesus could be described as the first psychoanalyst in the sense of Freud. But his liberating pastoral care points so decidedly in its fundamental form to analysis that Christians ought to be ashamed to have left the utilization of these shining footprints to a Non-Christian. The reason, undoubtedly, for this lies in the fact that the compulsive-neurotic bungling, which threatens, religion like any other form of the human spirit, has also covered up this beautiful trail, as in the materialism of a former psychiatry.

We could continue further in examining Jesus' elimination of compulsion and the refuting of its determinative power, we could prove how his father concept is free from all reaction symptoms towards an oedipal hatred – God is not to be appeased with sacrifices, but rather is to be loved in the brother – We could point out that brotherly love is in the deepest and broadest sense the mark and star of the Christian teaching. We could draw attention to the fact that the goal and highest good of all our longing and waiting does not consist of personal self-gratification, but rather of the Kingdom of God, in other words the reign of love, truth and justice in the individual, as well as in the universal community. However, we would get too far.

And is it not equally possible to say similar things about the religion of Echnaton, and to some degree even of Buddha? Is there not in the principle of Protestantism with its freedom of faith and conscience, but also with its call to love, a powerful liberating principle, and this not only in the sense of liberation from religious compulsion, but also as all-encompassing healing from compulsions?

It is very unfortunate that Freud leaves out precisely those highest expressions of religion. From a developmental-historical perspective it is not the case that religion creates compulsions and then keeps mankind in a neurosis. Rather it is true that pre-religious life creates neurotic compulsions, which then lead to corresponding religious concepts and rites. Magic that preceded religion is not yet religion. But then we find precisely in the greatest religious development, the Israelite-Christian development, again and again a religious inspiration (revelation), kindled by a higher, ethical, and therefore also social biological recognition, which attempts to eliminate compulsion and creates liberation, until under further circumstances, that nobody can understand better than the analyst, again and again through the predicament of the time new chains are forged, which a later religious conception is called to break. That this religious struggle for liberation corresponds to a humanization process, cannot be overlooked. Therefore, we see one follow the other, pre-Israelite animism and naturalism, the Mosaic religion, Baalism, the classical prophets, post-exilic nomism (finding its peak in the Pharisaic religion), the birth of Christianity, Catholicism, the Reformation, classical Protestant Orthodoxy, Pietism and the Enlightenment, in addition to all the present offshoots of the various Christian systems that either further or fight compulsion. It deserves our attention that a compulsion-free individualism at present is very strongly represented within Protestantism, which on the one hand through its social pathos, on the other hand through its rigorous critical-scientific work, has gained quite a reputation nong the other faculties.

One should also not forget that religion cannot, in any way, go through a development that is contained in itself! When Christians in particular centuries were competing in cruelty with the wildest barbarians, this did not happen because of a consequential living up to their religious principle, but due to neurotic illnesses, which were disfiguring and devastating the Christian religion, just as scientific research and artistic creativity were exposed and succumbed to the most horrible deformations. Therefore, I flatly deny that religion as such has a neurotic-compulsive character.

1.3 Religion as Wish Formation

For the thought that all religions only represent wish formations Freud rightfully does not claim any priority (p. 57). With an unsurpassable consistency Feuerbach almost ninety years ago followed through the thesis of theology as disguised anthropology and religion as a dream (p. 43). However, Freud with his microscope of the soul has refined strengthened these assumptions an extraordinary way in several aspects. Here we should not allow ourselves any illusions. The description of the latent wishes and their transformation for the purpose of making them conscious, as well as the unveiling of the oedipal situation, the repressed sadism and masochism make it absolutely impossible for us to deny wishful elements in the formation of religion. However, can we therefore explain every aspect of religious thinking from this? And is this mixing up of wishes and reality a special characteristic of religion only? And should the pushing back of wishful thinking by our reality thinking and the mobilization of reality thinking through! Wishful thinking in religion and science, and ultimately even in the arts and in morality, be the ideal towards which the development of the spirit, gasping, hoping and again and again painfully disappointed, is striving?

Before we continue in this examination, we would like to consider a common place from which to begin. I will never forget that sunny Sunday morning in the spring of 1909 in the Belvedere park in Vienna, where Prof. Freud pointed out to me in his lovely, fatherly manner the dangers of the scientific studies he was doing. Already at that time I was willing to give up the pastorate that meant a great deal to me, if truth would require it to proclaim a faith that was repudiated by reason, or to make one's head the place of unbelief, while having the heart as the place of faith, seemed to me like the tricks of jugglers, with which I did not want to have anything to do. I do not know what I could change in this position. One does not invest one's soul for illusions. To some extent I can meet Freud half way. was also applauded by theologians in his psychological critique of religious teachings that the conceptions of God and the life to come were often colored with the colors of a palette of wishes, I knew already. When for the first time I found the features of the father, various pastors etc., and behind that the influence of hatred, in a hallucinated conception of God the clarity with which this connection could be proven seemed fairly interesting to me, but I did not consider this as something radically new or unexpected.

THE ILLUSION OF THE FUTURE 127

That in the life to come of the Eskimos, which *is* filled with whales, that in the green Hunting-Grounds of the Indians, which is inviting for the hunting of scalps, that in the mead-blessed Valhalla of the Germanic people, which is filled with tournaments, we find the wishes of their originators in the same way reflected as in the prayer-hall heaven of the Pietist or in the afterlife of Goethe, with its ethical final decision, I knew already.

Nemesis furthermore wanted that also those atheists that I analyzed rather often were guided by wishful thinking. Which analyst did not find very often those atheists whose unbelief was only a disguised form of the elimination of the father? However, I would consider it a false assumption to press every rejection of religion into this wish scheme.

Let us look at those wishes that lead to religion more closely. It has to be acknowledged that in their initial stage they are predominantly of an egoistic nature, But would it be different with science? Could one expect a disinterested thirst for knowledge from primitive man? Already in the case of the so-called primitive man we see how an ethical need is awakened in the cult and in the faith, for instance the need for the atonement of evil that was committed (for instance of the death wishes against the father). In this ethical development we see at the same time a religious development. The selfish wishes more and more recede into the background, even if here and then we find again backlashes into an egoistic form of thinking, a sign of the fact that the wild and primitive element in man is very hard to eradicate. The classical prophets in the old Israel do without a personal continued existence after death; so strongly was their appearance and thinking wrapped up in the people,

In the Gospel we see those wishful drives powerfully fought, and this is true the more the development of Jesus proceeds in a continuous struggle with the tradition. The concept of reward, the idea of races, and the materially depicted and colored conceptions of the afterlife are pushed into the background, with the idea of reward pushed into the background *in* a much more skilled and wise way according to psychoanalysis than *in* the rigorous philosophy of the categorical imperative which pours out love without any understanding of its place. What Jesus demands *in* the name of his religion *is* to a great extent directly opposed to an Egotistic attitude, even though Jesus with great wisdom does not at all look down upon self-love, and thus *in* no way supports the masochism of the ascetics. The meekness and humility, the self-denial and rejection of the gathering of treasures, the devotion of one's own life to the highest ethical good, *in* short, the whole life attitude which the Crucified of Golgotha demanded from his disciples, *is* diametrically opposed to the desires of the original human nature. This corresponds, however, to a higher understanding of the human nature, as it definitely could not come from the lower demands of the instincts, but rather only from an ideal realism that was fought for in hard adversities and developed out of a magnificent intuitive anthropology and cosmology. In Jesus' prayer all egoistic elements disappear the petition for the daily bread, this subsistence, is no longer to be understood egoistically, rather the universal ethical ideals dominate, and at its highest we find the submission under the divine will ("Thy will be done.") This is no Buddhist wishlessness, nor a pathogenic introversion. The contention that according to a Christian understanding everything that this earthly life denies to the Christian is reflected in the conception of the life to come is wrong. The renunciation of sexual activity is compensated in the life to come according to the Islam, but definitely not according to Christianity. Jesus emphasizes explicitly that sensuous expectations of life after death be eliminated. (Matth 22: 30) His highest ideal, the Kingdom of God, has the earth here and now as the scene of action and ideal ethical and religious values, which have nothing to do with wishful instincts, as its content.

However, the opponent might ask whether religion does not at least correspond to wishes of some higher form? I would answer: One has to become aware of the difference between a wish and a postulate. A wish in a hallucination and other phenomena which Freud has helped us to understand is oriented towards gratification, without being concerned about the actual realities. In this sense we know many religious phenomena which make this illusionary leap from the desire to the assumption of some reality. However, nobody will declare that every wish is only capable in such an illegitimate way to find its gratification. It is very well possible to work in a way adequate to reality towards the gratification of one's wishes. Jesus felt in himself imperatives of love that were contradicting the sacred tradition. It is still possible to recognize the stage at which he thought it possible to harmonize the claims of this inner demand with those claims of the Mosaic law (Matth 5: 17–22). Yet, as we could see already before (Matth ew 5: 27ff. 33ff. 38ff.), this was not recognized in every place. Thus it had to end in the open break with tradition. The inner commandment had to overthrow the outer commandment. Then, however, this inner ethical necessity itself had to have its origin in God. And since it was oriented towards love, God himself had to be a loving God, and no longer the strict, jealous God of the Old Testament. At the same time this fear-producing compulsive character of the Torah broke down, as was shown above. If we want to translate this process, which happened intuitively and inspirationally in the soul of Jesus, into cumbersome knowing acts, then we get on the way of the postulate. This does not say: I wish this and that, therefore it is real. Rather it concludes: This and that exists; what therefore do I have to think as real in order that this particular existing reality becomes intelligible, could become

THE ILLUSION OF THE FUTURE 129

real and can be real? The postulate starts with an existing reality that is accepted and presupposed as certain, in order to conclude about other existing reality that follow from this first one in a logical and necessary way. The natural sciences with their hypotheses, which in the course of sufficient confirmation are further developed into theories, follow in some sense a similar way. Except that here we find existential from which one proceeds to other existential. In the postulate, however, the point of departure is a value or an imperative. Kant, for instance, considers the categorical imperative "Thou shalt" to be the Archemedean point and postulates from this a law-maker. I myself started from a different ethical certainty which had suggested itself to me precisely in the psychoanalytic, as well as the sociological observation: from the determination of love towards the neighbor, oneself and the absolute ideal. In this norm which follows from the particular nature of mankind, since in its being lies a demand of the ought, I found the place from which I had to deduce an absolute as the origin of both being and ought, as well as of all values. This philosophical operation is basically nothing else but the experiential-intuitive God-awareness of Jesus.

That in this a great deal of wishes of one's own liking and even many "needs" have to be sacrificed to the hard recognition of reality, is obvious. And if the ground of being of the determination of love in the highest sense is itself stated as spiritual and loving, is this then is really unreasonable.

Furthermore, we need to pose the question: Is not in science too the symbolic phantasy a charade-like disguised bearer of valid knowledge. Does not scientific thinking as well work with suggestive and at the same time much concealing harbingers of anthropomorphism?

I want to begin with the latter problem. I still remember the joyful surprise with which I read in the first year of the *Imago*, Robitsek' s important study on the scientific work of the chemist Ukulele von Stradowitz. Accordingly, the theory of structure and benzene originated from visual fantasies of dancing pairs and queues; nevertheless, the waking reasoning had to examine these dreams.

We ought to be careful not to look at all primitive conceptions that appear fantastic to us reality thinkers in the 20th century immediately as wish products. When the wild man suspects a living animal in the boiling water, which wish would guide him in that? Was it not close at hand for him to explain the unknown boiling analogous to the movement of the water known to him which was caused by a hidden animal? And when human-like forces and essences are projected on natural phenomena and events, is this a particular characteristic of religion, or do we not find this process which is based on analogy conclusions even in the proudest halls of the natural sciences, and even of the still more strictly disciplined philosophical thinking? We speak of "power," "cause," "effect," "law" and hundreds of other terms which long ago have been created by epistemology as rather crude, but still indispensable anthropomorphisms? Is this not also true of the term "censorship"?

The history of the sciences is a continuum with anthropomorphisms and other impermissible projections of known facts into unknown ones. Why should religion and theology here be an exception? The question, however, is whether theology which dealt with religion has stayed with one foot in the stage of wishes. If she did, I seriously would fear (or should I hope it) that she shares this depressing fate for any science with the other sciences, without excluding the natural sciences or the historical sciences. I can definitely say it about philosophy, and even if we can acknowledge a plus of pure objectivity to the rigorously exact natural sciences, they still lack that which an empirical criticism looked for with such passion, yet without any success: the pure experience from which all additions of human subjectivity could be eliminated.

On the contrary, the natural sciences end with the bitter recognition of only being able to perceive a little spot of the surface, that still has to be acknowledged only as a shining glaze. The colors dissolve in "etheric waves," whereby one still has to add in a resigned manner that the ether is a very doubtful auxiliary term, the sounds turn out to be oscillations of air whose combination into a melody or a symphony has no place in the documents and in the world of the natural sciences, the atom that during several thousand years of experimenting and reflecting had been looked at as downright simple and unchanging little block of reality and had been elevated to be supporter of a seemingly scientifically proven world view, suddenly one morning breaks into pieces like a piece of coal, and it even transforms itself into another element; the law of nature turns out to be the product of a wish according to newer critiques of the natural sciences, the wish that a process under the same conditions has to take its course always the same way. One only has to remember the embarrassment of the builders of machines and bridges, if this were otherwise ! If the revolutionary opinions of the newest and critical natural sciences have provided something that is certain, then it is the recognition that in their field we got stuck in wishes up to our necks, and pragmatism, as much as we might reject it by turning up our nose, at least has its positive side in that it revealed the interest of the practical American in the extensive benefiting of reality, and thus revealed the wish background of all knowing.

Theology has shown no small willingness and capability for the surrender of wishful thinking. However, it seems more useful to me to present this at the end of our friendly dispute. With theology religion, however, likewise subjected itself to the most drastic and for our wishing most painful sacrifices.

THE ILLUSION OF THE FUTURE   131

Furthermore, we should not overlook the fact that religion from its beginning was able to integrate the knowledge of nature and values quite extensively. Whoever laughs about the still-standing sun of Joshua, should have payed attention to the fact that the concept of a fixed closure much later. It entered the sciences, until it lost recently not insignificantly against some of its credit. Christianity fought too long, way too long, against Copernicus and the theory of evolution, but it finally got used to them. That it does not follow every scientific trend of the day should not be held against it. Quite a number a excellent scientists until the present do not find any difficulty in harmonizing religion and the natural sciences, while the half-educated very often much more easily than great researchers of the stature of Freud proclaim the incompatibility of both areas at the beer table. Nothing is thereby proven for the truth or falsehood of religion.

However, what about the contradictions in religious thinking? I already spoke about the sincere desire of the newer theology to overcome them. Whether it succeeded is hard to decide. I believe to have reached a religiosity that has mastered those contradictions, even though there still remain, like in every other field of human thinking, unsolved mysteries.

But now I would like to turn the tables and ask: Does not after all the empirical science abound in whopping contradictions? I do not even want to point to the terminological deformities like the ether, that is supposed to be a substance without consisting of atoms, but which nevertheless was greeted with most submissive bowing as lord by the most honest scientist. Yet it might make some impression that very important scientists of nature and of the soul, like for instance Herbart and Wundt, do not assign any other task to philosophy than to eliminate those contradictions inherent in the empirical terms and to reconcile those cleared up empirical terms with each other. In view of this it seems that one ought to be a bit more lenient with the religion of the uneducated and the theologians too. Since Freud did not enter into a discussion of the particular contradictions, but rather limits himself to declare as unprovable and irrefutable most of the religious teachings (p. 50, 52), I cannot enter into a defense of religious reality thinking in particular cases. If we consider how humbly today the natural sciences have learned to think about that area that can really be proven, then we have to acknowledge that in our problem the greatest caution is urgently required, lest one demand of other faculties what one does not fulfill in one's own, and accuse others of what one does oneself. With what exemplary caution Freud speaks of the proven-ness of his assertions! We furthermore have to be careful not to consider agreements between scholars as proof and validity of a theory. It is very often only a sign of fatigue, and the undertakers may already stand in front of the door. In this area, which makes our truly scientific assets look a little bit dubious in comparison to our liabilities, we have to be aware even more of the danger of cheating. Through wishful thinking and the allowing of contradictions one would not get a more favorable balance, but rather even more endanger one's credit. But one also does not see any reason to put all one's assets in the one bank of science and to declare all other cultural assets as superfluous. But more on this later.

When Freud accuses religion of hallucinatory confusion, he is undoubtedly right in terms of specific, yes even many forms of religion. However, is this true for all forms of piety? I do not see this. Once more it seems, that the great master has very specific forms in view and seems to generalize from those. I almost get the impression that he was a rare guest in protestant worship services and also hardly ever payed a visit to critical theology. Especially we analysts who take seriously for the first time the psychology of the ingenious in a total manner, know by the way very well that something very great and very deep can lie behind a hallucinatory confusion. When Paul confesses that his teaching of the cross is foolishness to the Gentiles (1 Cor 1:23), then this is no counter-argument for him. To me a creative, Dionysian or Apollonian fire spirit, which does not hand out its revelations as mellow wine, but rather as fermenting new wine, is much more precious than a sober scholar who consumes his life strength in a sterile juggling of terms and pedantic precision. The degree of reasonableness is not necessarily the measure of value. The stormy youth with its frenzy and follies has after all no small advantage in comparison to the prudent old age. You cannot wait with eating and drinking until the honored physiologists have carried out their food analyses and have worked out their nutrition theories to the satisfaction of many. The radium-containing baths provided for several centuries good services, before the radium and thus the cause for the healing successes was discovered. Is it so unconceivable that in the area of the spirit the knowledge of causes heavily panting hobbled after the possession of precious values? It honestly seems to me that we have kept rather not enough than too much of a Platonic frenzy and Pauline scandal in our modern Protestantism with its incredibly rigorous and sharp criticism. And yet I cannot do otherwise than to carry out the reality principle at my place with the utmost and uncompromising rigor, even though with a constant fear of losing precious values in the mesh of netting of a scientific abstraction. And be it not forgotten: Scientific hypotheses can be rejected; in our practical questions, on the answers of which depends our life development, we have to take a stance, even where stringent proofs are lacking. How else cold one marry or take a job? Similarly, there is inherent in religion a trust; but woe to the one who only gets married on the basis of wishes, who chooses a job and decides for a religion without meticulously taking account of reality!

THE ILLUSION OF THE FUTURE   133

1.4   *Religion as Hostile to Thinking*

What religion as such is hostile to thinking, I do not comprehend. Freud writes: "If we pose the question, on what the claims of religious teachings to be believed are based, then we receive three answers which in an odd way poorly agree with each other. First, they deserve our faith, since already our fore-forefathers believed in them, second, we have proofs, which have been transmitted to us precisely from that antiquity, and third, in principle it is forbidden to raise this question for confirmation." (p. 40)

I acknowledge, awful argumentations like that have emerged here and there. But which educated Christian today would want to be put off by these arguments? We Protestants definitely not. We criticize the Bible and dogmas as radically as we criticize Homer or Aristotle. and Catholics, at least they place before their dogmatics their apologetics which tries to satisfy the claims of reason. One may dispute its necessity a philosopher, diagnose it as rationalization as a disciple of Freud, reject at least part of it as order under the king's private seal but as a Protestant, there still remains a work of reason that deserves respect. We Protestants know too well how much we owe to thinking for our religion, that we could deny it full space. Even if Luther did not give reason its appropriate rights, nevertheless he was a theologian and a scientific thinker, otherwise he would have never become a Reformer. Zwingli went through the humanistic school, which not only gave to his theology and piety their gentleness, but also their clarity. And even the gloomy Calvin, Geneva's dreadful Grand Inquisitor, had made his legal thinking available to his fortress like theology. The religion of the Reformers also was the result of their scientifically trained professorial thinking. The newer theology which did and still does accomplish a great deal in its radical negation is aware of the fact that it serves an invaluable service to religion – precisely in its rigorous reality thinking.

In my environment I have never heard of the prohibition to think about religious matters. On the contrary, we Protestant ministers urge in our pupils free critical thinking. Among pastors of a free spirit this is self-evident, but it is also known to me among many conservatives. We calm frightened persons that have fallen into crises of faith with the assurance that God loves the honest doubter and that a faith that has been strengthened by thinking is much more worth than one that is simply taken over and learned. We urge and cherish free thinking also in the religion of adults.

Thinking according to Freud is supposedly weakened through religion. It is true, of course, that he adds that maybe the effect of the religious prohibition against thinking is not as strong as he assumes (p. 78). But nevertheless, he considers it worthwhile to try an education that is free from the sweet poison (p. 80) of religion. (p. 79) Historically, it may be pointed out that undisputedly a long line of the deepest and freest spirits which have greatly contributed to the spiritual and intellectual life of humanity at the same time approved of religion and science, and hear of religion very often with greatest fervor, and I cannot believe that Freud seriously thinks that they would have created even greater things, if they had never heard of religion. Physicians like Hermann Lotze, Wundt, Kocher, physicists like Descartes, Newton, Faraday, Robert Mayer, chemicists like Justus Liebig, biologists like Oswald Heer, Darwin, Pasteur, K,E, von Bar, mathematicians like Leibnitz, Pascal, Gauss, geographers like Ritter, historians like Johannes von Muller, Carlyle, Niebuhr, L. von Ranke, statesmen like Lincoln, Gladstone, Bismarck, philosophers like Kant, Fichte, Schelling, Hegel, Herbart, Ruskin, Eucken, Bergson, poets like Goethe, Schiller, Ruckert, Bitzius, Gottfried Keller, K.F. Meyer, Geibel – I only mention quickly a few out of a long line of excelling names – betray after all no intelligence defect, although they believe in God, and I really would not know what allows for the contention that their spirit could have risen to even higher and greater accomplishments, if they had not met religion. Quite a few of those that were named were certainly in religious fervor far above the average of the believers, while in view of their great intellectual accomplishments one actually should have expected the opposite, if the danger of becoming stupid were really so intimately connected with religion.

We already now would want to point out how still in the recent past important natural scientists precisely through their thinking reached an assurance or at least the probability of a constructive world will (Einstein, Becher, Driesch). But again we will not base the proof of the truth of religion on these authorities.

Freud used to formerly attach great importance to the idea that the urge of the thinking process in children was damaged, if one answered the question of the origin of natural objects by summarily referring to God. I concur with him, but I would like to ask whether the result is different, if one says: Nature has created them. I want to emphasize that one always points out in religious education in school how God works through natural, events and human activity.

I myself remember how my own thinking has been greatly encouraged and helped by religion. Innumerable thought problems, which after all some time will have to be dealt with, since one also cannot play the ostrich relating to life, were stimulated, magnificent historical figures were offered to me, the sense for greatness and ethical necessity was developed. I would consider it an irreplaceably grave loss, if one were to eradicate these religious memories from my life. Even that I was presented with the Bible as the infallible Word of God sharpened my thinking; I still remember how as a twelve-year-old after reading, the story of the Flood I ran to the zoological museum, in order to compare the

THE ILLUSION OF THE FUTURE 135

measurements of the ark with those of the glass cases and thus to construct a childish evolutionary theory, but at the same time to take a skeptical stance towards the Bible, that later developed into free criticism.

Regarding the proposed experiment of Freud of a religionless education at school we can say that this has been done already quite often and has been carried out in masses in communist circles for many years.

In my analyses I often dealt with persons educated *in* a religionless way, however I honestly cannot confirm that I found a plus in intelligence or respectively a more advantageous development of the thinking capacities, as well as I would not recognize those who deny God among the philosophers, like Karl Vogt or Moleschott (one can also in a qualified way include Hackel here), as the superior ones. History at least until now has given a different judgment.

1.5 *Religion for the Protection of Culture*

What remains is the examination of religion as the protection of culture. Freud is thereby assigning a police mission to religion. Religion apparently has offered a great service to human culture, contributed to the taming of asocial instincts a great deal, but not enough. If it had succeeded in making happy the majority of human beings, in comforting them, reconciling them to life, making them into bearers of culture, then nobody would get the idea to search for a change of the existing conditions. What do we see instead? That an alarmingly great number of human beings is dissatisfied and unhappy in this culture, experiences it as yoke which one has to throw off, that these human beings either invest all their energy in the change of this culture, or go so far in their hostility to culture that they do not want to know anything more about culture and the limitation of instincts." (p. 60)

I can fully agree with Freud that religion, as the police of culture, often did not prove very helpful at all; however, I would want to add: It appears to me to be fortunate that this is the case: for religion has more important things to do than to protect the mixture of grandeur and atrocity that today is called culture.

As culture Freud understands "all that in which human life has risen above its animalistic conditions and in which it is distinguished from the life *of* animals. (p. 6) The differentiation between culture and civilization is rejected."Culture on the one hand consists of all the knowledge and capability that human beings have attained in order to subdue the powers of nature and to gain from it all the goods for the satisfaction of human needs, on the other hand of all the institutions that are necessary in order to regulate the relationships between the human beings and especially the distribution of the accessible goods." (p. 6 f.)

I have to confess that in my view a great many abominable and destructive elements are found among that which puts the human person above the animal; the knowledge and ability, the goods for the satisfaction of human needs, the institutions for the regulation of social relationships and the distribution of the goods, all this appears to me to be so thoroughly saturated with cruelty, injustice, seeds of poison, that religion really has no reason to stand up for the preservation of the existing as it is. War, the spirit of Mammon, pleasure-seeking, mass poverty, exploitation, oppression and innumerable other miseries point to the necessity to distinguish in that which one calls culture between the good and that which is worth its protection, and the evil which has to be fought. It even seems to me that a seriously lived-out Christianity would have to search for radical changes over against our externalized and in inner values, especially emotional values, stunted culture, and the study of psychoanalysis has supported me in this opinion – not a preserving police, but a leader and light to true and authentic culture out of our mock culture religion should become for us.

It also would seem to me unworthy of religion, if with Freud one assigned to it the task to provide comfort for the renunciations of instincts that are required by culture, as it were to supply muzzles or handcuffs for the social masses (p. 60). The taming of animalistic instincts (as far as they hinder human well-being and human dignity) rather should only be the back side for the solution of a positive task: Religion should unleash the highest spiritual and emotional powers, further the highest accomplishments in the arts and in science, fill the life of all, even of the poorest, with the maximum of goods of truth, beauty and love, help overcome real life miseries, pave the way for new more substantial and authentic forms of societal living and thus create a higher, inwardly more fulfilled humanness which corresponds better to the true demands of human nature and ethics than our much praised non-culture, which already Nietzsche called a thin apple skin over a burning chaos. One totally misunderstands the essence of Christianity, if one thinks that it offers heaven as a substitute for the earth left to its misery. "To us thy Kingdom come" prays the Lord's Prayer and enjoins on us the demand to invest all our energies for this earthly Kingdom of God, as much as the commandments of the Gospel are very this-worldly. "Before you offer your offering on the altar, first go and be reconciled to your brother!" is demanded in the Sermon on the Mount (Matth 5: 24).

It is not the fault of Jesus that Christianity has often misunderstood this. Freud has given us the possibility to recognize why very often the intentions of the founder of the Christian religion were disfigured by compulsive-neurotic developments into a caricature. There is no more authentic realism than Christianity. Only we should not forget that to reality belongs not only that

THE ILLUSION OF THE FUTURE   137

which can be grasped and received by our smelling-organ and other little
windows of the soul, but also that which is found behind these little windows
in the depth of the soul and behind the stimulating sources of our senses.
However, we need a little bit a more deeply penetrating view of reality and
philosophy of value in order to recognize that the neglect of these higher realities that lie beyond toe manifest and massive only leads to a bad realism.
Therefore, we put aside for the moment this problem.

2   Freud's *Scientism*

2.1   *The Belief in Science as Beneficial to Humanity*

Over against a religious belief Freud puts the belief in the gladdening power of
science, which is understood by Freud only in the sense of an empirical science. In it illusion has given way to truth. In all this it seems that he is less
bothered by the question what science really is than Pilate was bothered by the
parallel concern what truth really is. Freud is a positivist, and we can be thank-
ful to God for this. Without his concentrated commitment to the empirical, he
would not have become the great pioneer. We can pardon such a successful
and ingenious pioneer for setting up in the moment that he tries to strangle
the religious illusion the messiahship of science, without realizing that in the
same way illusion spreads itself out in this belief.

But let us hear first the word of the master! Freud is way too intelligent to
entrust himself blindly to the vulgar uncritical belief in the omnipotence of
the natural sciences. He does not shy away from the question "whether our
conviction, that through the use of observation and reflection in scientific
work we can come to know something about our external reality," has a sufficient basis (p. 54). In a truly philosophical manner he continues: "Nothing
should keep us from welcoming the use of observation for our own reality and
the use of reflection for its own critique. A number of distinctions come up
here which have to become crucial for the formation of a 'world view'. We also
suspect that such an endeavor will not be wasteful and that it will offer at least
partially some justification for our suspicion."(p. 54f.) But the ability, of the
author forbids such a comprehensive endeavor, therefore out of necessity he
will limit his work to the pursuit of a single one of these illusion, namely the
religious illusion." (p. 55)

Later on, however, the empirical sciences are accorded an optimism, which
is elevated to daring perspectives of the future. After the abandonment of
religion humanity will then extend its power through the help of science and
learn how to bear the great necessities of the human fate with submission

(p. 81). However, Freud immediately acknowledges that perhaps this hope too may be of an illusionary nature (p. 85). How? So we possibly only would have to exchange the religious illusion with the scientific one? The difference would be that one assuredly, the other one perhaps fools us? So we still remain in a state of uncertainty, and the last word belongs to skepticism which at least has no doubts about this one thing, namely that doubt has its full logical justification?

However Freud shows that not only religion is able to comfort. Chivalrously he breaks a lance for the intellect: "The voice of the intellect is soft, but it does not rest until it has been heard. At the end, after countless repeated rejections, it is still heard. This is one of the few aspects in which one can be optimistic for the future of mankind, but as such it is not unimportant. Connected with it can be other hopes. The primacy of the intellect, to be sure, seems still far, far, but probably in spite of all not infinitely far away. And since the intellect probably will have as its goals the same that you expect to be realized by your God – in human moderation, of course, as much as the external reality, the *anagke* (fate), allows it – namely the love of mankind and the reduction of suffering, we can say to each other, that our enmity is only a temporary one, and none that could not be reconciled. We hope for the same, but you are more impatient and – why should I not say it? – more selfish than I and those around me. You want to have supreme happiness start right after death..."(p. 87) "We believe that it is possible for scientific work to come to know something about the reality of the world, whereby we increase our power and according to which we can organize our life. If this belief is an illusion, then we are in the same boat as you are, but science has proven through countless and important successes that it is no illusion."(p. 89) "Science will further develop and become more refined, However, it would be an illusion to believe that we could get from elsewhere what it cannot give to us." (p. 91)

With this magnificently logical statement Freud concludes his prediction of the downfall of religion and the glorious absolute rule of science. God the Logos overthrows the God of religion and reigns in the kingdom of necessity, the meaning of which is not at all clear yet.

2.2 *Historical Elucidation*

Only in passing should it be remembered, that this ideal of science too, as it is certainly well-known to Freud, looks back to an honorable past. Only it seems that the founder of psychoanalysis perhaps has undertaken a certain sharpening of the position, when he isolated the concept of science more emphatically from philosophy in his positivism than used to be the case. His empiricism is radically different from the one of the English empiricists, who with greatest

THE ILLUSION OF THE FUTURE

precision took hold of the empirical world, on the other hand however in their actions allowed their natural instincts and their conscience, and not anymore science, to guide them, or even, like the absolutely irreligiously brought up John Stuart Mill, finally, after this, still sought the contact with religion; the "future of an illusion" also radically differs from a positivism of Auguste Comte, who first destroys the mythological, and then the metaphysical level of reflection, in order to sing his praise of the only-saving individual sciences, then however, nevertheless, wants to explain the world out of the ethical feeling of the human being and constructs a highly romantic and fantastic religion for mankind, a rather amusing witness to the fact that he does not seem to get by with his decidedly broadly-based scientism. Likewise, David Friedrich Strauss, who gets very close in his position to Freud with his mechanical materialism, and who only in his assumption of a "reasonable and benevolent universe" moves somehow into the area of philosophy, which the opponent of the religious illusion could hardly follow, insists on an ethic that in no way is fully satisfied by scientific production. Closest to Freud among those philosophers known to me is Baron von Holbach, who already derives the formation of the idea of God from the wish to make the natural powers accessible to the influence of prayer and sacrifice through their humanization, who, denies any utility to religion, tries therefore to put an end to it and elevates continuous happiness as the goal of all our endeavors. That Freud highly surpasses the materialists of the 18th century as an empiricist and refuses to be taken in by his banal metaphysics, is self-evident. He is fully satisfied by scientific production. Closest to Freud among those philosophers known to me is Baron con Schoolbag, who already derives the formation of the idea of God from the wish to make accessible the influence of prayer and sacrifice through their humanitarianism, denies any utility to religion, tries therefore to put an end to it and elevates coninuous happiness as the goal. Freud surpasses all 18th century materialists as an empiricist and refuses to be taken in by his banal metaphysics, is self-evident. all of our endeavors.

2.3   *Freud's Optimism about Science*

We now are faced with the task to examine Freud's optimism about science. First we should clearly consider what he understands by science and how far his optimism goes.

To the first point we do not get any clear hints. So far the attitude of the greatest of the newer pathfinders in the area of the life of the soul was definitely negative towards philosophy. Now however I hear to my satisfaction that Freud allows for the basic justification of epistemology as far as it is its task to give an answer to the question whether we can get to know something about external reality. Certainly, as we heard before, Freud shies away from this task in his modest way; however, he still declares that science has to limit itself to the description of the world as it has to appear to us according to the characteristic nature of our organization (p. 91) and that the problem of the constitutional structure of the world without due consideration of our perceptual psychic apparatus is an empty abstraction (p. 91).

Here it seems that Freud nevertheless is offering epistemological conclusions without a preceding epistemology. He assumes as self-evident that we are only dealing with the phenomenal world. But is it not of the essence of science everywhere to disentangle this phenomenal world and to set it against abstractions that alone mediate understanding to us of this world of the senses, Optics breaks up colors, as we already heard before, into oscillations of colorless "bodies," which again are deprived of their "corporeality" by physics and chemistry and are divided into electrons and other abstracted concepts – causation we do not see or smell anywhere, rather we read it into the phenomena.

We ought to be clear about the fact that this "perceptual psychic apparatus, that according to Freud all analysis of the constitutional nature of the world has to take into account, is in no way a concept that is very clear and safe from deception. Can I measure temperatures with the thermometer without being certain about the reliability of the instrument, can one simply ignore all of the more recent history of philosophy which started in Descartes with and weighing is a form of abstraction, since numerical terms are of course, like other terms, abstract. Philosophy, which immediately starts where experience ends, reaches into the empirical sciences, and whoever does not seriously want to deal with philosophical problems, does it anyway in an unprofessionally confused way.

In addition, how could one settle the religious problem, if one excludes fundamental epistemological questions? Is it not simply a form of negative dogmatism to declare in some declaration of might that a world will and world meaning do not exist?

If one thinks that philosophy is some spleen of heads remote from life and reality, then it should be pointed out that the history of philosophy nevertheless shows a number of excellent names of people who have accomplished enormous things in physics, mathematics, astronomy etc. When still in our days a natural scientist of the caliber of Driesch, who for twenty years has gloriously contributed to the natural sciences, changes over to philosophy, then psychiatrists follow the same way, then it should help us recognize that philosophy is not simply a matter of whims and wild notions, but deals with a reality whose existence cannot be brushed aside with the wave of a hand. In my

THE ILLUSION OF THE FUTURE

141

view this world of the spiritual order, which can be deduced from the phenomenal world, stands more secure in front of us than the very certainly deceptive world of the senses. Of course one can take it easy and advocate agnosticism. But even this declaration of bankruptcy of thought is not that easy.

Therefore, from Freud's rather popular concept of science how far this knowledge can reach, which degree of reliability it can attain, and which chances it has. How then could I know whether or not there is a spiritual primal ground and ordering, thus thinking world will? How can I know whether the expansion of power through knowledge signifies an extra of happiness for humankind?

Now we can also look at Freud's science prognosis. We cannot say that he is offering us a rose-colored *Eos* (goddess of the dawn). Freud is much too serious and honest a man to give promises that he is not convinced he can keep. The human person will expand his power with the help of science – how far we are not told – and learn how to bear the great necessities of fate in submission. This is all, really all, But has not Freud already said too much with this? Could it not be that culture will soon collapse? Has it not been predicted to us by a man whose rich knowledge has been acclaimed everywhere that there will be the downfall of the Occident? Is it so unthinkable that a culture that is only guided by science will succumb to wild passions, after the World War has revealed to us the deep-seated barbarity of the nations? Do not Eduard von Hartmann and many others assure us that the development of the sciences only increases our misery? Is it so certain that the advancement of the sciences has so far increased the total sum of human life enjoyment, and if it was that way so far, is it certain that it will always remain that way? Is it certain that we are happier than a hundred years ago? Is it at least the case among the scholars? Do the workers feel more satisfied because of the blessings of science than a few generations ago? Or the craftsmen? Or the farmers? What will happen to the most marvelous accomplishments of technology, if they are forced into the service of human greed for money, human cruelty and inhumane pleasure-seeking?

Freud's scientific prognosis is based on a simple conclusion of analogy which I do not consider to be certain. It says: Since so far the progress of science has brought mankind certain advantages, this will also be the case in the future, Or to put it more succinctly, there is in the background of this a belief in science whose basis Nietzsche in his falcon view recognized and expressed in these words: "It will be understood that it is still a metaphysical belief on which is based our belief in science, – that we knowing people of today, we godless and anti-metaphysical people, as several millennia had ignited, that Christian belief, which was also the belief of Plato, that God is truth, that the truth is divine.

But what if this becomes more and more untrustworthy?" Shall we still take our fire from the blaze that a belief is as old as this? Do we know through the pronouncement of an oracle that knowledge will always contribute to the enhancement of human happiness, even if evil passions dominate, Byron complains: "The tree of knowledge is not the tree of life!" can exact knowledge prove him wrong? And if we are consumed by a Faustian desire for knowledge, can the natural sciences and medicine today (philosophy and theology are excluded) satisfy us, or will even a Faust of today almost be consumed in his heart?

Freud predicts that one will learn how to bear the great necessities of fate in submission. Well, many were able to do this of old even without science, and even though I bow before the great soul of that religionless one who can find this submission, who says to me that and why submission ought to be the last word? Some shot themselves despairingly in the head, even though they stood on the proud pinnacles of science. Others got lost in wild hatred against life and tried to numb themselves in excesses, others became introverted with and without a pleasant invitation in some mysticism hostile to the world etc.

Do we not find behind Freud's belief in the final victory of the intellect the wish and does not his prediction of the end of an illusion include the parade of a new one, namely the illusion of science? That the parade of this does not happen with drums beating and waving of flags in Freud, but rather very subdued and with groping steps, fits his humility; however, I cannot join him, precisely because the reality principle is a warning in my way.

2.4   *Freud's Belief in the Sufficiency of Science*
However, reveals that here as before (p. 81) he is also thinking of the fully valid substitute for that which religion offered to its believers. As much as I happily and enthusiastically like to follow Freud on the marvelous paths of his empirical science, at this place it is impossible for me to keep pace with him. Here Freud's shining intellect goes so far as to become intellectualism which enamored by its successes forgets its limits.

We human beings are not just thinking apparatuses, we are living, feeling and volitional beings. We need goods and values, we need something that satisfies our emotions, that enlivens our volition. Our thinking too has to give us values, logical ones, but also others. Do we not very frequently deal with clearly thinking human beings in our analyses who are almost starving to death and radically despairing? Do we not carry in ourselves a conscience that judges or rewards us? Is not precisely through psychoanalysis the power of guilt-feelings proven? Does not Freud more clearly than any other in the world show the crucial importance of value, emotions, affects and instincts? As is known, the intellect does not know how to make value judgments. The sharpest reasoning

THE ILLUSION OF THE FUTURE

143

process is unable to indicate whether a symphony of Mahler or a painting of Hadler is beautiful. The most educated human person can welcome a vile betrayal and laugh at the death of a hero for the sake of truth without any inner opposition. A heartless scoundrel can possess a clear-sighted intellect, and a mentally weak person can be upset over some perfidy. Science lacks the ability to assess aesthetics and ethical entities. Truly, one still seems to hear Aristotle's definition of the brain as a cooling apparatus echo, when thinking not only in Spinoza – is characterized and praised as an emotion-suppressing function. That Freud has to find some place for emotional values, of which his own life shows such a beautiful richness, somewhere in his scientific life work, is clear. But I cannot find that place in his definition of science.

I also cannot see where he keeps the temples of the arts. Is art really only a sign of not having been analyzed and of weakness? Could science replace to us the loss of the symphonies of Beethoven or the sonatas of Reger? And should we sacrifice the gorgeous works of Egyptian, Hellenistic and Christian art for scientific propositions and discoveries? The magnificent domes and cathedrals, which constitute the pride and enjoyment of our generation, those paintings inspired by Christian emotions by a Fra Angelico, Leonardo da Vinci; Albrecht Dürer, Holbein, up to Gebhardt, Thoma, Steinhausen, the Pieta of a Michelangelo, the Thief or the Prodigal Son of a Meunier etc., all this should disappear, The fountain of Christian poetry, as it emits its silver waves in Lessing's Nathan, Goethe's Faust, Dostojewski's The Idiot, Tolstoy' The *Resurrection* etc., would have to dry up, and in place of the green pastures only the heather of theory would remain, on which the ghosts of error menacingly float around? To the sceptic who is not even capable of sighing with Faust: "How happy, who can still hope to emerge from this ocean of error!" to him one would stubbornly present the glorious future of science for the coming millenias.

For me art is still that herald, blessed with the vision of a seer, of deep secrets and revealer of precious treasures which elude the glasses of the scholar again and again, a feeding miracle for hungry souls, a message of peace from the world of ideals, which no thinking fist can ever tear down, since they belong more securely to true reality than those material things at hand and other delusions of our senses. To elaborate on this more thoroughly would require more explanations, in which the intellect would only be given the role of that which explains, which pays homage to and serves the creative genius. How frightened would I be in a state of scholars devoid of art!

And even less can inventive science replace for us the realm of ethical values and forces. Science itself has to be integrated into an ethical purpose, lest it degrade itself to some doubtful endeavor. Who would want to question that in Freud it fits into an ethical plan and helps to fulfill it? But in his little book, if I see this correctly, I find no mention of this all-encompassing observation. We do no longer stand on a Socratic ground that understands that knowledge itself is already power. The alcoholic who knows that he will ruin himself with his addiction, nevertheless still does not have the strength to break with it. Also the analytical insight into the dynamics of the unconscious and its deep roots does not, as we know today, help already as such in the liberation from its ban; Freud has taught us that through transference the obstructed instincts have to be liberated as well.

Is it really so certain that with an increasing progress of science the attitudes of human beings will be cleansed too? Has not Alexander von Ottingen shown how exactly the highly educated percentage-wise have more criminals than the intellectual middle-class? Do we not find now and then among academicians incredible pettiness in attitude? When almost a hundred years ago the public school was founded, one expected a rapid decline in crime. And today?

From where do we take the assurance that in the future the increase of knowledge and technology will magically bring about an increase in ethical forces? In the fight against alcoholism I experienced often enough and very clearly how little can be accomplished with scientific arguments. And even if our repressions were overcome, that morality which gives to life its dignity and true inner health could still not be reached through science.

Here I have also presented the reason why I do not believe in the replacement of religion by science. Religion is the sun that caused the most glorious blossoming life of art and the richest harvest of ethical attitude to come forth. All truly great, magnificent art which for the philosopher of religion is the ground of the reality of ideals, is for the pious the ideal ground of his reality-based creativity, the Spirit of Pentecost, who descends on earth in flames, the revealer whose "Let there be light" also can enlighten the darkness of the human spirits with glaring clarity. Whoever wants to destroy religion, at the same time cuts through the roots of the great arts which reveal the deepest meaning and the highest forces of life.

In the same way we see in religion a foundational pillar of morality. We do not want to overlook that pious faith took over moral insights again and again, as for instance the history of Christianity shows. However, we also do not forget that the most daring and exalted ethical progresses could only start as religion. The great progresses in ethics cannot be attributed to scientists, but thankfully to the founders of religion. Even Kant, who with his exclusion of love represents a dubious regression behind the ethics of Jesus, is basically only the educated speaker of a Protestantism diverted into Puritanism.

THE ILLUSION OF THE FUTURE

145

It is in no way even clear that ethics itself is following a progressing line. I cannot concur with Freud's statement that the moral always understands itself on its own. As is known, we cannot rely without further qualifications on conscience and in the moral sciences the most varied theories gesticulate against, each other. Plain utilitarianism seems an abomination to the follower of Kant, eudemonism with its glaring lack of clarity irritates the follower of Nietzsche who looks for and canonizes the will for power as the norm for good and evil. In the particular ethical problems we find a chaos of contradicting opinions; one only has to think of the moral evaluation of war, excessive accumulation of capital, free love, abortion etc. The positivistic thinking of science as Freud seems to have it in mind very certainly cannot help us much further, even though, as I described elsewhere, it can provide us with highly valuable building-blocks for ethics, which will always remain a philosophical discipline, namely besides sociology primarily the psychoanalysis of Freud. Most recently I hear in a public discussion from the lawyer Kelsen from Vienna how positivism could not even formulate law (Kelsen is himself a positivist); how could he then create an ethical theoretical system!

The empirical sciences therefore let us down in the formulation of ethical concepts. And what is more important: the generation of ethical living has never been achieved by dry theories and smart concepts. It would be pedagogy of the worst kind to overlook this fact. Religion with its partly exalted, partly lovely symbols, with its poetic magnificence and heart-stirring interpretations of reality, with its fascinating personalities, who through their heart-winning actions and sufferings are able to captivate us and through their imperfections and weaknesses partly warn, but then also encourage, the fallen human being once again to strive with new strength for his ideal, religion with its enormous metaphysical backgrounds and perspectives of the future, with its divine sanction of the ethical commandment and its message of salvation, which anticipates, some of the most important achievements of psychoanalysis, with its demands which overcome all opposition from the empirical world through the assurance of a higher obligation and covenant community, in short, all this world of ideals, which after all is only the expression of a higher, highest reality, and which easily can integrate all the gifts of science in itself, but also adds to it an incredible fullness of other valuable goods, life goods and life forces, is an educator whom science with its theories very certainly could not replace. But if faith were untrue, we would have to fight it in spite of its achievements. Better to go to hell with the truth than to heaven with the prize of lies! Freud in his tolerance praised religion as a neurosis.

Previously he explained that since the weakening of the religions neuroses had drastically increased. Could it be that Freud's gallantry led him too far here? I see even among the crowd of the intensely pious people quite many hysterical and compulsive-neurotic people; besides the fact that all orthodox-ies have to be considered as collective compulsive neuroses, we find among the very pious Christians many who are psycho-neurotic. After all, it depends a great deal on the nature of piety itself, how much it serves a repressive func-tion. However, that the free air of a genuine Gospel creates an indispensable protection against the danger of neurosis cannot be denied.

Nevertheless, the area of religion is thereby in no way yet fully described. Re-ligion cannot be dissolved in an enthusiasm of the arts, in morality and the pro-tection against neurosis. In addition to this we find many other elements. Reli-gion deals with the question of the meaning and value of life, with the integrative search of reason for a universal conception of the world that encompasses both being and a sense of ought, with the longing for a homeland and for peace, with the urge for a *unio mystica* (mystical union) with the absolute, with the fetters of guilt of the soul and the thirst of freedom for grace, with the need for a love that is removed from the unbearable insecurity of earthly reality, with innumerable other questions which in the case of not having been dealt with strangle and frighten the soul, yet through the religious compensation elevate human life to a height of indescribable views, strengthen the heart and through the imposi-tion of very difficult ethical obligations in the spirit of love increase the value of existence. The irreligious person cannot understand this, as the musically in-competent cannot understand the content of a musical composition of Brahms.

Religion is far from being as aristocratic as the arts and the higher sciences, however. It is itself a stream of water in which lambs can swim and elephants can drown. But it is true again what the New Testament says: "Not everyone has faith." (2 Thess 3:2). However, we do not conceive of faith only in the sense of imagining, rather in the sense of the whole inner person being moved.

How limited is science in comparison to this plenitude, of which we could only indicate a very small part, for we did not have enough room to elaborate on it and words cannot capture the unspeakable after all! I am not surprised at all that many of the most important researchers considered their endeavors to be worship and many of the greatest artists and poets humbly put down their wreaths of laurel before the altar of God.

Conclusion

How should we then think of this future of an illusion which Freud objects to, That it has to fall and disappear, if it only is an illusion, is also my conviction.

THE ILLUSION OF THE FUTURE   147

However, Freud did not intend to ask the question of truth; he explicitly emphasizes that this illusion could be true (p. 49). Therefore it is my conviction that our reality thinking has to be extended as far as the nature of reality allows it in any way. How this could happen I sketched in my brief hints in my essay "Weltanschauung und Psychoanalyse" (worldview and sychoanalysis). I indicated an empirical science there follows as a necessary logical supplementation a metaphysic, and how even more – and this is even more important for religion out of an ethical determination conclusions in terms of world meaning and a world will are possible and even necessary. A reflected religion can only come from a harmonious combination of faith and knowledge, from a mutual interpenetration between wishful thinking and reality thinking, whereby however the content of reality thinking should not be falsified by wishful thinking in its content and coherence. But does not the specific content of religion in this synthesis get lost? Freud suspects it (p. 52); yet I cannot agree with this conclusion. In my view the substance of Christianity is in now way attacked, if we deny the miracles in the sense of God's intervention in the course of nature; at least it is a fact that millions of Christians have done this for centuries and yet have been able to see the most Holy in their religion.

This God who is free from crude anthropomorphisms in a philosophically reflected modern theology, this world will which strives for the realization of love in the highest ethical sense is far more sublime than the God who strolls about in the cool of the evening and with his own hands closes the door of the ark, also far more sublime than the God who uses the earth as his footstool, and the parabolic language of piety should not contain wishful thinking. Ethical precepts, which we however no longer simply have dictated to us out of holy documents, but rather derive as autonomous children of God from the nature of human beings and human community, in which we reverently examine the ethical insights of former times and reserve to ourselves every right of disagreement and objection, are not less holy to us than the precepts of any religious documents.

The Bible has not become less significant, but rather more magnificent, since we do not suspect it as a paper Pope and infallible oracle, as legal, basis for the inquisition of heretics, but in view of Protestant freedom submit it to the most inexorable criticism. Reward and punishment we have put aside as dangerous educational methods long ago, even if we cannot deny the fact that inherent in the ethical commandment there is also a form of hygiene, which informs us about the dangers threatening individual and social health. and therefore points to an inherent regularity which decides about happiness and suffering and is crucial for the structuring of life.

This ethical world order is for us no given condition, but rather a normative in the above-mentioned sense, a disposition and inherent regularity the tendency of which we can know from the observation of the reality of life and try to express in ethical precepts, which we formulate ethically as the expression of the highest cosmic developmental aspiration and recognize because of its relationship to the will of a creator as the will of God and holy.

Therefore, morality is not based on some heteronomous authority, but on the autonomy of the individual and sociality, yet not on its arbitrary will, but rather on its basic essence which again points to an ultimately and absolutely conceivable authority.

Can we dispense with this religious deepening of reality? Will the advance of the exact sciences make it superfluous? The present turn to the right in the direction of the orthodoxies shall not be decisive for our judgment. Simply out of the nature of the human person and the narrow limitation of the intellect will I have to contrast Freud's prophecy of the future of an illusion with the no more prophesying, but psychological substantiated contention of the illusion of such a future. I am very pleased that basically Freud himself strives for the same goal as I do, he with his ingenious view of a researcher, I with my limited means. He is driven by his God Logos, which he understands as intellect, "presumably" towards the goal of the love of humanity and the limitation of suffering (p. 87). I am driven by my God Logos, which however in reference to the first chapter of the Gospel of John, I look at as divine wisdom and love, towards the same goals, to which I only would want to add more strongly than Freud's indication echoing Schopenhauer the creation of positive inner and external values and goods. Not the religious confession is the true criterion of the Christian, John 13:33 gives us another one: "In this everyone will know that you are my disciples, if you love each other." Risking to be joked at by loose tongues, I dare again to say that Freud, in the light of this word, is ahead of many Church Christians, who, – as he himself does – consider him to be a heathen, with his conception of life and his life work. And so *The Future of an Illusion* and "The Illusion of a Future" are united in a strong faith the credo of which says: "The truth will make you free."

CHAPTER 9

The Fifth Commandment

Sandor Rado

Abstract

Rado notes in this short article the unique features of the Fifth Commandment. It is the only one that includes positive result. In an "if" "then" format it suggests that honoring one's parents will result in a long life. In Rado's concern for adapting to one's environment, the commandment promises a long (and probably a happy) life results from honoring one's parents. Implicit in this commandments is the honoring one's father will mean obedience to him guarantees he won't kill you and honoring one's mother implies not engaging in incest with her. Rado generalizes this pattern to conclude that sublimation of impulse results in progressive and successful farming. [Editors]

Of the ten commandments, it is known that only the fifth promises a concrete reward. All the others are simply put as apoptotic commands or speak in general of the intention of Jahweh to punish and to reward. The text of this commandment is found in two places in the biblical text as handed down. First in Exodus (20,12), where Moses, coming down from the mountain, proclaims it, among the other commandments, to the people: "Honor your father and your mother, that you may live long in the land which Jahweh, your God, will give you"[1]. Then it will be repeated, again by Moses (Deuteronomy 5:16): "Honor your father and your mother, as Jahveh, your God, has commanded you, that you may live long and that it may go well with you in the land which Jahweh, your God, will give you"[2]. The two versions go back to different sources; probably the first is the older, but in any case they differ only a little.

Now, what could the prospect of long life mean? We believe this reward betrays the hidden meaning of this commandment if one transforms it back into the threat of death, from which it presumably arose in the course of time. Then it is no longer difficult to restore the entire commandment to its original form, which perhaps could have gone: Observe the priority of the father, in that you steer clear of the mother, otherwise the father will kill you.

---

1 According to E. Kautzsch, Die heilige Schrift des alten Testaments. 1909, Bd. (vol.) 1, p. 112.
2 Ibid., p. 250.

If our assumption is correct, the distortion of the text is doubt less to be seen as the result of progressing secular repression. It hid the actual meaning of the commandment, in that it turned the wording after the analogy of a dream into the opposite of the literal expression in two decisive places (in the actual event and in the penal sanction). Thus the original sentence of punishment is converted into a formula of reward, and the mention of incest is circumvented.

The text as handed down contains, however, outside of this distortion, an addition for which there is nothing which corresponds to the original commandment as we have construed it: "(... so that you can live long) on the ground that Yahweh your God will give you." We strongly assume that this part of the text corresponds to a new development in the time which came between, an important step on the path of drive sublimation. In that here the Old Testament adds to the dropping of the incestuous love—wish the hope of a fruitful piece of mother earth,[3] and thus signifies the discharge of the forbidden sexual impulse in farming, it has preserved for us the memory of one of the most significant events of the development of culture.[4,5]

Background

Sandor Rado (1890–1972) was a Hungarian psychoanalyst who became secretary of the Hungarian Psychoanalytical Society in 1913, two years before he met Freud and almost a decade before he, himself, was analyzed. Obviously, Rado was identified as a good record keeper because he quickly became the secretary of the German Psychoanalytic Society and was very involved in planning the Society's training program.

In 1931 Rado moved to the U.S. Where he organized the New York Psychoanalytical Institute on the model of the Berlin model. He was eventually appointed professor of psychiatry at Columbia University.

However, Rado was not a classical psychoanalyst. He has serious doubts about spending an inordinate amount of time in treatment on the past and advocated focusing on using the past in adapting to the present and future. He used the term "adaptational psychodynamics" and felt that analysis should be a form of reeducation. He major work was *Adaptational Psychodyamics:*

---

3 The "land which Jahweh your God will give you".

4 This interpretation is in close agreement with the deductions of Reik, who understood the Sinai episode as the initiation of males (*Probleme der Religionspsychologie*, 1919).

5 It is Canaan, the land from 'which the nation comes, the land of the fathers, [which is] consequently the mother.

THE FIFTH COMMANDMENT

Motivation And Control published only three years before his death. One of his students, Jean Jameson, suggested that Rado's approach attempt to distinguish the theory of psychoanalysis from the treatment of psychoanalysis. This led to a focus on helping patients improve the patterns of their interactions with the environment within which they chose to live. Rado's theory was an anticipation of ego psychology.

CHAPTER 10

The Three Foundational Elements of Religious Feeling

Wilhelm Reich

Abstract

Reich conceives of religious feeling as arising in those who are the lower social class economically or who have been trained as children to conceive of the divine. He postulates further that the God 'concept' arises out of the relationship with the father. The elemental composition of the divine is integrally related to basic sexual drive, particularly the orgastic drive. [Editors]

I do not wish to give a detailed investigation of religious feeling here, but rather merely to summarize what is already known. The appearance of orgastic excitations touches at a particular point the problem of religious excitation from the most simple trustful devotion to fully developed religious ecstasy. The concept [of] religious excitation is not to be limited to the sensations which tend to appear in those who believe deeply in God, say, they attend devotions. Rather we must add to this all excitations which are commonly characterized by a particular situation of mental and physical excitation; those the excitation of the listening masses when they are influenced by the speech of a beloved leader; obviously also the excitation which one feels when one is overwhelmed by natural phenomena. We first will summarize what has become known up to [the time of] sexual economic research[1] on religious phenomena. Social research could show that the *forms* of religion and even the contents of different religions are conditioned by the stages of development of socio-economic relations. Such as, say, the animal religions [were conditioned] by the life-style of primitive hunting peoples. As a rule, the manner in which people conceive the divine, supernatural being is determined by the condition of the economy and culture. Sociologically, religious concepts also are determined very fundamentally by the capability of people to master nature and social difficulties. Helplessness in the face of the forces of nature and elemental social

---

1 Here the word economic pertains to Freud's use of the word vis-a-vis quantities of excitation or energy. (Freud, *Introductory Lectures on Psychoanalysis*)

THE THREE FOUNDATIONAL ELEMENTS OF RELIGIOUS FEELING

catastrophe is conducive to the production of religious ideology in the respective cultural circle. The sociological explanation of religion thus has to do with the *social-economic* foundation in which religious cults arise. It asserts nothing about the dynamic of the religious ideology nor about the psychic process which precedes it in the person sublimated to this religious ideology.

The formation of religious cults is thus dependent of the will of individual people; they are sociological formations which spring *from the relationships between people* and [from] the relation of these people to nature.

The psychology of the unconscious would add to the *sociological* frame of religion a *psychological* one; if previously one comprehended the social conditioning of the religious cults, now one would research the psychological process *in the people* submitted to the objective religious cults. In this way psychoanalysis could determine that the God-concept is Identical with the *father*-concept, the idea of the *Mother of God* is identical with the *mother* of every individual religious [person]. In the *trinity* of the Christian religion, the triangle directly reflects father, mother and child. The psychic contents of religion are taken from early childhood familial relations.

The psychological explanation thus would grasp the contents of the religious culture, but not the energy by means of which they [the concepts] establish themselves in people. Where religious concepts wealth of affect and accentuation of feeling come from remains above all unclear. It also remains unclear why the concepts of the super-powerful father and the kind mother changed into the mystical, and what relations they had to the sexual life of individuals.

The orgastic character of many patriarchal religions has long been established by many sociologists. Likewise, it has become clear that the patriarchal religions are always politically reactionary. They are always at the service of the interests of the powerful strata of class society, and *to all practical purposes* prevent the elimination of the distress of the masses in that they always represent it as the will of God, and console [them] with the claim of happiness in the hereafter.

Now, sexual-economic research adds the following questions to the current knowledge of religion:

1. *How* do the concept of God, the ideology of sin and the ideology of punishment which are produced by society and reproduced by the family establish themselves in the individual person? In other words: What compels people not only to accept these fundamental religious concepts and not experience them as a burden, but, to the contrary, often to affirm them ardently and to uphold and defend them at the sacrifice of the most primitive vital interests?

2. *When* does the establishment of religious concepts occur in people? With the help of what *energy* does this occur?

It is clear that without an answer to these questions a sociological and psychological interpretation of religion is indeed possible, but a real change of the structure of the person is not. For if religious feelings are not forced upon the person, but rather are taken up structurally from himself and adhered to even though it goes against his own vital interests, then it is a matter of an energetic structural change in the person himself.

In all patriarchal religions there is always the fundamental religious idea of sexual need. There is no exception to this if we do not take into account the sexually affirmative primitive religions in which the religious and the sexual were still a unity. In the transition of social organization from natural law and matriarchy to patriarchy, and therewith to a patriarchal class society, the unity of the religious and sexual cult was split; the religious cult became the antithesis of the sexual. With this, the sexual cult ceased to exist in order to make room for the sexual unculture of brothels, of pornography, and of backstairs sexuality. It requires no further substantiation than in the moment when sexual experiences no longer displayed unity with the religious cults but rather with their opposite, religious excitation had to become at the same time a substitute for the lost (socially affirmed) way of handling pleasure. Only from this contradiction within the excitation of the religious feeling, namely that it is simultaneously anti—sexual and a substitute for sexuality, can the power and tenacity of religion be comprehended.

The affect-structure of the genuinely religious person can be described briefly as follows. Biologically he is just as subject to states of sexual tension as all other people and organisms. Yet through his acceptance of sexually negative religious concepts, and particularly through the fear of punishment which he acquired, he has lost any capacity for natural sexual tension and gratification. Thus, he suffers a chronically exaggerated state of physical excitation which he is continually obliged to master. Happiness on earth IS not attainable for him, but rather appears to him instead as not even desirable. As he awaits pardon in the hereafter, he is overcome by a feeling of being incapable of happiness in earthly things. But as he is a biological organism and under no circumstances can renounce happiness, release of tension, and gratification, he searches for the illusory happiness which the religious pre-pleasure tensions are able to give him, that is, the vegetative currents and excitations known to us in the body. Thus together with his fellow believers he will arrange meetings and create institutions which can both ease his state of physical ex-citment and mask its actual nature. His biological organism then builds an organ whose tones are able to evoke that sort of current in the body. The mystical darkness

THE THREE FOUNDATIONAL ELEMENTS OF RELIGIOUS FEELING 155

of the church heightens the effect of a super-personally understood sensitivity to one sinner self and to the tones of a sermon, a chorale, etc. tailored to it.

The religious person actually has become completely helpless, since the capacity for happiness and aggressiveness the difficulties of life have been lost to him through the suppression of his sexual energy. In reality helpless, he must believe all the more in supernatural forces which support and protect him. We understand from this that in many situations he is able to develop an unbelievable power of conviction, indeed of passive courage in the face of death. He draws this power from the love of his own religious conviction which indeed is sustained by very heightened pleasurable physical excitations. He believes surely the power comes from "God". His longing for God and to God is thus in reality the longing which comes from his sexual pleasure excitation and which calls for release. Deliverance is and can be nothing other than deliverance from the unbearable physical tensions which can be pleasurable only so long as they can be mixed with a fantasized turn on with God; that is, with the gratification and release of tension. The inclination of fanatically religious people to self injuries, to masochistic behaviors, etc. confirms what we have said. The sexual economic clinic could show that the desire to be beaten (Geschlagenwerdenwollen) or self—punishment (Sichselbstzuchtigen) arises from the instinctive wish for release without one's own culpability. There is no physical tension which would not produce ideas of being beaten or tortured as soon as the person in question feels incapable of bringing about the release of tension himself. Here lies the root of the ideology of passive suffering of all genuine religions.

The urge for solace, support and stability comes from the outside, from real helplessness and physical pain, above all over against one's own evil instincts; as it says, over against the "sins of the flesh". Now if religious people fall into strong excitations with the help of their religious concepts, then the state of vegetative attraction intensifies with physical excitation which approaches gratification, yet without actually bringing a physical release. It is known from the treatments of sick priests that at the peak of religiously ecstatic states, involuntary ejaculations of semen occur very frequently. Normal orgastic gratification is replaced by a state of general physical excitation which excludes the genitals and which, against one's will, by coincidence, brings about partial releases.

Sexual pleasure was originally and naturally the good, the beautiful, the happy; that which connected people with universal nature. With the split of the sexual and the religious feeling, the sexual had to become the bad, the hellish, the devilish.

I have attempted elsewhere to explain how the fear of pleasure (and thus fear of sexual excitation) arises and works itself out. I repeat in brief: In the end, people who are incapable of release (of tension) must perceive sexual excitations as tormenting, burdensome and destructive. Sexual excitation is in fact destructive and tormenting if release is not permitted. Thus we see that the religious concept of the sexual as a destructive, devilish power which works toward a person's ruin is rooted in real physical processes. Now the attitude toward sexuality has to split: the typically religious and moral valuations "good", "bad", "heavenly", "earthy", "divine", "devilish" etc. become symbols of sexual gratification on the one hand and punishment for sexual gratification on the other.

At the same time the deep longing for release and redemption consciously from "sins," (unconsciously from sexual tension) is defended against. Religious, ecstatic states are nothing other than states of inescapable sexual excitation of the vegetative nervous system. Without the contradiction which dominates it, the religious excitation cannot be understood at all, and thus also not mastered. It is not simply anti sexual, but is itself [at the same time] sexual to a great degree. It is not simply moral, but is at the same time deeply perverse, [it is] in the sexual—economic sense unhygienic.

In no social class do the hysterias and perversions of this sort blossom as in the circles of the ascetic church. One may not draw the false conclusion from this—that one should treat them as perverse criminals. In conversation with religious persons it happens that with their denial of the sexual they also make a very good case for their state. They are, like all other people, divided into an official and a very private personality. Officially they consider sexuality a sin, privately they know very precisely that they could not exist without their substitute gratifications. Indeed they are amenable to the sexual solution of the contradiction of sexual excitation and morality. They understand very well, if one makes contact with them and does not eject them as human beings, that that which they describe as union with God is the real connection with the universal operation of nature, that their ego is a piece of nature, that their ego is a piece of nature, that they feel, like all people, like a microcosm of the macrocosm. One must admit their deep conviction has a kernel of truth, that what they believe really is true, namely the vegetative current of their body, and the ecstasy into union they are capable of lapsing. Religious feeling is absolutely genuine particularly by people from poor social strata. It only become inauthentic if it denies its own origin and the unconsciously desired gratification and deceives itself. Through this there arises the contrived benevolently-acting self-control of priests and religious people.

This presentation is incomplete. Yet in the fundamental sense we can say in summary:

1. Religious excitation IS a masked vegetative, sexual excitation.
2. Through making excitation mystical, the religious person negates his sexuality.
3. Religious ecstasy is a substitute for the orgastic excitement.

THE THREE FOUNDATIONAL ELEMENTS OF RELIGIOUS FEELING   157

4. Religious ecstasy brings no sexual release, but at most a muscular and mental fatigue.
5. Religious feeling is subjectively genuine and physiologically grounded.
6. The negation of the sexual nature of this excitation causes chacteriological inauthenticity.

Small children do not believe in God. Faith in God establishes itself in them as a rule first when they have to learn to suppress their sexual excitations. Through this they acquire fear of pleasure. Now they begin to actually believe in God, to develop fear of him and not only to fear him as all knowing and all seeing, but at the same time to call upon him as protection against their own sexual excitation. All of this has the function of avoiding onanism. The establishment of religious concepts thus occurs in early childhood. Yet these religious concepts could not bind the sexual energy in children if they were not connected to the real figures of father and mother Whoever does not honor the father is sinful; in other words, whoever does not fear the father and abandon his sexual pleasure, will be punished. The living, strict, refusing father is the God's representative on earth and his (God's) organ of enforcement in the imagination of the child. Should awe for the father fall victim to real insight into his weakness and human inadequacies, he nonetheless persists in the figure of the abstract, mystical God concept. As patriarchal authority invokes God and means the real paternal authority, so the child in reality invokes the real father when it says God. In the structure of the child, sexual excitations, the concept of father, and the concept of God naturally form a unity. It confronts us tangibly in treatments as a state of genital, muscularity. As a rule, the concept of God and fear of the father recedes with the loosening of the state of cramps in the genital musculature. Thus the state of genital cramps not only represents the physiological structural establishment of religious fear, but at the same time it produces the fear of pleasure which becomes the core of any religious morality.

I must leave it to further investigations to work through the very complicated [and] detailed relations between the manner of religious cultus, socio-economic social organization and human structure. For all sexually-negative patriarchal religions, aversion to genitalia and fear of pleasure remain in force as their energetic core.

Background

Wilhelm Reich was a controversial German psychoanalyst who was born in 1897 and died in a US prison just short of his possible parole in 1957. He is best know for Character Analysis. While he received a medical degree, he never practiced the type of classical analysis as seen in Freud. Even before he received his medical degree, he became a worker, and soon deputy director of Freud's out-patient clinic. Early in his tenure he began to visit in the homes of the clientele. He began to reason that the symptoms he saw were due to a large part on the social conditions in which the clients were living. He theorized that Marxism and psychoanalysis could be combined. Quite likely he influenced Freud's mechanism of defense that came to be a part of classical psychoanalysis.

Reich was a large, robust man who was imposing socially. He was a force both in his demeanor and appearance. He coined the term "orgone" to combine what classical analysis would call the libido and orgastic sexuality in what he termed "character analysis." His own relations evidenced no effect of his theoretical understanding but he, nevertheless, had remarkable success in convincing others of the need to use the contraption that he designed with which persons could stimulate their energy and sexual vitality. He evoked some strong criticism for selling the instrument and was sentenced to prison in the United States. He died there shortly becoming up for parole.

CHAPTER 11

Freud's Journal IMAGO – 1912 to Present

"IMAGO" has been a preferred name of psychoanalytic journals since Freud established the first such journal is 1912. As can be seen in the history of the movement, variations on the use of that label have appeared in other publications since this Vienna publication was first off the press. It was edited by Freud along with Otto Rank and Hans Sachs as a vehicle for applying psychoanalysis to the humanities, arts, and social sciences. In the initial year, Freud himself wrote four articles that became *TOTEM AND TABOO*. Religion was included as can be seen in the articles of this volume. Even Freud, in spite of his conviction that religion was an illusion embedded in neurosis, published several of the chapters that later appeared in *MOSES AND MONTHEISM* in the pages of IMAGO.

IMAGO came into existence only two years before the outbreak of the First World War. Its pages reflected the end of many of the centuries old European countries and their reformation into post war conglomerates. An social psychological article on statehood by Hans Kelsen was published as was Erich Fromm's analysis of crime and punishment. Articles by Melanie Klein and Ernst Kris led psychoanalysis into child analysis and art history. The growing crisis in Germany swept IMAGO into concern for the existence of the journal. Anti-Semitism became pervasive and Freud himself had to abandon Vienna for London.

The German IMAGO published until 1938 when problems between Nazi Germany and Austria made publication impossible. Freud, in turn, had fled from Vienna to London and hoped that IMAGO could continue in German. Sachs convinced Freud that continuation of IMAGO was only possible if he agreed to change to from German to English. Thus the AMERICAN IMAGO came into existence and its one hundred years of publication was celebrated in 1938. Unfortunately, Freud died before the first issue was printed. Interestingly, Freud's daughter and others succeeded in the publishing of the old German IMAGO outside Austria until 1941.

The centennial of the German language IMAGO was celebrated in 2012.[1] In the meantime, Freud had launched the *Jahrbuch fur Psychonalyse and*

---

1 Brian J. Shea of The John Hopskins University Press (publisher of the AMERICAN IMAGO) wrote an account of the 100th anniversary of Freud's founding of Imago in July 2012. It can be read by dailing (410) 516–7096 or bis@.press.jhu.edu.

Zentralatt fur Psychoanalyse and yet a third interdisciplinary journal IMAGO. ZEITSCHRIFT FUR DIE ANWENDUNG DER PSYCHOANALYSE AUF DIE GEISTESWISSENSCHAFTEN. The publisher stated that the other two publications had been primarily oriented toward clinical applications of psychoanalysis, but that was only partially true. The real uniqueness of this new periodical was its interdisciplinary character. This periodical sought to introduce dialogue between psychoanalysis and neighboring fields such as anthropology, literature and linguistics.

After the break with Freud, Jung initiated his own journal using IMAGO in the title (IMAGO DEI ON THE PSYCHOLOGICAL PLANE). Here Jung relates the self to the Biblical image of God within the psyche. Jung develops an ego psychology in this periodical that is quite different from classic al psychoanalysis.

Finally, the issue of writings about religion within the field of psychoanalysis both during the time of the German IMAGO and later psychoanalytic writings is considered more fully in Chapter 1, *The Psychoanalytic Study of Religion: Past, Present, Future* in this volume.

CHAPTER 12

The Future of an Illusion, The Illusion of the Future: An Historic Dialogue on the Value of Religion between Oskar Pfister and Sigmund Freud

H. Newton Malony and Gerald O. North

This is an account of the Freud-Pfister dialogue.* Sigmund Freud was the well-known Viennese neurologist who founded psychoanalysis. Oskar Pfister was a Reform Church pastor in Zurich, Switzerland. Pfister was the first religious professional to embrace psychoanalysis. Pfister began writing to Freud in 1908. They corresponded with each other until Freud's death in 1939. Pfister kept all his letters from Freud. Freud preserved a number of his letters from Pfister. They have been brought together in a book entitled *Psychoanalysis and Faith* (Meng and Freud, 1963).

In addition, in 1973 several organizations, including the Institutes of Religion and Health, sponsored a symposium to celebrate the centennial of Pfister's birth. Several of the presentations from this symposium have been published in *The Journal of Religion and Health* (cf. Stettner, 1973; Bonhoeffer, 1974; Irwin, 1973; Jager-Werth, 1974; Stettner, 1974).

The issues are re-presented here in the form of quotations from the correspondence followed by concluding remarks. It is hoped that a reconsideration of this historic debate will enliven appreciation for the spirit of intellectual dialogue and evoke a new appreciation for the spirit of intellectual dialogue and evoke a new awareness of the major concerns. The points of view expressed by Pfister and Freud are by no means dead.

1 Overview

Both Freud and Pfister wrote many articles and books about psychoanalysis in general and about religion in particular. Pfister was influential in such clinical areas as the splitting off of the emotions and the question of lay analysis. In the area of religion they differed radically. Although Freud affirmed Pfister's use of

---

* Reprinted with permission from *The Journal of the History of Behavioral Sciences*, 15(2), 177–186, 1979.

psychoanalysis in pastoral work, he was a confirmed atheist who felt that religion was a collective neurosis without which society would be better off. Pfister, in turn, was a perennial optimist who was convinced of the value and the power of religion. He saw this exemplified in the love of Jesus. He thought that Jesus' love would one day bring all persons together in brotherhood and peace (cf. Pfister's book *Christianity and Fear*. 1944, 1948).

The two men remained friends to the end. This is more than can be said of many other colleagues of Freud (cf. Jung and Adler, for example). They debated civilly and openly. In 1927 Freud notified Pfister of his forthcoming book The Future of an Illusion and said he hoped that Pfister would not find it inappropriate. Pfister responded with a review article entitled "The Illusion of A Future" (1928) and sent it to Freud for perusal before publication. Freud was both more pessimistic and more optimistic than Pfister. Pfister was an was an old-line liberal who was convinced that the love of Jesus could conquer evil. Freud was pessimistic with regard to human nature and suggested that Pfister did not truly acknowledge evil in persons. Yet Freud had a naive faith in science and reason. According to Freud, persons needed no religious figure to follow. They could trust rationalistic science to lead them to Nirvana. Pfister felt that Freud's trust in science was unproved and ill founded.

2 The Freud-Pfister Correspondence

The afore-mentioned issues are the heart of the letters between Freud and Pfister. Excerpts from this correspondence follow. Although their ideas about religion are of prime interest, references to many other historical events can be noted. The correspondence is grouped into three periods:

> An Early Period of Cordiality from 1909 to 1922;
> The Era of Serious Debate from 1925 to 1928; and last,
> An Era of Reflections encompassing 1929 to 1939.
> Occasionally, due to the excerpting of and/or the loss of letters, *two* letters from the same source (Freud or Pfister) may appear in sequence.

3 Early Period of Cordiality 1909–1922

This section begins with Freud's first reply to a letter from Pfister. Pfister sent Freud one of his many articles. He was a prolific contributor to psychoanalytic literature. The reference in Freud's August, 1909 letter to the "journey across the barren waste of waters" is to his trip to the twentieth anniversary of Clark

THE FUTURE OF AN ILLUSION   163

University in Massachusetts at the invitation of G. Stanley Hall. The death of Hermnn Rorschach, a Swiss psychiatrist who invented the Rorschach Ink Blot Test, is referred to in the 1922 letters. This period is marked by great cordiality and civility. It precedes the publication of Freud's The Future of an Illusion in 1927.

3.1   *Freud to Pfister January 18, 1909*
Dear Dr. Pfister:

I cannot content myself with just thanking you for sending me your paper Delusion and Suicide among Youth.

I must also express my satisfaction that our psychiatric work has been taken up by a minister of religion who has access to the minds of so many young and healthy individuals... Your name has often been mentioned to me by our common friend C.G. Jung, and I am glad now to be able to associate a more definite idea with it...

3.2   *Pfister to Freud February 18, 1909*
Dear Professor:

Your letter has made the pleasure I take in the science initiated by you even greater. It was a great satisfaction to me to gather from your remarks that basically I have correctly understood the application of psychoanalysis to pastoral work. The (ethical) difference between your outlook and mine is perhaps not so great as my calling might suggest.

3.3   *Freud to Pfister August 16, 1909*
Dear Dr. Pfister:

Yes, you can come and see me at any time, and I am delighted to hear from you before undertaking the journey across the barren waste of waters. You always make one cheerful, because you call into consciousness the things which because of the unhappy human disposition are hidden behind small miseries and fleeting cares. I do not know what promises you left behind with my children, because I keep hearing things like next year I'm going with Dr. Pfister, I'm going climbing with him, and so on and so forth. I dare not mention your 10,000 foot climb with your son, because it would rouse my boys' blackest envy, they would wish they had a father like you, who could still climb with them instead of being tormented by his Conrad and picking strawberries in the woods down below.

3.4   *Freud to Pfister October 9, 1918*
As for the possibility of sublimation to religion, therapeutically I can only envy you. But the beauty of religion certainly does not belong to psychoanalysis. It is natural that at this point in therapy our ways should part, and so it can remain.

Incidentally, why was it that none of all the pious ever discovered psychoanalysis? Why did it have to wait for a completely godless Jew?[1]

3.5   *Pfister to Freud October 29, 1918*

...you ask why psychoanalysis was not discovered by any of the pious, but by an atheist Jew. The answer obviously is that piety is nor the same as genius for discovery and that most of the pious did not have it in them to make such discoveries. Moreover, in the first place you are no Jew, which to me, in view of my unbounded admiration for Amos, Isaiah, Jeremiah, and the author of Job and Ecclesiastes, is a matter of profound regret, and in the second place you are not godless, for he who lives the truth lives in God, and he who strives for the freeing of love 'dwelleth in God' (First Epistle of John, 4:16). If you raised to your consciousness and fully felt your place in the great design, I should say of you: A better Christian there never was.

3.6   *Pfister to Freud April 3, 1922*

Dear Professor Freud:

I had hoped to give you a little pleasure by sending you a new book, but now the pleasure is overshadowed by a great sorrow. Yesterday we lost our ablest analyst, Dr. Rorschach ... He had a wonderfully clear and original mind, was devoted to analysis heart and soul, and threw in his lot with you down to the smallest details. His diagnostic test, which would perhaps better be called analysis of form, was admirably worked out. His intention was to become a university teacher. He was a poor man all his life, and a proud, upright man of great human kindness, and he is a great loss to us.

3.7   *Freud to Pfister June 4, 1922*

Rorschach's death is very sad. I shall write a few words to his widow today. My impression is that perhaps you overrate him as an analyst; I note with pleasure from your letter the high esteem in which you hold him as a man. Of course, no one but you shall write the tribute to him in the journal, and please write it soon.

4   Era of Serious Debate 1925 to 1928

This period begins with a letter to Freud from Pfister who is spending Christmas in Bethlehem. He uses the occasion to suggest that Berggasse (Freud's

---

1   [Footnote by Freud.] This personification of the body in Spitteler's Imago impressed me greatly. (Imago was a novel published in 1906 by the Swiss writer Carl Spitteler)

THE FUTURE OF AN ILLUSION   165

residence) had a holiness about it, too. The October 16, 1927 letter from
Freud is addressed to Pfister while he is on vacation in Scandinavia. Pfister
was a frequent traveler. The letter's importance is in its announcement that
"pamphlet of mine" would soon appear. This was the monumental *The Future of an Illusion* which was to become the focus of the serious dialogue
between the two men. Note how the plot thickens but also note how the
debate remains gentlemanly and cordial. Freud welcomes Pfister's review
and critique in *Imago*, which was the journal that was the organ for the psychoanalytic movement. Pfister eventually wrote an article delineating his
position in a 1928 article which turns a phrase on Freud's title, i.e. "The Illusion of a Future".

4.1   *Pfister to Freud December 23, 1925*
One gladly rakes refuge from the turmoil of Christmas in the quiet of Bethlehem to rest, reflect and meditate, free from dogma and science ... There I derive gladness and strength, and science awakens memory, not of deprivation
and hardship but of germinating greatness, succor and growth. You will smile,
but in your neighborhood too I feel something of the clarity of the Lord, and
in any case in thinking of you I am filled with an infinite gratitude and hope.
Love is the greatest safeguard against intellectual envy, and after it realization
of the blessing of humility and of the beauty of the honest labor of fetching
and carrying, which in the case of your Titanic building is magnificent
enough....

4.2   *Freud to Pfister October 16, 1927*
Dear Dr. Pfister:

Thanks to your letters, I have been following with intelligible interest your
triumphal progress through the Scandinavian countries. The very gratifying result must largely be attributed to your personality, because the resistance to
analysis of these Scandinavians is particularly deep-rooted.

...In the next few weeks a pamphlet of mine will be appearing which has a
great deal to do with you. I had been wanting to write it for a long time, and
postponed it out of regard for you, but the impulse became too strong. The
subject-matter – as you will easily guess – is my completely negative attitude to
religion, in any form and however attenuated, and, though there can be nothing new to you in this, I feared, and still fear, that such a public profession of my
attitude will be painful to you. When you have read it you must let me know
what measure of toleration and understanding you are able to preserve for the
hopeless pagan.

Always your cordially devoted, Freud

4.3   *Pfister to Freud October 21, 1927*

...As for your anti-religious pamphlet, there is nothing new to me in your rejection of religion. I look forward to it with pleasurable anticipation. A powerful-minded opponent of religion is certainly of more service to it than a thousand useless supporters. In music, philosophy, and religion I go different ways from you. I have been unable to imagine that a public profession of what you believe could be painful to me; I have always believed that every man should state his honest opinion aloud and plainly. You have always been tolerant towards me, and am I to be intolerant of your atheism? If I frankly air my differences from you, you will certainly not take it amiss. Meanwhile my attitude is one of eager curiosity.

4.4   *Freud to Pfister October 21, 1927*

Such is your magnanimity that I expected no other answer to my "declaration of war." The prospect of your making a public stand against my pamphlet gives me positive pleasure, it will be refreshing in the discordant critical chorus for which I am prepared. We know that by different routes we aspire to the same objectives for poor humanity.

Dear Professor Freud:

If I express my sincere thanks for the warmth of your dedication, please do not regard it merely as a conventional reaction to a friendly gift. That you care for me a little gives me uncommon pleasure and makes me almost a little proud. As for what I think of your work, it is exactly as I foresaw. If anything surprised me, it is that I was so little surprised...

What you say about the contradictions of religious and theological thought you yourself describe as a repetition, a repetition psychoanalytically developed in depth, of long familiar ideas. But what surprises me is that you pay no regard to the voices of those defenders of religion who bring out those contradictions just as sharply and resolve them in a higher philosophical-religious context. Let me mention von Euckan, and Brunstad, who concerns himself with conflicting values, and it is significant that deeply intelligent men have gone over from philosophy to theology. My friend Albert Schweitzer, the distinguished philosopher, professor of theology, organ virtuoso, etc., thinks just as pessimistically as you do about the optimistic-ethical interpretations of the world (*Civilization and Ethics*, 2, Introduction. p. xiii, 1932); but in his view that is only the beginning of the real problem, and he does not shut himself off from insight into the philosophy of life of those without a philosophy of life. (*Decay and Restoration of Civilization*, p. 53, 1932).

Your substitute for religion is basically the idea of the eighteenth century Enlightenment in proud modern guise. I must confess that, with all my pleasure

THE FUTURE OF AN ILLUSION

in the advance of science and technique, I do not believe in the adequacy and sufficiency of that solution of the problem of life. It is very doubtful whether, taking everything into account, scientific progress has made men happier or better. According to the statistics, there are more criminals among scholars than in the intellectual middle class, and the hopes that were set on universal education have turned out to be illusory. Nietzsche summed up your position in these words: The reader will have realized my purport; namely that there is always a metaphysical belief on which our science rests – that we observers of today, atheists and anti-metaphysicians as we are, still draw our fires from the blaze lit by a belief thousands of years old, the Christian belief, which was also that of Plato, that God is truth and that the truth is divine.... But supposing that I do not properly understand your outlook on life. It is impossible that what you reject as the end of an illusion and value as the sole truth can be all. A world without temples, the fine arts, poetry, religion, would in my view be a devil's island to which men could have been banished, not by blind chance, but only by Satan. In that case your pessimism about the wickedness of mankind would be much too mild; you would have to follow it through to its logical conclusion. If it were part of psychoanalytic treatment to present that this grew less believable and nothing divine was left, save errors, blindness, lies? despoiled universe to our patients as the truth, I should well understand it if the poor devils preferred remaining shut up in their illness to entering that dreadful icy desolation.

Have you as much tolerance for this frank profession of faith as I have for your long-familiar heresies? I hold it as a piece of good fortune that you had to deprive yourself of so much in order to do such tremendous work in your science (with which your faith or lack of faith has nothing whatever to do). But allow me to add two questions. Would you agree to my dealing with your views in Imago? Perhaps I might be able to offer a little aid to many who now, according to your own expectation, run the risk of rejecting the whole of psychoanalysis, and thus I might be doing a service to the psycho-analytic movement?

...Well, I have come to the end of a long letter. In writing it I have had your picture in front of me, listening to what I said with indulgence and friendliness. I hope that speaking out like this has only strengthened our friendship. It has, has it not?

With cordial greetings, Yours, Pfister

P.S. As you quoted statements by a number of important men on our problem, you will certainly be interested in what Bleuler wrote to me:

> I promptly devoured your Future of an Illusion and enjoyed it. Starting from quite different standpoints one comes to the identical conclusion,

but your argument is not only particularly elegant, it of course goes to the heart of the matter.

4.5   *Freud to Pfister February 24, 1928*

Dear Dr. Pfister,

It (you reply to me) has already gone to the editorial office. It was very necessary that my Illusion should be answered from within our own circle, and it is very satisfactory that it should be done in such a worthy and friendly fashion. What the effect on me was of what you have to say you have no need to ask. What is to be expected if one is judge in one's own cause? Some of your arguments seem to me could be poetical effusion, others, such as the enumeration of great minds who have believed in God, too cheap. It is unreasonable to expect science to produce a system of ethics – ethics are a kind of highway code for traffic among man kind and the fact that in physics atoms which were yesterday assumed to be square are now assumed to be round is exploited with unjustified tendentiousness by all who are hungry for faith; so long as physics extends our dominion over nature, these changes ought to be a matter of complete indifference to you. And finally-let me be impolite for once-how the devil do you reconcile all that we experience and have to expect in this world with your assumption of a moral world order? I am curious about that, but you have no need to reply.

4.6   *Freud to Pfister November 25, 1928*

Dear Dr. Pfister,

In your otherwise delightful letter there is one point I cavil at, namely your finding something surprising and gratifying in the attitude of the International Journal (editor and staff) on the subject of the Illusion. Such tolerance is no merit.

In both works which have recently reached me from the publishing house, one of which contains a reprint of your Discussion, I note with satisfaction what a long way we are able to go together in analysis. The rife, not in analytic, but in scientific chinking which one comes on when the subject of God and Christ is touched on, I accept as one of the logically untenable but psychologically only too intelligible irrationalities of life. In general I attach no value to the 'imitation of Christ.' In contrast to utterances as psychologically profound as 'Thy sins are forgiven thee; arise and walk "there are a large number of others which are conditioned exclusively by the time, psychologically impossible, useless for our lives. Besides, the above statement calls for analysis. If the sick man had asked: 'How knowest thou that my sins are forgiven?'" the answer

THE FUTURE OF AN ILLUSION   169

could only have been: 'I, the Son of God, forgive thee.' In other words, a call for unlimited transference. And now, just suppose I said to a patient: 'I, Professor Sigmund Freud, forgive thee thy sins.' What a fool I should make of myself. You are quite right to point out that analysis leads to no new philosophy of life, but it has no need to, for it rests on the general scientific outlook, with which the religious outlook is incompatible. For the point of view of the latter it is immaterial whether Christ, Buddha, or Confucius is regarded as the idea l of human conduct and held up as an example to imitate. Its essence is the pious illusion of providence and a moral world order, which are in conflict with reason. But priests will remain bound to stand for them. It is of course possible to take advantage of the human right to be irrational and go some way with analysis and then stop, rather on the pattern of Charles Darwin, who used to go regularly to church on Sundays. I cannot honestly see that any difficulties are created by patients' demands for ethical values; ethics are not based on an external world order but on the inescapable exigencies of human cohabitation. I do not believe that I behave as if there were 'one life, one meaning in life,' that was an excessively friendly thought on your part, and it always reminds me of the monk who insisted on regarding Nathan as a thoroughly good Christian. I am a long way from being Nathan, but of course I cannot help remaining 'good' towards you.

5   Era of Reflections 1929 to 1939

In this period, we see Pfister beginning by espousing both lay analysis and lay ministry. He was an old line liberal who emphasized function over position. He also expresses his continued appreciation for Freud over and beyond their differences on the value of religion. Freud's seventy-third birthday is noted in an affectionate letter to Pfister dated May 26, 1929. The loss and rediscovery of the box containing Freud's letters is mentioned along with Pfister's remarriage after his first wife's death. Freud's chronic problem with cancer of the jaw and the beginning of his many operations is noted. Pfister also writes about the death of Ferenczi and the growing problems of Nazi rule in Germany. The section concludes with the couching letter to Mrs. Freud after Freud's death in 1939.

5.1   *Pfister to Freud February 9, 1929*
...Please allow me to return to your remark that the analysts you would like to see should not be priests. It seems to me that analysis as such must be a purely 'lay' affair. By its very nature it is essentially private and directly yields no higher values. In innumerable cases I have done nothing but this negative work,

without ever mentioning a word about religion. The Good Samaritan also preached no sermons, and it would be tasteless to have a successful treatment paid for in retrospect by religious obligations. Just as Protestantism abolished the difference between laity and clergy, so must the cure of souls be laicised and secularized. Even the most bigoted must admit that the love of God is not limited by the whiff of incense.

...If no priest should analyze, neither should any Christian or any religious or morally deep-thinking individual, and you yourself emphasize that analysis is independent of philosophy of life. Disbelief is after all nothing but a negative belief. I do not believe that psychoanalysis eliminates art, philosophy, religion, but that it helps to purify and refine them. Forgive a long-standing enthusiast for art and humanitarianism and an old servant of God. Your marvelous life's work and your goodness and gentleness, which are somehow an incarnation of the meaning of existence, lead me to the deepest springs of life. I am not content to do scientific research on their banks, but have to drink and draw strength from them...At school my cleverest master used to say that music was a pitiful row. I did not try to convert him, but took refuge in Beethoven and Schubert. At heart you serve exactly the same purpose as I, and act 'as if there were a purpose and meaning in life and the universe,' and with my feeble powers can only fit your brilliant analytical discoveries and healing powers into that gap. Do you really wish to exclude from analytical work a "priesthood" understood in this sense? I do not believe that that is what you mean...

5.2   *Freud to Pfister May 26, 1929*
Dear Dr. Pfister,

So far you are the only one whom I have not thanked for sending me birthday greetings. Now I do so, and I am glad that it is done. Life is in any case not easy, its value is doubtful, and having to be grateful for reaching the age of seventy-three seems to be one of those unfairnesses which my friend Pfister puts up with better than I. However, if you promise never to do it again, I shall once more forgive you, just as you seem to forgive me a lot of things, including *The Future of an Illusion.*

5.3   *Freud to Pfister February 7, 1930*
I shall deal with only one point. If I doubt man's destiny to climb byway of civilization to a state of greater perfection, if I see in life a continual struggle between Eros and the death instinct, the outcome of which seems to me to be indeterminable, I do not believe that in coming to those conclusions I have been influenced by innate constitutional factors or acquired emotional

THE FUTURE OF AN ILLUSION
171

attitudes. I am neither a self-tormenter nor am I cursed and, if I could, I should gladly do as others do and bestow upon mankind a rosy future, and I should find it much more beautiful and consoling if we could count on such a thing. But this seems to me to be yet another instance of illusion (wish fulfillment) in conflict with truth. The question is not what belief is more pleasing or more comfortable or more advantageous to life, but of what may approximate more closely to the puzzling reality that lies outside us. The death instinct is not a requirement of my heart; it seems to me to be only an inevitable assumption on both biological and psychological grounds. The rest follows from that. Thus to me my pessimism seems a conclusion, while the optimism of my opponents seems an a priori assumption. I might also say that I have concluded a marriage of reason with my gloomy theories, while others live with theirs in a love-match. I hope they will gain greater happiness from this than I.

5.4 *Pfister to Freud July 31, 1930*

I am writing a lecture for the psycho-analytical society in New York on "The Origin and Conquest of Anxiety and Obsession in Judaeo-Christian Religious History." It is a subject which has been in my mind for years, and it first attracted my attention because it provided such magnificent corroboration of your theories.

...It always gives me great pleasure to see the great stream that bears your name growing stronger, deepening its bed, and widening.

My wife had a piece of news for me on her arrival that gave me great pleasure. I had carefully preserved your letters since 1909 and kept them in a box in the attic. After my first wife's death I had a house-maid who inexcusably burnt some of my most valuable papers and robbed me dreadfully. After her departure I hunted for the box in vain and gave it up for lost. Now the letters have fortunately been found. I cannot tell you how much my correspondence with you has meant to me, and how much stimulus I have derived from it. I am greatly looking forward to seeing your kind and sagacious letters again when I return to Zurich in the middle of November....

5.5 *Freud to Pfister May 12, 1931*

Dear Dr. Pfister,

After another major operation I am fit for little and un-cheerful but, if I have go back to some kind of synthesis again by the end of the month – that is what I have been promised – am I to miss the opportunity of seeing my old but by God's grace rejuvenated friend here? certainly not, I count on it. (*A reference to Pfister's remarriage*)

5.6   *Pfister to Freud May 24, 1933*

Dear Professor Freud,

I heard the news of Ferenczi's death last night. I am deeply grieved at the loss of your distinguished champion, and I wish to share my sorrow with you. With Abraham he was the man who most thoroughly imbibed, nor only your ideas, but also your spirit and, thus impelled and qualified, planted the banner of psychoanalysis in more and more new countries. In particular his brilliant discoveries about the psychology of philosophical thought, and metaphysical thought in particular, made me a grateful admirer of the modest man,

I paid a brief visit to Germany last week, and it will be a long time before I am able to get rid of the feeling of disgust I got there... Cowardly towards the-outside world, it wreaks its infantile rage on defenseless Jews, and even loots the libraries. Good luck to him who in the face of such crass idiocy still has the strength to be a doctor-of souls.

5.7   *Freud to Pfister June 13, 1934*

Dear Dr. Pfister,

I congratulate you on your honorary degree, but cannot agree your passing on to me the honour conferred on you; as the champion of religion against my *Future of an Illusion* you have the sole right to it. The fact that the Geneva theological faculty was not deterred by psychoanalysis is at least worthy of recognition.

5.8   *Freud to Pfister March 12, 1931*

My daughter will certainly gladly accept your report; she will hardly dispute that her files are incomplete. Actually I do not deserve your reproach for not writing anything. I have finished a sizeable piece about some significant matters, but because of external considerations, or rather dangers, it cannot be published. It is again about religion, cf. (Moses and Monotheism) so again it will not be pleasing to you. So only a few short papers have been usable for the Almanac and Imago.

With cordial greetings, Yours, Freud

5.9   *Pfister to Frau Freud December 12, 1939*

Last Saturday the Swiss Psycho-Analytic Society held a memorial meeting in honour of your great husband ... The occasion was not for the purpose of doing homage to the dead man to whom we have such a tremendous amount to be grateful for, but a profession of loyalty to the living Freud, to whom we can pay off a small part of our debt of gratitude, not by expressing our admiration and veneration, but only by cultivating his work.

THE FUTURE OF AN ILLUSION

173

In examining your husband's letters it was with both grief and pleasure that I was once again reminded of how infinitely much his family meant to him. I vividly remember his introducing me to you, his three fine sons, the vital Sophie, and the little mother of the lizards on April 25, 1909. I, who grew up fatherless and suffered for a life-time under a soft, one-sided bringing up, was dazzled by the beauty of that family life, which in spite of the almost superhuman greatness of the father of the house and his deep seriousness, breathed freedom and cheerfulness, thanks to his love and sparkling humour. In your house one felt as in a sunny spring garden, heard the gay song of larks and black birds, saw bright flower-beds, and had a premonition of the rich blessing of summer. To the visitor it was immediately evident that a large part of that blessing was to be attributed to you, and that you, with your gentle, kindly nature, kept putting fresh weapons into your husband's hands in the fierce battle of life ... His letters show that his friends also meant much to him, and the fact that I had the privilege of counting among his closest friends cheered me in the sad business of paying him tribute. Now and in later years it must be a satisfaction to you and your children to remember how much you contributed to mitigating your husband's internal and also external sufferings and the tragedy of his old age by your goodness and piety.

From the letter of your daughter Anna to our president we learnt with pleasure how capable of enjoyment the great tolerator remained to the end. For that he was indebted to all of you.

...At any rate his wish for mental rest after dying in the royal harness of the thinker has now been fulfilled.

Your husband's letters are among my most cherished possessions. As long as I live I shall always have them by *my* side.

With cordial greetings to you and your children, and especially Fraulein Anna and Dr. Martin. With deep devotion.

6 Conclusion

Freud and Pfister continually interacted with one another over their views of religion and the significance of a religious experience to life. Three issues appear to be foremost in their interchanges.

The issue of religious experience was one of the focal points between them. Freud contended that there was only one "variety of religious experience," that being obsessionalism with its basis in the totem. Pfister, on the other hand, was of the belief that the Judaeo-Christian religious experience removed the neuroses and created freedom for the individual. For him there was no room for obsessionalism in true religion.

Another issue was the testing of the reality of a religious experience. Freud contended that it was necessary to see with one's own eyes to accept something as reality. Religion had an incontrovertible lack of authentication due to the reliance of primal fathers' beliefs and the forbidding of raising questions concerning the belief of the fathers. Thus, it was impossible to test the reality in the here and now and "see" what the religious experience really was. Pfister's contention was that much of reality could not be validated directly, even such an accepted institution as the family. He emphasized that "in practical questions on whose answers the structure of one's life depends, one must take a stand even where stringent proofs fail." Even so, there was also a need for trust in religion.

Finally there was the issue involved in Freud's *Future of an Illusion* and Pfister's "Illusion of a Future." For Freud, religion was an illusion that had no future. "Is it possible for mankind to endure the hardships of life without the consolations of religion?" Freud asked. Perhaps, but only if in the process of growth the religious phase is replaced by the higher order of science. His premise for hope in the future was science. He stated, "our science is no illusion. But an illusion it would be to suppose that what science cannot give us we can get elsewhere." Pfister opined that Freud "takes it as self-evident that we have only to do with the world of appearance." Citing his own experience with empirical criticism that proved unfulfilling, he stated, "In my opinion the world of spiritual order ... stands more securely ... than the whole deceptive world of the senses." Further "In my view there can be no such thing as a pure empiricist, and a man who sticks rigidly to the data is like a heart specialist who ignores the organism as a whole."

In conclusion, perhaps Pfister's comments to Freud best express the basis for their differing views on religion, "Our difference derives chiefly from the fact that you grew up in proximity to pathological forms of religion and regard these as religion; while I had the good fortune of being able to turn to a free form of religion which to you seems to be an emptying of Christianity of its contents, while I regard it as the core and substance of evangelism" (Meng and Freud, p. 122). It just could be that life experience, even more than well reasoned logic, led both men to their positions. Such an anti-Semitic milieu as that in which Freud existed must have contributed to his bitter anti Christian feelings. He reported I'll never forgot the insults of Christians to his father.

Moses became his prototype. This faithful, lonely, determined Jew who led his people out of slavery was an inspiration for Freud. Freud saw himself as a modern atheist Moses with a somewhat messianic mission. This atmosphere was quite distinct from the idyllic, pastoral, supportive upbringing of Pfister.

THE FUTURE OF AN ILLUSION

175

For whatever reason, nevertheless, the two men represented opposing views on the dynamics and values of religion that still persist. A reconsideration of their interaction is a testimony to scholarly dialogue and a crisp restatement of the concerns for contemporary discussion.

References

Thomas Bonhoeffer, "Christianity and Fear Revisited," *Journal of Religion and Health,* 13:4 (1974):239–250.

Sigmund Freud, *The Future of an Illusion.* Translated by W.D. Robson-Scott (Garden City, N.Y.: Doubleday, 1958–published in German in 1927).

Sigmund Freud, *Moses and Monotheism* (New York: A.A. Knopf, 1939).

John E.G. Irwin, "Pfister and Freud: The Rediscovery of a Dialogue." *Journal of Religion and Health* (1973) 12:4:315–324.

Hans Ulrich Jager-Werth, "Oskar Pfister and the Beginning of Religious Socialism." *Journal of Religion and Health* (1974) 13:1:53–61.

Heinrich Meng and Ernest L. Freud, *Psychoanalysis and Faith: The Letters of Sigmund Freud and Oskar Pfister* (New York: Basic Books, Inc., 1963).

Oskar Pfister, "Delusion and Suicide among Youth" (Wahnvorstell ungen und Schuler-sel bstmord), Schweizer Blotter fur Schulgesundheitspflege 1 (1909).

Oskar Pfister, "The Illusion of a Future" (Die Illusion einer Zukunft), *Imago 14* (1928):149–184.

Oskar Pfister, *Christianity and Fear; A Study in History and in the Psychology and Hygiene of Religion.* Translated by W.H. Johnston (London: G. Allen and Unwin, 1948-publ. in German in 1944).

Albert Schweitzer, "Civilization and Ethics" (Kultur und Ethik) in *The Philosophy of Civilization* (London: Black, 1932, 1946).

Albert Schweitzer, "Decay and Restoration of Civilization" (Verfall und Wiedera uffaau der Kultur) in *The Philosophy of Civilization* (London: Black, 1932, 1946).

John W. Stettner, "Pfister as Pastoral Theologian." *Journal of Religion and Health* (1973) 12:3:211–222.

John W. Stettner, "What to do with Visions." *Journal of Religion and Health* (1974) 13:4:229–238.

Index

Abel 115, 117–118
Abraham 116
Abraham, Karl 34–35, 172
abstraction 11, 123, 132, 140
Acts of the Apostles 69
Adam 108, 116
Adaptational Psychodynamics: Motivation and Control (Rado) 150–151
Adler, Alfred 162
adoptionist theory 69, 72–74, 81, 91–93
Am Ha-aretz 57–58, 67
Amon 117
Anabaptists 79, 88
Anthanasius 92–93
apocalypse 62–63, 72, 78
Archelaus 59
Arianism 81, 93
Arius 92–93
Athanasius 81, 93

Baalism 125
baptism 104, 108, 113
Beyond the Pleasure Principle (Freud) 9
Birth of the Living God, The (Rizzuto) 25
body openings 30–31
    See also genitalia
Bowlby, John 107
Breasted, J. H. 37
breath 110
brotherhood 67–68, 162
Buddhism 125, 128

Cain 6, 115–118
castration 12, 84, 87, 111–112, 115
Catholicism 84, 87, 90
Catholic Mass 8, 11, 108
causality 6–13
Celsus 64–65
childhood 14–16, 40, 46–47, 52–54, 103–104
Christianity
    as class movement 71n36
    early 55–73
    Gnosticism and 88–89
    and Homoousion dogma 73–86
    Montanism and 88
circumcision 115–118

Civilization and Its Discontents (Freud) 6
clinging 107
Colyridians 86n52
Communion 109
compromise, unconscious 5, 5n6
compromise formations 5–6, 5n4, 5n6
conflict
    unconscious 6, 23
creation 110–111, 116–117
crocodile 111
crucifixion 70, 72, 76n42, 82–83, 87, 92, 108–109, 127
culture
    defined 135
    in Freud 20, 22, 135
    Freudian theory and 4
    human nature and 123
    illusion and 17
    nature and 123
    phylogeny and 7
    as reflection of mental contents 4
    religion for protection of 122, 135–137
    transmission of 1

Daniel, Book of 62
Darwin, Charles 7, 169
delusion, religion as 2, 17
Deuteronomy, Book of 69, 149
double possibility 4
dove 112
drives 48–49

ecstasy 15, 156–157
ego 9, 14, 18, 48–49, 51, 123, 127
Egypt 36–42, 111, 117
Eleutherius 110
embryology 6n8, 9
Enlightenment 125, 166
Enoch, Book of 62–63
Epiphanius 86
essentialism 4
Exodus, Book of 149
experience
    in psychoanalysis 45–46
    religious 13–15, 22, 24, 26, 173
Ezekiel, Book of 117–118

178 INDEX

Ezra, Book of   70

faith   4–5, 14, 17, 20, 54–55, 67–69, 71–73,
    78–82, 88, 91, 96, 119–121, 157
fantasy(ies)
    in applied psychoanalysis   2
    castration   111–112
    dogma and   98
    early Christianity and   70–73, 81–85, 99
    of Jesus   86–87
    of Mary   86–87
    number three in   30
    Oedipal   104
    psychological conflict and   3
    rescue   32
    and satisfactions of religion   51, 54
    science and   129
father   7–8, 10–13, 16, 32, 103–106
    fertilization and   110–111
    Fifth Commandment and   149–151
    God as   15, 52, 68, 71–73, 82–85, 92, 110,
        153, 157
    Holy Spirit and   108
    See also Oedipus complex; patriarchy
female genitalia   34, 104, 110
fertilization   110–112
    See also creation
feudalization   77–78
Feuerbach, Ludwig   16, 23, 126
Fifth Commandment   149–151
1 Clement   76n42
1 Corinthians   74, 132
1 John   164
fratricide   115
Freud, Sigmund
    Abraham and   34–35
    assumptions of   4
    causality in   6–13
    culture in   20, 22, 135
    on individual vs. social psychology   43
    as initiator of discourse   1–2
    instinct in   17–21
    Jung and   5n4
    on limitations of psychoanalysis   2
    Moses in   36–42
    ontogeny in   13
    Pfister and   119–148, 161–175
    phylogeny in   6–13
    positivism and   4n3, 5

    religion in   1, 3–6, 8, 13, 18–19, 21–22,
        121–137
    religious experience in   13–15
    religious ideas in   15–17
    science and   137–146
    totem in   7–8
Fromm, Erich   159
Future of an Illusion, The (Freud)   6, 52,
    119–148, 165, 174

gender   20, 112
Genesis, Book of   113, 116–117
genetic fallacy   16
genitalia
    female   34, 104, 110
    male   30–31, 34, 112
Gnosticism   88–90, 97
God
    as father   15, 52, 68, 71–73, 82–85, 92, 110,
        153, 157
    in Gnosticism   89–90
    images of   11
    kingdom of   65–66

Hall, G. Stanley   163
Heracles legend   32
Hermann, Imre   107
hermeneutics, in psychoanalysis   3–4
hero   38–40
Herod   59
Hippolytus   75n41
historical epochs   7
"History of Egypt" (Breasted)   37
Holy Spirit
    crocodile as   111
    as feminine   108
    psychological meaning of   112–113
    as replacing mother   112–113
Homoousion dogma   73–86
hydrophobia   104

id   5, 9–10
ideas, religious   15–17, 24
illusion(s)
    culture and   17
    religion as   5, 16, 20–21
    religious ideas as   15, 53
    and renunciation of instinct   18
    wish fulfillment and   25

INDEX

images, of God   11
Imago (journal)   38, 119, 129, 159–160, 165
impotence   52–53, 111
incest   33, 108, 115, 117
    See also Oedipus complex
inheritance   9, 22
instinct, renunciation of   17–21, 122–123
Ishmael   118
Israel   116

Jacob   12–13
Jael   117
James, Epistle of   67, 75
Jansenism   104
Jesus Christ   11
    in adoptionist theory   69, 72–74, 81,
        91–93
    dogma of   43–100
    in early Christianity   55–73
    ego and   127
    in Gnosticism   89
    and kingdom of God   65–66
    Logos and   90–91
    love and   124, 128
    monoarchianism and   91–92
    as son   69–70, 82–83, 85, 110
    tradition and   127
John, Gospel of   148
John the Baptist   63–64
Jones, Ernest   20, 113–114
Judaism   10–11, 58, 98
Jung, Carl   5n4, 160, 162

Kant, Immanuel   144–145
Kedar   118
Kelsen, Hans   159
Klein, Melanie   159
Kris, Ernst   159

Lamarck, Jean-Baptiste   9
Leviticus, Book of   117
Logos   90–91, 93, 111, 148
Lot   117
love   68–69, 77, 84–87, 95, 99, 112, 119–120,
    123–129, 144–146
Luke, Gospel of   66

Maccabees   62
male genitalia   30–31, 34, 112, 115

    See also castration; circumcision;
        impotence
Mark, Gospel of   69
Mark of Cain   115–118
Mary   85–87, 86n52, 108
Mass   8, 11, 108–109
materialism   4, 71n36, 124, 139
Matthew, Gospel of   66, 123–124, 128, 136
Mill, John Stuart   105–106, 139
Mithra   109
Moab   117
Mohicans   73
monoarchianism   91–92
monotheism   10–11
Montanism   88
Moses   149, 174
    as Egyptian   36–42
    etymology of, as name   36–37
    as father   12–13
    in Freud   36–42
Moses and Monotheism (Freud)   6, 10–13, 21,
    159
mother   33–34, 86–87, 104n1, 108, 110–112
    Fifth Commandment and   149–151
    Holy Spirit as replacing   112–113
    object cathexis with   14
    in pagan cultures   86n52

necrophilia   33
neurosis
    Oedipus complex and   11
    reality and   46–47
    religion and   5–6, 9–10, 22, 121–125
    taboo and   7
Nicene Council   81, 92–93
Nietzsche, Friedrich   141, 145

"Obsessive Actions and Religious Practices"
    (Freud)   5–6
Oedipus complex   4–5, 7–16, 21–25, 47, 52,
    82, 101, 104, 106, 109, 122–126
ontogeny   13, 23
original sin   10, 109, 112

Pascal, Blaise   101–106
patriarchy   113, 153–154, 157
    See also father
patricide   7, 11, 108
    See also Oedipus complex

Paul 74–75, 76n42, 78, 132
penis. *See* male genitalia
Pfister, Oskar 17, 119–148, 161–175
phantasy. *See* fantasy(ies)
Pharisees 56–58, 64, 66–67
Philippians, Epistle of 76n42
"Phylogenetic Fantasy, A" (Freud) 13
phylogeny 6–13, 15, 18, 22, 26
Pietism 125, 127
Plato 132, 141, 167
pleasure principle 17, 49
positivism 4n3, 5, 137–139, 145
Protestantism 125, 132–133, 144
proximate-causal theory 6
Psalms, Book of 69
psychoanalysis
    applied 2
    experience in 45–46
    Freud on 2
    as hermeneutical method 3–4
    method of 3
    and social psychology *vs.* individual
        psychology 43–47
psychoanalytic impulse 1–3
punishment 6, 56, 64, 86, 111, 115, 147, 150,
    153–156, 159
Puritanism 144

Rado, Sandor 86–87, 150–151
Rank, Otto 159
reality(ies)
    neurosis and 46–47
    principle 19–20, 49, 52
    sex drives and 48–49
    social construction of 4
    social situation and 49
    transcendent 2, 4
recapitulation 7, 9
Reich, Wilhelm 157–158
Reik, Theodor 6, 48, 52, 71, 94–98, 115, 118,
    118n1
religion
    childhood and 52–54
    as delusion 2, 17
    as enemy 20
    in Freud 1, 3–13, 18–19, 21–22, 121–137
    as hostile to thinking 133–135
    as illusion 5, 16, 20–21

instinct and 17–21
neurosis and 5–6, 9–10, 22, 121–122
as neurotic compulsion 122–125
Oedipus complex and 8–9
ontogeny and 13
phylogeny and 8
for protection of culture 135–137
social-psychological function of 48–55
as wish formation 126–132
religious ecstasy 15
religious experience 13–15, 22, 24, 26, 173
religious feeling 152–158
religious ideas 15–17, 24
rescue fantasy 32
Revelation, Book of 75
revolution 58–65, 71n36
Ricoeur, Paul 4
Ritvo, Lucille 22
Rolland, Romain 14
Rorschach, Hermann 163–164

Sachs, Hans 159
salvation 78n44, 145
Sargon of Agade 38–39
science 20–21, 36, 91, 105–106, 119–121,
    126–127, 129–132, 137–146
2 Thessalonians 146
self-punishment 6, 86, 115, 155
sex drives 48–49
sexual constitution 45, 45n3
sexual economic research 152–154
sexual ethics 52
sexual excitation 155–157
sexual intercourse 104, 110
sexuality
    ego and 123
    primacy of, in human motivation 10
    religious feeling and 154–156
    renunciation of 128
sexual symbolism 115–116, 118
Short History of the Development of the Libido,
    Viewed in Light of Mental Disorders, A
    (Abraham) 34–35
Simmel, Georg 44n2
sin 81, 109, 118, 153
Sisera 117
social psychology 43–45, 44n2, 46–47
social stability 50–51, 54

INDEX

son   10–11, 69–72, 82, 85, 103–105
Spitz, Rene   107
Strauss, David Friedrich   139
subjectivity   4, 130
sublimation   150, 163–164
sun   112
super-ego   5n6, 6n6, 9, 18,
    24–25

taboos   7
Talmud   57
three (number)
    Oedipus legend and   32–35
    symbolism of   30–32
Three Essays on Sexuality (Freud)   23
tilling   116, 118
totem   7–8, 13, 51
Totem and Taboo (Freud)   6, 10–11, 21, 51–52,
    159
transcendent realities   2
transference   3, 49, 124, 144, 169
trinity   30, 153

ultimate-causal theory   6
unconscious, the
    acquired characteristics and   9
    dogma and   98
    father in   8
    necrophilia in   33
unconscious compromise   5, 5n6
unconscious conflict   6, 23
urination   104

Vedic Literature   110

wind   110–111
wish formation   126–132
wish fulfillment   14–15, 21, 25–26, 31, 52–53,
    106, 171
"Woes of the Messiah"   62

Zealots   59, 61, 63–64, 67–68, 70
Zeno of Verona   110
Zeus   112
Zweig, Arnold   12